Feasting Through *the* Seasons *of a* Cajun Life

BAYOU

MELISSA M. MARTIN

PHOTOGRAPHS BY DENNY CULBERT

ARTISAN | NEW YORK

Library of Congress Cataloging-in-Publication Data is on file.

ISBN 978-1-64829-140-1
ISBN 978-1-64829-495-2 (signed edition)

Design by Nina Simoneaux

Artisan books may be purchased in bulk for business, educational, or
promotional use. For information, please contact your local bookseller
or the Hachette Book Group Special Markets Department at
special.markets@hbgusa.com.

The publisher is not responsible for websites (or their content) that are not
owned by the publisher.

The Hachette Speakers Bureau provides a wide range of authors for speaking
events. To find out more, go to hachettespeakersbureau.com or email
HachetteSpeakers@hbgusa.com.

Published by Artisan,
an imprint of Workman Publishing,
a division of Hachette Book Group, Inc.
1290 Avenue of the Americas
New York, NY 10104
artisanbooks.com

The Artisan name and logo are registered trademarks of
Hachette Book Group, Inc.

Printed in China on responsibly sourced paper

First printing, September 2024

10 9 8 7 6 5 4 3 2 1

for Saga & Jackson

Man is nostalgia and a search for communion.
—Octavio Paz, *The Labyrinth of Solitude*

Good cooking is the result of a balance struck
between frugality and liberality. . . .
It is born out in communities where the
supply of food is conditioned by the seasons.
—Patience Gray, *Honey from a Weed*

CONTENTS

COOKING TO THE
BEAT OF LIFE

The seasons on the bayou are not necessarily summer, fall, winter, and spring. They are marked by nature, traditions, and distinct emotions. They are rituals playing out on a stove every day. We mark years with dishes and celebrations—some so small they are personal to my own table, and some, like Fat Tuesday, world-renowned. We commemorate, reminisce, and harvest through the year. We celebrate holidays and memorialize the days life marks for us, like the passing of a loved one or the date a hurricane made landfall. We never need an excuse to gather and toast to life, love, and supper.

There are countless versions of Cajun life and Cajun food. But all the parishes that make up Cajun country sit on delta soil and have bayous running through them, old pathways and tributaries of the Mississippi River that appear as arteries through South Louisiana.

On the bayou, folks are tethered to the heart of Cajun life: food, family, and the rhythms of a year. Neighborhoods, homes, and industry flank the bayous. Directions are given as "up the bayou," "down the bayou," and "across the bayou," and folks identify themselves by the bayou they come from. Chauvin is nestled on Bayou Petit Caillou; Montegut and Bourg are to the west of us on Bayou Terrebonne. Lower south is Bayou Pointe-aux-Chenes, an epic, lush Amazon-like area, and Isle de Jean Charles, an island cut off from the mainland that is near extinction and home to American Indian tribes. To the west of Chauvin is Dulac on Bayou Grand Caillou. Louisiana is home to countless bayous; they all spill into the barrier waters of the Gulf of Mexico and all are home to fishing communities. The bayou is part of our identity and a lifeline to our culture.

The variations in dialect and in food are vast in this tiny twenty-mile radius, but we all start our New Year feasting with family. In my case, it's a simple meal of black-eyed peas and cabbage rolls to digest the holidays and preceding year. We look forward with great hope that life's cycles of solitude and resilience will restore us in our complicated world. It takes a bit of grace and fortitude to call South Louisiana home, but these qualities become us. Our work in kitchens breathes life back into us, we contemplate and create, then we bring together our family at tables to share in the act of communion, to fill our inner state with the love around us. Communion with others restores us; gathering in small groups on a birthday or in large groups for Carnival brings equilibrium, the abundance of love, laughter, and pure joy. These moments create stocks of resilience and jubilation. Time alone is precious, but time together is warm and restorative. There is a certain euphoria to each.

After the New Year comes Carnival, spring, and Lent, events of both feasting and fasting. When yellow sprays of butterweed bloom, blanketing our landscape after our patchy winter, we know spring is coming. February rain arrives to fill swamps and ditches, and crawfish come out to feed on the flowers; the cycle of life continues. Purple irises and spider lilies fringe the edges of the bayou; soon crawfish are ready for harvest along with spring's first peas. There is abundance and simplicity as we make our way out of winter, masking and parading ourselves and our shrimp boats, from Epiphany through the Blessing of the Fleet.

When swamp mallows are in full bloom, we're in summer. We don't need their brilliance to alert us—we are well aware of the heat. Summer means blackberries, muscadines, okra, shrimp, seafood boils, and stocking the larder. Filling freezers with fish and shrimp is as important as picking up milk at the grocery store. Water lilies congest the bayou to signal hurricane season, and a bit of anxiety sets in. The heat is thick and life is stripped down to mere basics: Stay cool and calm and feast on the sea's offerings.

Fall is marked with tradition as we drive through a sea of sugarcane and boats are adorned with roseaus and palmettos. In October we trudge through heat and summon cooler weather. Citrus and pecan trees hang thick with fruit; okra, peppers, and tomatoes still line the bayou; and Cajuns ready themselves to hunt alligator, squirrel, duck, deer, and turkey. Fall means boucheries; big fairs like the Andouille Festival in Laplace, Louisiana; and small-town Cajun fairs where folks gather for things like the Black Pot cookoff, to see who can make the best gumbos, stews, and desserts in cast iron, then two-step the night away to Cajun and zydeco bands. Sometimes there is no rhyme or reason to these traditions—but if it resonates, you respect it and keep the ritual going year after year.

We surround ourselves with love and sharing during the holidays stretching from Allhallowtide through the ringing in of New Year's. I mark the winter solstice as my mother's birthday. We take a break and head home for Christmas to tables surrounded with family and filled with food. An air of celebration and fellowship envelops the bayou over the winter holidays. We gather in cemeteries to clean our loved ones' tombstones and light candles. We go to church. We bake pies for no other reason than to give them away to neighbors. We eat *a lot*. Then we prepare for New Year's and let the cycle begin anew.

Food at my family's table in Chauvin, the bayou community where I grew up, is marked by consistent flavors and timeless dishes. Our tastes mirror our lives and our relationships to the seasons and the extreme conditions we face—one minute we're having watermelon under the gazebo to cool off and the next we're packing up our lives to evacuate. Our foods are marked by simplicity, resilience, and a fortitude that runs deep. A commitment to this tradition preserves our culinary identity and roots: An achingly simple shrimp okra gumbo brings me straight home and can also illustrate a world history lesson.

I'm often asked if I ever get bored cooking traditional Cajun food, if I feel penned in. How much creativity can one really have within a genre, especially while running Mosquito Supper Club, my traditional seafood restaurant in New Orleans? The answer is that I never feel limited. The discipline itself is liberating. Maintaining a commitment to sustainable seafood in South Louisiana means that I cook with an abundance of ingredients directly from farmers in my region. I carry on food heritage with shrimp, flounder, and crab and create new dishes with sustainable seafood and seasonal produce. Many of the most satisfying preparations of food the world over are based in "peasant" foods, cuisines created by people making the most of their terrain, ingredients, and climate. Homes are where peasant cuisines started, and peasant cuisines are the basis from which all other foods have evolved. I take the raw materials and recipes from home kitchens and the bayou and thrive in that discipline.

No matter how many books we publish about traditional cuisine, it's the act of cooking food that keeps it alive, as we learn from elders the nuances and complexities of a dish, a time, and a season. Cajun food will therefore never bore me. I feel a privilege and responsibility to bear these foods like a peasant queen. I continue to be a student of this culture and cuisine, and my job is to record, practice, and share. Anyone cooking Cajun food across South Louisiana (or preparing these foods in their homes across the world) is continuing this culinary tradition. The old ways are being lost, and salt water is washing away our roots. When I peer into the future, I know that cooking this food and sharing these recipes are acts of radical historical preservation. I am a daughter of the bayou. If not me, then who? When you cook and serve and savor these foods, you, too, are keeping the Cajun spirit of communion alive. I invite you into a year of cooking in South Louisiana: a place where communion is at church, but also at the table, on a boat, and anywhere we gather, tethered together, bayou to bayou, by the rhythms of life.

MY CAJUN TABLE

If a kitchen is the heart of a home, then a table is its arteries. Cooking, eating well, and nourishing ourselves bring us to the table of life. "It's the table and the bed that count in life," the author Marlena de Blasi writes. "And everything else we do, we do so we can get back to the table, back to the bed." The table is sacred space. We come together in communion and acknowledgment of labor, bringing food from farms to our homes, from stoves to our tables. To share a meal with family after a long, hard day—or a leisurely Sunday—is to participate in and savor the greatest riches this life has to offer.

I grew up on Bayou Petit Caillou, where my family cozied up at a Formica snack bar and then later a round table from Pier 1 Imports. We preferred the kitchen to the dining room and never had an heirloom piece passed down from generations. Even if we had, the hurricanes would have certainly carried it away. It's not important that your table be laid with fine china or decked out worthy of a social media post. What's important is that your table be a place of togetherness, presence, and love; mine is marked by a pile of freshly boiled seafood on news-paper, unbreakable Corelle bowls steaming with a perfectly cooked gumbo, or a strong hot cup of coffee and a sweet treat.

The idea of a table is not limited to furniture; a table can be a picnic blanket, an overturned bucket, or a bar corner you stand around polishing off a dozen raw oysters. A table can expand to accommodate anyone; it's the Cajun way to make room for another and feed folks. I invite you to create your own table with these recipes. But first, here are some cooking guidelines to get you set up that have helped me along the way.

A PASSION FOR POTS AND PANS

Almost all the recipes in this book feed six to eight people, which requires one good, large heavy-bottomed pot. You can easily cut a recipe in half and cook for fewer, but if you're putting in the effort, you'll want leftovers. I use my trusty **Magnalite pot** for almost everything I cook at home: soups, gumbos, stews, dips, and smothered chicken. I use my Magnalite so much that it rarely leaves the stove: I wash it and return it to its place, ready for action. You don't need a Magnalite, but you do need a heavy-bottomed pot. Any nice wide heavy-bottomed pot with a tight-fitting lid will do the trick. It's imperative you get to know your pot and its cook times. Aluminum-based Magnalites need constant heat, but because they're dense on the bottom with thinner sides, the heat is distributed quickly. I'm amazed how yellow onions cook down in stainless steel versus aluminum. Same number of yellow onions, same heat: widely different cook times. Enameled cast iron makes great heavy-bottomed pots; a Dutch oven (9½ to 15 quarts/9 to 14 L) is perfect. You can also find pots used; a nice heavy copper one can be passed down through generations and remain achingly beautiful.

A **boiling pot** is essential for boiling pasta, corn, and shrimp. It needs to hold a good amount of water. Get something that is heavy and spacious and use it for all boiling needs. Having *two* boiling pots can speed things up: When making potato salad, for example, you can boil your eggs and potatoes at the same time, maybe choosing a slightly smaller pot for the eggs. Or simply boil the eggs in one pot, remove them with a slotted spoon, then add the potatoes to the same water.

Get yourself a solid **cast-iron skillet** with a lot of surface area. Cast iron heats up slowly but maintains its temperature with ease. It is second to none for searing fish, steaks, pork chops, chicken, shrimp, and more. It also goes from stovetop to oven seamlessly and is not as difficult to clean as some people make it out to be. I've even finished pasta in my cast iron—when I'm making a quick pan sauce, pasta goes straight from boiling water into the cast-iron pan. I have never been one for a nonstick pan; seasoned cast iron works just as well. Look for an old one with history that you can season and give new life to. You can also buy lightweight cast iron—a great option for tired arms.

I've worked with stovetop **cast-iron fryers** all my life, and my mother always kept one ready to go with oil, but they take up a lot of space on a cooktop. If you prefer them, by all means cook in a cast-iron fryer, but use it with an appropriate thermometer and learn the heat levels of your stove. In my growth as a chef, I have come over to the side of a **tabletop fryer** because of its ability to regulate temperature. If I were to recommend one thing that plugs in, it would be a tabletop fryer. I like the simple Winco or Galaxy countertop commercial fryers, and my mom swears by the FryDaddy. The recipes in this book will suggest a tabletop fryer.

I cook on a gas stove, but of course these recipes will work on any range. I don't have a lot of experience on an electric range, but if you cook on electric or induction, knowing the power of your stove and its abilities to sear and be brought to its lowest temperature for simmering and smothering is critical. When I make gumbo or anything smothered, I use a **cast-iron diffuser**, a disk placed over the flame on a gas stove. This ensures that the pot does not heat up too much on the lowest flame. Often, you cannot bring the flame down really low without it shutting off. The diffuser acts almost like a French cooktop, shielding the pot from high heat and keeping it at a steady low cooking temperature. Smothering in a sense creates a stovetop pressure cooker, keeping the heat as low as possible while building up steam.

When I'm baking, I use minimal equipment. A **stand mixer** and **food processor** are helpful, as are **silicone spatulas**, **offset spatulas**, a **whisk**, and a **Silpat mat** for baking. Pan spray is a great invention, but you can also grease with a paper towel and cooking oil. For all the baking in this book, I used **aluminum baking pans**. Know that baking times in a glass, cast-iron, or enameled cast-iron pan will differ from those of an aluminum, metal, or nonstick baking pan. If you love baking, you probably have a lot of vintage and beautiful pans that present well, from oven to table. Get to know their best cooking times and make adjustments to my recipes accordingly. Glass and ceramic pans retain heat very well, but the bottoms of foods will brown much faster than with metal, and that can sometimes leave you with burnt biscuit bottoms if you're not paying attention.

ON INGREDIENTS

All butter will be unsalted in these recipes. Cream and milk should be the best quality; you will taste the difference. I mostly use raw, unrefined cane sugar because it is readily available in the sweet state of Louisiana. Meat should be free of antibiotics and raised properly. If possible, your fruits and vegetables should come from a garden, farmers' market, or reputable grocery, preferably without stickers—aren't stickers on our fruits and vegetables the worst? If you buy from the farmers' market, you will be astounded at how long your greens, vegetables, and fruits last. All onions are yellow, unless otherwise stated. Expect to finish a dish with flat-leaf parsley and green onions. Bell peppers are green, unless specified otherwise. Fish is sustainable and preferably line caught. It is urged strongly for the sake of bayou Cajun culture that seafood be domestic and from your own fisheries—always shop local if possible, and I refer you to online resources (see page 359) for domestic wild-caught seafood.

ABUNDANCE

WE PARTY AND THEN WE FAST. It may come as a surprise to people converging on South Louisiana for debauchery that Mardi Gras is a religious holiday dating back to pagan festivals of revelry and excess, followed by forty days of fasting. Today we move from one delicious religious season to the next— -Allhallowtide to Christmas, Christmas to Epiphany, Epiphany to Mardi Gras, and then Ash Wednesday to Good Friday and finally Easter.

Once we reach Epiphany, we say, "It's on, pecan," and embrace the season of parties, parades, and hangovers that all culminate in Fat Tuesday. It's a marathon, best taken slow and steady. The consumption of crawfish, Popeyes chicken, and king cake ramps up as Carnival season rolls on, and the urge to eat and live abundantly with a little extravagance is our daily norm.

Throwing backyard crawfish boils, making entrées of crawfish fettuccine, decadent crawfish po'boys, or traditional crawfish étouffée, is an extravagance best enjoyed with company. Seafood platters and dishes like oyster and Herbsaint soup, barbecue shrimp, and jambalayas filled with chicken and sausages can satisfy a hungry parade-going crowd. There is no dieting during Carnival season, only a desire to fill yourself to the brim with ritual, culture, and food—a living feast, reveling through the greatest party on earth.

Carnival Crawfish Boil

SERVES 12 TO 24

Some say that if you roll down your windows while driving in Cajun country, you can hear the hum of propane burners. That's because folks up and down the bayous and across South Louisiana are gathering for crawfish boils. Newcomers are always invited, but you may want to eat before you arrive—peeling crawfish is an art form best learned in childhood, and a rookie will need to learn quickly to fill up.

Unlike shrimp, which can be frozen and stored, crawfish must be boiled while alive; freezing them is not an option. When crawfish fishermen start offering sacks for sale, everyone gets excited. For connoisseurs, the beginning of the season, in January, is too early because the crawfish are still a bit soft and so peeling them is challenging. By the end of the season, in May and June, the crawfish are too hard. The best crawfish come in the middle, right around Mardi Gras and early spring.

NOTES: *Soaking crawfish is important to imparting flavor—do not skip this step. You want them to be flavor-forward and spicy, but not too spicy.*
Peel these and use the tails for recipes calling for boiled crawfish tails.

In a pot large enough to hold 20 gallons (75.7 L) of water set over a large propane burner, combine the onions, lemons, salt, celery, garlic, hot sauce, boil seasoning liquid, paprika, cayenne, vinegar, oil, and bay leaves. Fill the pot halfway with water using a hose. Bring the water to a full boil over high heat, then reduce the heat to low and simmer until the stock is fragrant, 1 hour.

Empty the crawfish into an ice chest or tub large enough that the crawfish won't be crowded and with enough space to add water to cover them. Use a hose to fill the ice chest with water, then continue to run water through it for about 45 minutes, until the water is clear and the crawfish are clean. If some of the crawfish make it to the top and escape, just wrangle them back into the water. →

10 pounds (4.5 kg) yellow onions, quartered

4½ pounds (2 kg) lemons, halved

4½ pounds (2 kg) kosher salt, plus more as needed

2 pounds (910 g) celery, chopped into 4-inch (10 cm) pieces

1½ pounds (680 g) garlic heads, halved

2 cups (480 ml) hot sauce, preferably Original Louisiana Hot Sauce

1 cup (240 ml) Zatarain's crab and shrimp boil seasoning liquid

1 cup (120 g) paprika

½ cup (45 g) cayenne pepper, plus more as needed

½ cup (120 ml) white vinegar

¼ cup (60 ml) canola oil

10 bay leaves

60 pounds (27 kg) live crawfish

10 gallons (38 L) ice

Potatoes (see page 28)

Shucked corn (see page 28)

Dipping sauces, for serving

Crackers, such as Ritz and saltines, for serving

Return the stock to a rapid boil over high heat. Use a large strainer or net to remove 30 pounds (13.6 kg) of the crawfish from the ice chest and add them to the stock, pressing them down firmly. (Leave the rest of the crawfish in the water in the ice chest until you're ready for the second batch.) Bring the water back up to a rolling boil, then cook the crawfish for 5 minutes. Turn off the heat and add 5 gallons (19 L) of the ice to cool the crawfish. Let them soak for 30 minutes, tasting one crawfish after 20 minutes. Does it need more salt or more heat? If so, stir in more salt or cayenne. Don't remove the crawfish until you really love the flavor; remember that crawfish will be only as good as the stock it's cooked in. Use a spider to transfer the crawfish from the pot to a big platter. Bring the water back up to a rolling boil, and repeat with the remaining 30 pounds (13.6 kg) crawfish.

Boil the potatoes and corn to round out the meal (see below).

Get your table ready: Cover it with newspaper and set out your favorite dipping sauces and crackers. You'll need lots of paper towels and some ice-cold beer, alcoholic and non-alcoholic, please. Crawfish also go well with white wine, rosé, and champagne.

Transfer the crawfish to the newspaper-covered table for eating, with the potatoes and corn alongside.

HOW TO BOIL POTATOES AND CORN

After boiling crawfish, crabs, or shrimp, reserve the boiling stock to cook the potatoes and corn. You can put the potatoes and corn in a strainer directly in the shellfish pot or you can transfer some stock to a smaller boiling pot. For **5 pounds (2.3 kg) small red potatoes**, boil for 10 minutes, or until a knife or fork can easily be inserted. For **8 to 12 whole corncobs**, break them in half and boil for 5 minutes, until they turn bright yellow.

Crawfish Rolls

SERVES 6

A crawfish roll is decadent, the kind of sandwich that earns audibly voiced approval. Make these during Carnival season and put them out for your friends. What makes a crawfish roll so special is knowing the amount of work that went into peeling the crawfish. To give someone a roll slathered in spicy mayonnaise and filled with buttery crawfish is a bit extravagant and a celebration unto itself. If you're feeling extra, top this roll off with caviar.

In a medium bowl, gently mix together the crawfish, melted butter, and a small squeeze of lemon juice. Taste the crawfish and season with the salt, a crack of black pepper, and a touch of cayenne.

In a small bowl, mix together the mayonnaise and hot sauce.

Toast the rolls. Butter the rolls with the butter from the bottom of the crawfish bowl. Then spread the spicy mayonnaise in the rolls. Fill the rolls with the crawfish and garnish each with a bit of the green onion.

½ pound (225 g) peeled boiled crawfish tails (from about 3 pounds/1.4 kg of crawfish; see page 27)

2 ounces (60 ml) unsalted butter, melted

Juice of 1 small lemon wedge

½ teaspoon kosher salt

Cracked black pepper

Cayenne pepper

⅓ cup (80 ml) homemade mayonnaise (page 338)

2 tablespoons hot sauce, preferably Original Louisiana Hot Sauce

6 soft rolls, such as split-top hot dog buns

2 tablespoons finely chopped green onion

Soft-Shell Crawfish Po'Boys

MAKES 4 PO'BOYS

The po'boy I dream about when I'm not at my mom's table is one from the long-gone soft-shell crawfish po'boy stand at the New Orleans Jazz and Heritage Festival. That po'boy was dressed with lettuce and mayo, loaded with deep-fried crawfish and fried jalapeños, and served on French bread. I never crave white bread until we start talking about po'boys. I did not grow up in New Orleans, so I never lean toward the kind of French bread that is crumbling around you as you eat it, nor do I prefer the hard-shell, airy variety used for most po'boys and banh mis. I want a soft French bread, the kind baked at Clement's in Chauvin, the kind my mother uses for our homemade po'boys, and the kind most of the shops on the bayou and prairies choose for their sandwiches.

Soft-shell crawfish are a real delicacy. If you come across some while crawfishing in the wild, you are lucky. LTE in Ethel, Louisiana, is the only remaining producer in the state that packages them for sale. If you purchase from them, the crawfish will already be cleaned (Louisiana Direct Seafood carries LTE crawfish online; see Resources, page 359).

NOTE: *You'll need to soak the jalapeños overnight.*

Place the crawfish in a bowl and pour in enough of the buttermilk to cover them completely. Add the hot sauce, gently stir, and let marinate overnight in the refrigerator.

Place the jalapeños in a small bowl and pour in enough buttermilk to submerge them. Let soak overnight. Pro tip: Use a plate or jar lid as a weight to keep the jalapeños submerged.

When you're ready to make the po'boys, prepare a tabletop fryer with oil and heat to 350°F (180°C). Alternatively, fill a large heavy-bottomed

24 soft-shell crawfish (about ¾ pound/360 g)

2 cups (480 ml) whole-fat buttermilk, or as needed

2 tablespoons hot sauce, preferably Original Louisiana Hot Sauce, plus more for serving (optional)

2 pickled jalapeños from a jar, sliced into ½-inch (1.3 cm) pieces

Canola oil or peanut oil, for frying

4 cups (500 g) all-purpose flour, plus more as needed

2 teaspoons kosher salt

¾ teaspoon finely ground black pepper

¼ teaspoon cayenne pepper

Sea salt

1 loaf soft French bread or similar

Homemade mayonnaise (page 338)

1½ cups (90 g) shredded iceberg lettuce

pot with 4 inches (10 cm) of oil and heat the oil over medium-high heat to 350°F (180°C).

In a large shallow bowl, combine the flour, kosher salt, black pepper, and cayenne.

Remove each crawfish from the buttermilk and dredge liberally in the flour mixture. Be sure to get flour into all the crevices, then place on a sheet pan. Dredge the remaining crawfish.

Now repeat the steps. This is called double battering. Dip the crawfish in the buttermilk and then the flour mixture. If you need to add more flour to the flour mixture, go right ahead; you do not want a gummy coating.

Working in batches of 6 to 8, place the crawfish in the hot oil and fry until crispy and golden, about 3½ minutes. Use a slotted spoon to transfer the crawfish to brown paper bags or a paper towel–lined plate to absorb excess oil. Season the fried crawfish with sea salt. Repeat with the remaining crawfish.

Now fry the jalapeños. Remove them from the buttermilk and batter them with the remaining flour mixture. Fry for 30 to 40 seconds, until golden brown. Use a slotted spoon to transfer them to a brown paper bag or paper towel–lined plate. Sprinkle on a little sea salt.

Assemble the po'boys. Using a bread knife, cut the loaf of French bread into 4 pieces. Cut the pieces lengthwise in half. Liberally spread some mayonnaise on the bottom of each sandwich, then layer on some crawfish and jalapeños and top with shredded lettuce. If you want your crawfish a bit spicier, hit them with a couple dashes of hot sauce.

Mim & Eunola's Étouffée

SERVES 8 TO 10

Deep in Breaux Bridge, they tell a legend of two fierce Cajun friends named Eunola and Mim who fished the Atchafalaya Basin, of locals trying to ride their tails and learn their secrets, and of them speeding away in their outboard. Eunola's family remembers a time when folks would go deep into the woods to boil crawfish. This is when it was a faux pas to eat "mudbugs," and Cajuns wanted to hide the delicacy they knew about. Peasant food has always evolved with a little bit of humiliation on the back side, such as how lobster was once considered a desperate person's food. It wasn't until Breaux Bridge started holding an annual crawfish festival that the rest of the state, country, and world caught on to the exquisiteness of crawfish. Cajuns know how to handle crawfish, and the crustaceans are wild and plentiful in the Atchafalaya Basin. Mim and Eunola's étouffée requires a bit of crawfish fat to thicken and make this dish rich and extravagant. The friends created the recipe at home in Breaux Bridge while staying up late playing cards.

NOTE: *Carrying on Mim and Eunola's recipe traditions, Eunola's daughter takes boiled crawfish and lets them sit in a strainer with a bowl underneath. The fat on the crawfish will seep off and collect in the bowl below. You can also just use your fingers to lift off the beautiful bright orange fat from the heads and tails. You'll need some fat to give your étouffées and bisques a beautiful golden hue and rich, complex notes.*

4 ounces (110 g) unsalted butter

1 pound (455 g) yellow onions, finely diced

3 pounds (1.4 kg) peeled boiled crawfish tails, with about ¼ cup (2 ounces/ 60 g) fat reserved (see page 27 and Note)

2 tablespoons all-purpose flour, plus more as needed

1 cup (240 ml) chicken stock (page 348) or crawfish stock, plus more as needed

1 tablespoon kosher salt

½ teaspoon cracked black pepper

½ teaspoon cayenne pepper

Cooked rice, for serving

¼ cup (15 g) finely chopped flat-leaf parsley, for garnish

¼ cup (15 g) finely chopped green onions, for garnish

Warm a heavy-bottomed 5-quart (4.7 L) Dutch oven or pot over medium-high heat for 1 minute. Add the butter and yellow onions and cook, stirring frequently, until the onions start to take on a golden hue and become translucent, about 10 minutes. Stir in the crawfish fat. Cook for 10 minutes more, stirring often and reducing the heat if the fat and onions start sticking.

In a small bowl, stir the flour into the stock and mix well. Add this mixture to the onions and simmer until the mixture starts to thicken

and resemble a loose cheese sauce, about 5 minutes. You may need to add a little more stock to thin the mixture or a little more flour to thicken it. You want a consistent sauce that's thicker than gumbo and more on the stew side. Continue cooking until the onions are completely translucent, 10 to 15 minutes more. You are not looking for color on the onions.

Stir in the crawfish, salt, black pepper, and cayenne and cook for 2 minutes. Reduce the heat to medium-low and cook for 3 minutes more so the flavors marry.

Taste and adjust the seasoning and consistency, if necessary. Serve over rice, garnished with the parsley and green onions.

Crawfish Fettuccine

SERVES 8 TO 10

I updated our bayou crawfish fettuccine recipe for a lighter, quicker version that eliminates processed cheese. The best method for making a perfect fettuccine is to follow the Italian way, tossing the pasta with some of its cooking water on warm platters to make a quick, velvety sauce. Adding crawfish tails and Parmesan cheese makes a filling recipe. It's a good way to use up those extra tails from a crawfish boil, and it feeds a crowd, too. This pasta with all its cheese and butter goes well with a bitter, acidic green salad to help cut the fat.

Place a large platter, casserole dish, or cast-iron skillet in the oven on the warming setting; the dish should be warm enough to melt butter but not warm enough to cook food.

Taste the crawfish: Does it need more salt? More pepper or heat? Add salt, black pepper, cayenne, or hot sauce to your liking. Boiled crawfish tails are usually seasoned already and do not need additional seasoning, but peeled crawfish tails from a store will need doctoring up.

Bring a large pot of water to a boil over high heat. Add enough salt (about 2 tablespoons) so that the water tastes as salty as the sea, then cook the fettuccine according to the package directions. Drain the pasta, reserving 1 cup (240 ml) of the cooking water.

Scatter the butter in the warm platter. Add the fettuccine and top with the Parmesan. Using tongs, quickly combine the fettuccine, butter, and Parmesan, thoroughly lifting and folding the pasta and adding ¼ to ½ cup (60 to 120 ml) of the reserved cooking water until a beautiful velvety sauce forms. Add more cooking water if needed. Once the sauce has coated the pasta, stir in the crawfish and season to taste. Serve immediately, garnished with the parsley and green onions.

2 pounds (910 g) peeled boiled crawfish tails and fat (see page 27), at room temperature

Kosher salt

Cracked black pepper

Cayenne pepper

Hot sauce, preferably Original Louisiana Hot Sauce

1 pound (455 g) quality fettuccine noodles, dried or fresh

8 ounces (225 g) unsalted butter (with highest fat content available), cut into 10 square flat pieces

8 ounces (225 g) freshly grated Parmesan

¼ cup (15 g) finely chopped flat-leaf parsley, for garnish

¼ cup (15 g) finely chopped green onions, for garnish

THE INTENSITY AND THE
REVERIE OF CARNIVAL

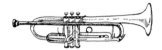

Carnival shakes off the holiday season. A certain euphoria takes over from indulging in king cake at Twelfth Night (Epiphany) to joining in the last parade on Mardi Gras day. You can't keep still. A trance sets in at the first parade. The tunes of Professor Longhair and Jon Batiste ring out everywhere, so you break open your costume box, glitter your face, and hit the streets. It's time to "rôder," as Cajuns say, parade yourself around town. You may assemble your own krewe and join a parade, party on the fringes, or make your way to neutral ground and wait for some good loot. Either way, you buckle in for the ride.

Carnival is intoxicating and addictive. You lust for the cadence of marching bands and live for costumes, feathers, and beads. You forget you have a job or responsibilities, your home becomes a disaster, and you heed a wild call to get lost in celebration until Fat Tuesday rings its closing bells. You let yourself get swept away. A king cake adorns your kitchen island, a butter knife tucked inside the box at the ready. Your coffee is anointed with liquor, Bloody Marys become a new food group, wine travels in a go-cup and tastes great on ice, and a dark beer fulfills your breakfast food group. Biking becomes your best mode of travel. You can easily find one-pot meals of beans, gumbo, and jambalaya as you walk down the street from folks leaving their doors open or those preparing and selling the dishes in makeshift kitchens under tents. You will feast like royalty.

When Rebirth Brass Band sings "Do Whatcha Wanna," they mean it. Carnival is a no-judgment zone. If your Carnival is Uptown with tricolored vests and golf shirts, extravagant balls, and silver cups engraved with your family's initials, then this is Carnival. If you participate in mock pageantry, call yourself a king, queen, duke, or knight, dress in the fashions of a long-ago era, and join a krewe that calls itself by a god or goddess name, this is Carnival. If your Carnival is a flutter of glitter and boxes of wine, Battle of the Bands, and a chase to catch our cultural bearers, Mardi Gras Indians, this is Carnival, too. If a brass band showing up at your favorite bar at two a.m. seems normal, it's Carnival time. If you try your hardest to get to Jackson Street at some ungodly hour to see Zulu, catch a coconut, and have a drink at famed bartender Chris Hannah's house, this, too, is Carnival. If you are an esteemed Zulu member and have been carrying on a tradition that started in 1909, remembering that Louis Armstrong was once your king, this is Carnival. If you are a reveler who costumes every year, struggling over which feathers and fabric to buy and deciding that spending that extra fifty dollars is okay, even if you need it for rent, this is also Carnival. And if you are a paradegoer with your children in a wagon, cursing ladders and spending your whole Sunday afternoon saying, "Throw me something, mister," this, too, is Carnival.

From the first bite of king cake to getting ashes on Ash Wednesday, South Louisiana knows how to throw a party. The feasting and parading prepare you for the solemn time of Lent. That's when you clean your home the best you can, the costumes make their way to the attic, and a simpler rhythm rolls in. You recover and reminisce, and you just might begin imagining what you'll wear next year, vowing to start your costume earlier this time.

Hearty Oyster, Herbsaint, and Fennel Soup

SERVES 8

New Orleans was considered an absinthe capital before Prohibition. Following the dry years, New Orleanian J. Marion Legendre is credited with distilling the first Herbsaint, an anise-forward liqueur that "replaced" absinthe but did not include the possible wormwood side effects. Herbsaint is herbaceous and was extremely popular in its heyday. It remains an important base spirit for many New Orleans cocktails. This soup is a handshake between the liqueur and fennel, an ingredient that has a short growing season in South Louisiana and must be celebrated in timely fashion. The Herbsaint lends subtle yet complex notes to the soup, and the fennel helps balance it and keep it earthy. Try adding a couple drops of Herbsaint to finish the soup also.

Make this decadent soup when celebrating Carnival. Have a dinner toasting the season with a bit of crawfish, and slot this in as a course along with barbecue shrimp and king cake. It's a meal fit for Carnival royalty—and by that I mean your friends.

NOTES: *Be careful when deglazing a pan with alcohol because it may flame up. Not to worry, though: The flame will go out as soon as the alcohol burns off.*

If you would like your soup thinner, add another cup (240 ml) of oyster liquor or stock.

Warm a heavy-bottomed 5-quart (4.7 L) Dutch oven or pot over medium heat, then add the oil and heat for 1 minute. Add the salt pork and cook, turning as needed to brown on all sides, about 8 minutes. Add the yellow onions and stir to coat them with the pork fat, then cook, stirring occasionally, until translucent, lightly caramelized, and golden, about 20 minutes. Add the celery and fennel bulb and stalks and cook until they are just starting to get soft, about 10 minutes.

2 tablespoons canola oil

¼ pound (115 g) salt pork, diced into ⅝-inch (16 mm) cubes

2 pounds (910 g) yellow onions, finely diced

½ pound (225 g) celery, cut into 1-inch (2.5 cm) pieces on a bias

½ pound (225 g) fennel bulb and stalks, cut into 1-inch (2.5 cm) pieces, fronds reserved for serving

¼ cup (60 ml) Herbsaint or Pernod, plus more for serving

1 pound (455 g) shucked oysters, liquor reserved

2½ cups (600 ml) oyster liquor or chicken stock (page 348)

1 bay leaf

½ teaspoon to 1 tablespoon kosher salt (depending on the saltiness of the oysters and oyster liquor as well as the salt pork)

¼ teaspoon freshly ground black pepper, plus more as needed

Cayenne pepper

10 ounces (285 g) red potatoes, peeled and diced into 1-inch (2.5 cm) cubes (about 2 cups)

1 cup (240 ml) heavy cream

1 cup (240 ml) whole milk

Stir in the Herbsaint to deglaze the pot and scrape up any bits stuck to the bottom. Add the oyster liquor, bay leaf, ½ teaspoon of the salt, the black pepper, and a pinch of cayenne. Bring to a simmer, then add the potatoes, cover the pot, and simmer until the celery and fennel are al dente and the potatoes are easily pierced with a fork, about 20 minutes.

Reduce the heat to low and pour in the cream and milk. When the soup comes to a slight simmer, stir in the oysters and cook just until they start to curl and seize up, about 2 minutes. Taste the soup: Does it need salt, black pepper, or heat? Season to your liking.

Ladle the soup into bowls. Sprinkle nutmeg over the top and, if you like, stir in a teaspoon of Herbsaint. Garnish with the fennel fronds, parsley, and green onions and swirl in a drizzle of olive oil.

Freshly grated nutmeg

¼ cup (15 g) finely chopped flat-leaf parsley, for garnish

¼ cup (15 g) finely chopped green onions, for garnish

Good finishing olive oil, for drizzling

Shrimp Sauce Piquant

SERVES 8

If you were crowned queen of the Sauce Piquant Festival, a community fair in Lafourche Parish in the 1970s, you were judged on your cooking abilities, too. Beauty and swagger only going so far, the stove and pots were the real deciding factor. You had to know how to make a sauce piquant. There are many sauce piquant recipes gracing tables all over South Louisiana, from home kitchens to well-established fine-dining restaurants. Here's a simple one to build up some good heat and satisfy a hungry crowd.

Warm a heavy-bottomed 5-quart (4.7 L) Dutch oven over medium heat for 2 minutes, then add the oil and heat for 30 seconds. Add the yellow onions and cook, stirring often, until they are soft, translucent, lightly caramelized, and taking on a golden hue, about 20 minutes. If the onions start to stick to the pot, deglaze the bottom with 1 tablespoon of water at a time.

Add the bell pepper, celery, garlic, and bay leaf and stir to combine. Reduce the heat to low, cover, and let the vegetables smother together until the celery and bell pepper have lost their bite, about 20 minutes. Add the tomatoes, tomato paste, and Worcestershire (if using), then smother the tomatoes for 20 minutes more, breaking them apart with a wooden spoon and mashing them against the sides of the pot.

In a medium bowl, season the shrimp with the salt, black pepper, cayenne, and hot sauce. Add the shrimp to the pot and increase the heat to medium-low. Stir well so the shrimp get coated with the sauce and cook for 5 minutes. Pour in the stock, bring to a simmer, cover, and cook for 5 minutes. Turn off the heat and let the shrimp rest for 10 minutes.

Taste, adjust the seasoning to your liking, and serve over rice, garnished with the parsley and green onions.

¼ cup (60 ml) canola oil

3 pounds (1.4 kg) yellow onions, finely diced

¼ cup (35 g) finely diced green bell pepper

¼ cup (25 g) finely diced celery

3 garlic cloves, finely chopped

1 bay leaf

1 (14½-ounce/410 g) can whole tomatoes

1 (6-ounce/170 g) can tomato paste

1 tablespoon Worcestershire sauce (optional)

3 pounds (1.4 kg) peeled medium shrimp

2 tablespoons kosher salt

½ teaspoon cracked black pepper

½ teaspoon cayenne pepper

2 tablespoons hot sauce, preferably Original Louisiana Hot Sauce

1½ cups (360 ml) chicken stock (page 348) or shrimp stock (page 345)

4 to 6 cups (800 to 1,200 g) cooked rice, for serving

¼ cup (15 g) finely chopped flat-leaf parsley, for garnish

¼ cup (15 g) thinly sliced green onions, for garnish

New Orleans–Style Barbecue Shrimp

SERVES 8

Pascal's Manale is located a couple blocks away from Mosquito Supper Club. The team there has helped us with many last-minute restaurant needs, and there is no finer place to eat raw Louisiana Gulf oysters in the city of New Orleans. Legend has it that this recipe was invented at Pascal's Manale in the 1950s and spread like wildfire, each chef in New Orleans creating their own version and putting it on their menu.

We call this preparation "barbecue" shrimp because the sauce is sweet, spicy, and tangy. It's prepared in a flash, so the key is to have all your ingredients ready. This is a dish to share—beautiful shrimp that asks you to be present—plus I love a dish that requires you to dig in and viscerally eat with your hands, sopping up the sauce with crusty bread. If you imbibe, wash it down with a dry white wine or a pilsner.

NOTE: *You'll need a very large sauté pan or brazier, at least 16 inches (40 cm) in diameter, to cook this amount of shrimp; if you have only a large sauté pan, consider cutting the recipe in half.*

In a large bowl, combine the shrimp, hot sauce, salt, black pepper, cayenne, and bay leaf.

Warm a very large heavy-bottomed sauté pan or brazier over high heat. Let it get very hot. At this point, things are going to move really fast, so have all the other ingredients ready to go. If you have a hood fan, now is the time to turn it on and maybe open a window or door. This preparation can cause some smoke.

Add the oil to the pan, then stir in the green onions and garlic and cook for about 30 seconds. Do not let the garlic burn—keep moving it with a wooden or stainless steel cooking spoon. Add the honey, hot water, and Worcestershire and cook for 30 seconds. →

3 pounds (1.4 kg) head-on medium-to-large shrimp

2 tablespoons hot sauce, preferably Original Louisiana Hot Sauce

1 tablespoon kosher salt

½ teaspoon cracked black pepper

⅛ teaspoon cayenne pepper

1 bay leaf

3 tablespoons canola oil or olive oil

2 cups (110 g) finely chopped green onions

8 garlic cloves, finely chopped

⅓ cup (80 ml) honey

⅓ cup (80 ml) hot water

⅓ cup (80 ml) Worcestershire sauce

Juice of 1 large lemon, about ¼ cup (60 ml)

½ cup (120 ml) Coca-Cola, beer, or white wine

8 ounces (225 g) unsalted butter, cut into cubes and kept in the freezer

¼ cup (15 g) finely chopped flat-leaf parsley

Crusty bread and lemon wedges, for serving

Making sure your pan is still hot, add the seasoned shrimp and lemon juice, then pour in the Coke to deglaze the pan and scrape up any bits stuck to the bottom. Cook the shrimp for 2 minutes in the sauce that forms in the pan, stirring and shaking the pan to keep the shrimp moving.

Remove the butter cubes from the freezer, reduce the heat to medium, and add the butter slowly, cooking for 2 minutes, stirring constantly. This technique is called mounting with butter; it will help the butter emulsify in the sauce, creating a lovely buttery, tangy broth for the shrimp.

Reduce the heat to its lowest setting. Using tongs, remove one shrimp and carefully but quickly peel it, blowing on it so you don't burn yourself. Taste the shrimp for doneness; it should be firm and seasoned but not mushy. Usually the shrimp are done at this point, as they will continue cooking with residual heat for a few more minutes, but depending on the size, you may need to cook them for 1 minute more.

Taste again. Does the shrimp need more salt, pepper, or heat? Adjust the seasoning, top with the parsley, and serve immediately from the pan. Put out the crusty bread and lemon wedges, then tuck away your cell phone, grab a sturdy napkin, and enjoy this treat.

Apex Jambalaya

SERVES 8 TO 12

Apex jambalaya is a nod to Avoyelles Parish, located at the "apex" of Cajun country. There you can find great butcher shops where they break down whole hogs, process boudin and andouille, and fry cracklins daily. This jambalaya has chicken and sausage. Growing up, I never saw my mom make a jambalaya that was not seafood-based, but in most prairie parishes chicken and sausage are more common.

This is a perfect dish to fill up a large crowd of people while partying before or after a parade. Enjoy the rich, silky jambalaya with a crunchy salad.

Remove and discard the chicken skin and place the thighs in a large bowl. Season with the salt, hot sauce, black pepper, and cayenne. Let the chicken come to room temperature so that it browns more easily.

Warm a heavy-bottomed 12-quart (11 L) Dutch oven over medium heat for 2 minutes, then add the oil and heat for 30 seconds. Add the salt pork, turning as needed to brown it on all sides, about 8 minutes. Transfer the pork cubes to a bowl or plate and set aside. Add the andouille and brown on all sides, about 4 minutes. Transfer the andouille to the bowl with the salt pork.

In the pot with the rendered pork and andouille fat, brown the chicken on all sides, about 4 minutes per side. Reduce the heat to low and cook the thighs for 8 minutes more, covered. Transfer the thighs to a plate or bowl. Add a touch of the stock to deglaze the pot and scrape up any bits stuck to the bottom; pour the liquid into the bowl with the andouille.

Wipe out the deglazed pot and add the duck fat. Let warm over medium-high heat for 2 minutes, then add the yellow onions and stir, stir, stir. This starts the very long process of browning the onions. After 5 minutes, turn down the stove to medium heat. Cook the

8 to 10 chicken thighs, about 3 pounds (1.4 kg) (I prefer bone-in, but you can use boneless)

1½ teaspoons kosher salt

1½ teaspoons hot sauce, preferably Original Louisiana Hot Sauce

¼ teaspoon freshly ground black pepper

¼ teaspoon cayenne pepper

1 tablespoon canola oil

½ pound (225 g) salt pork, diced

½ pound (225 g) andouille, cut into ½-inch (1.3 cm) pieces

5 cups (1.2 L) chicken stock (page 348) or water, plus more as needed

¼ cup (60 ml) rendered duck fat, lard, or oil

1½ pounds (680 g) yellow onions, finely diced

½ cup (50 g) finely diced celery

½ cup (75 g) finely diced green bell pepper

1 bay leaf

2 cups (370 g) long-grain white rice, rinsed under cold running water

½ cup (30 g) finely chopped flat-leaf parsley

½ cup (30 g) finely chopped green onions

onions for about 1½ hours, depending on how hot your stove runs, watching them very closely and stirring every 2 minutes. If the onions start to stick too much, add a tablespoon or two of water or stock at a time to loosen them, then stir to incorporate the browner onions and scrape up any stuck-on bits from the bottom of the pot. Stir, stir, stir until the onions are deeply caramelized. If you're worried about the onions burning, reduce the heat (see Cooking Onions, page 306).

Add the celery, bell pepper, and bay leaf to the pot and stir. Cover and cook over low heat for 15 minutes, stirring every 5 minutes.

Add the rice to the pot with the vegetables and stir to combine. Raise the heat to medium and cook for 5 minutes, letting the flavors mingle and marry. Add the chicken, andouille, and salt pork and stir to incorporate them.

In a separate saucepan, bring the rest of the stock to a boil, then add it to the jambalaya pot. Bring the jambalaya to a boil, then reduce the heat to low and simmer until the liquid has almost completely evaporated or looks like little puddles, about 8 minutes. When it's at the point of puddling—this is a judgment call based on temperature, pot size, and your stove—put the lid on the pot and reduce the heat to its lowest setting. From here, the cooking time is going to be 45 minutes total, and you can't remove the lid the entire time. This is a tough, long 45 minutes. But trust yourself. You'll want to peek, but don't.

Set a timer for 20 minutes. When it goes off, turn the heat off and let the jambalaya sit, covered, for 25 minutes before you lift the lid.

After the 45 minutes is up, uncover the pot. Add the parsley and green onions, stir, and serve.

CAJUN MARDI GRAS

There is a stark contrast between the pageantry of Fat Tuesday in New Orleans and the celebration of rural Mardi Gras. Cajun country holds on to medieval traditions centered on community and food. When Cajuns hear the minor chords of "Courir de Mardi Gras," something changes in them. A dance dating back to pagan times is near.

Like the medieval French tradition, the Cajun parade is also a run through the community. Everyone participates in a begging ritual, asking folks for ingredients to make gumbo and feed the village. A captain leads men and women in mandatory masks and fringed costumes to ask for rice, onions, flour, fat, parsley, green onions, and, of course, a (live) chicken. The chicken is the star of the day. It is offered up, let loose, and chased by runners all through the countryside until it is caught. You run, fueled by adrenaline, in a haze of beer, through rice fields, unfenced yards, and stunning countryside. With a captain who's carrying a whip and the day's permission to imbibe, this pursuit can become a chase of cinematic proportions. The captain keeps order, even when the run lasts hours and hours. It's a bonding experience for all. Just when you think things couldn't get any more magical, everything stops. You've arrived at the halfway point—no houses to be seen, just wide-open prairie and folks handing out boudin. You nourish yourself and then the journey continues. At the end of the run, a fais-dodo, a dance, awaits, as well as a feast of chicken gumbo.

Breakfast Ring

SERVES 8

Making breakfast ring is a weekend treat. As kids, my siblings and I made it with canned biscuits rolled in butter, cinnamon, and sugar and cooked it in the microwave. Nowadays, I make my breakfast ring in the oven with a yeasted dough, adding a touch of cardamom for an adult version. Cardamom can be a bit pricey, so I suggest getting it from the bulk bins at the grocery store and buying only as much as you need. If you purchase whole pods, put one in your coffeepot or French press in the morning when you're brewing coffee for a real treat.

Everyone will love breakfast ring; turn it out of the Bundt pan onto a large plate, place it hot on a table, and watch how fast it is delicately pulled apart and disappears.

NOTE: *You can mix the dough the night before, wrap it in plastic wrap, and refrigerate it for a slow rise.*

Make the dough: In a small bowl, combine the lukewarm milk and yeast and let stand until foamy, about 10 minutes. Add the honey and stir.

In a large bowl, sift together the flour and salt. Use your fingers to smudge the lard through the flour until you've combined the two. You may still see pea-size bits of lard. Make a well in the flour mixture and add the yeast mixture. Use your hands to mix and to form a craggy ball.

On a clean, lightly floured surface, knead the dough until it becomes cohesive and a bit shiny, 6 to 8 minutes. Let the dough sit for a minute while you wipe out and grease the dough bowl.

Place the dough in the greased bowl, cover with a clean dish towel or plastic wrap, and let it rise for about 1 hour or until doubled in size. →

FOR THE DOUGH

1½ cups (360 ml) lukewarm whole milk

1½ tablespoons active dry yeast

2 tablespoons honey

3½ cups (440 g) all-purpose flour, plus more for dusting

2 teaspoons kosher salt

3 tablespoons cold lard or unsalted butter, cut into small cubes

FOR THE BUNDT PAN

Baking spray or canola oil

3 tablespoons raw sugar

FOR THE CINNAMON-SUGAR MIXTURE

½ cup packed (110 g) dark brown sugar

½ cup (100 g) raw sugar

2 teaspoons ground cinnamon

¼ teaspoon ground cardamom

½ teaspoon kosher salt

4 ounces (115 g) unsalted butter

Prepare the pan: Use baking spray or about 1 tablespoon canola oil (which can handle high temperatures) to liberally grease a Bundt pan, then coat it with the raw sugar. Do not skimp on the greasing and sugaring step.

Turn the risen dough out onto a clean, lightly floured surface and roll it into an 8 by 16-inch (20 by 40 cm) rectangle. Using a pizza cutter, cut the dough into eight 4-inch (10 cm) square pieces; then cut each of those into four until you have 32 bite-size pieces (these will ultimately double in size).

Make the cinnamon-sugar mixture: Using a fork, combine the sugars, cinnamon, cardamom, and salt in a bowl. Roll each piece of dough in the mixture, then place the dough layer by layer in the prepared Bundt pan.

Place the remaining cinnamon-sugar mixture and the butter in a saucepan over medium-low heat and bring to a simmer. Immediately pour the hot butter-sugar around the sides of the dough in the pan, being careful not to pour directly on top of the dough, which would hinder the rise. Set the pan in a warm, draft-free spot and let the dough rise, uncovered, until doubled in size, about 45 minutes.

While the dough is rising, preheat the oven to 350°F (180°C).

Bake for 45 minutes, or until the ring is no longer doughy in the center and the internal temperature registers 190° to 200°F (90° to 95°C) on an instant-read thermometer. (If you are using a convection oven, the cooking time may be shorter.) Remove the pan from the oven, let cool for about 2 minutes, then turn out onto a cake stand or large flat plate. Be sure to turn the breakfast ring out of the pan while it is warm, otherwise the sugars will cement it to the pan and the residual heat will keep cooking it. Enjoy immediately—but don't burn the roof of your mouth.

King Cake

SERVES 12

My mom's king cake recipe is tricked out from a Tupperware bread recipe. She tacked it up inside our kitchen cabinet when I was a kid and she used it frequently. The recipe became so torn and tattered that we could hardly make out any of the ingredients or the method, and at some point, I put the very important Tupperware bowl with a sealable lid on a hot stove, which ended its reign as the king cake and bread bowl.

To make a modern version of the cake, you'll braid a yeasted dough with cinnamon, sugar, butter, vanilla, and salt. After the cake is baked, you'll be eager to eat it, but you must let it cool before icing it with cream cheese frosting. Consume it the same day; it's a bready dough so it goes stale quickly (you may want to slightly warm up any leftovers). To serve king cake like a true Cajun, you must leave the cutting knife sitting with the cake at all times.

Make the cake: In a small saucepan, warm the water and milk over low heat just until lukewarm. Transfer to a large bowl and add the yeast and 1 tablespoon of the raw sugar. Let stand until bubbles form on the top, 5 to 10 minutes. Add the remaining raw sugar and the kosher salt, egg and egg yolk, 1 teaspoon of the vanilla, and the lard. Mix together. It's okay if lumps of lard remain; they will be incorporated with the flour during kneading.

Add the flour to the bowl ½ cup (65 g) at a time and bring the dough together first with a fork and then with your hands, using just enough flour to create a dough ball. The dough will stick to your hands; just use some flour to remove it.

Turn the dough out onto a clean, lightly floured surface and begin kneading, adding flour a little at a time as needed so the dough doesn't stick to the surface. I like to knead my dough for 8 to

FOR THE CAKE

¾ cup (180 ml) water

¾ cup (180 ml) evaporated milk

2 tablespoons active dry yeast

⅓ cup (65 g) raw sugar

1 teaspoon kosher salt

1 egg plus 1 yolk, at room temperature

2 teaspoons pure vanilla extract

4 ounces (115 g) lard, at room temperature

4 cups (500 g) all-purpose flour, plus more for dusting and kneading

2 ounces (60 g) unsalted butter

FOR THE SUGAR MIXTURE

¾ cup (150 g) raw sugar

¾ cup packed (165 g) dark brown sugar

1 tablespoon ground cinnamon

1 teaspoon sea salt

Pinch of freshly grated nutmeg

FOR THE EGG WASH

2 egg yolks

1 tablespoon heavy cream

→

10 minutes (or two or three songs on my favorite playlist). The dough will become cohesive and a bit shiny. Resist the urge to add too much flour, even though that would make the dough easier to work with. Let the dough sit for a minute while you wash and dry the bowl. Grease the bowl.

Put the dough in the greased bowl, loosely cover the bowl with plastic wrap or a clean dish towel, and set it in a warm, draft-free place to rise until doubled in size. Depending on the weather and strength of your yeast, this could take from 45 minutes to more than an hour. (In summer in Louisiana, things can move dangerously fast.)

In a small heavy-bottomed skillet over medium heat, heat the butter until it melts and starts to brown, about 5 minutes. Set aside to slightly cool, then stir in the remaining 1 teaspoon vanilla.

Prepare the sugar mixture and egg wash: In a medium bowl, combine the sugars, cinnamon, sea salt, and nutmeg. In a small bowl, whisk together the egg yolks and cream to make an egg wash. Set both bowls aside.

Assemble the cake: Transfer the dough to a clean, *very* lightly floured surface—you do not want to incorporate too much flour into the dough. Using a kitchen scale or simply your best judgment, divide the dough into three even pieces. Roll out each piece into a 4 by 20-inch (10 by 50 cm) rope.

Use a pastry brush to generously coat the ropes with the melted butter mixture, then sprinkle on all but ⅓ cup (75 g) of the sugar mixture. Brush the edges with some of the egg wash to help seal them.

To braid the dough, attach the three ropes at one end by pressing them together, then braid the three ropes. Form the braid into a rough circle or oval and tuck the ends together. Don't worry, this is all very rustic. Place the cake on a large sheet pan, then brush the top with the remaining egg wash and sprinkle with the reserved ⅓ cup (75 g) sugar mixture.

FOR THE CREAM CHEESE ICING

1 (8-ounce/225 g) package cream cheese, at room temperature

2 tablespoons unsalted butter, at room temperature

⅓ cup (35 g) powdered sugar, sifted

½ cup (120 ml) heavy cream, chilled

1 tablespoon fresh lemon juice

¼ teaspoon fine salt

Zest of 1 orange

¼ cup (45 g) each purple, green, and gold decorating sugar

Set the cake in a warm, draft-free spot, cover loosely with a dish towel, and let the dough rise until doubled in size, 45 to 60 minutes. When the dough feels taut and springs back when you press on it, it's ready to bake.

While the dough rises, preheat the oven to 375°F (190°C).

Bake for 20 minutes, or until the internal temperature registers 200°F (95°C) on a point-and-shoot or instant-read thermometer. Let the cake cool completely.

In the meantime, make the cream cheese icing: In the bowl of a stand mixer fitted with the whisk attachment or in a large bowl using a handheld mixer, cream together the cream cheese, butter, and powdered sugar until smooth and fluffy, starting on low speed and gradually moving to high speed so you don't wind up in a cloud of powdered sugar. Reduce the speed to low and gradually add the cream, then the lemon juice, fine salt, and orange zest. Whip until completely smooth, about 5 minutes.

Use an offset spatula to spread the icing just on top of the cooled cake (we don't frost the sides of a king cake). The icing is delicious but also the glue for the decorating sugar. Sprinkle the icing with the colored sugars and you're ready to start slicing.

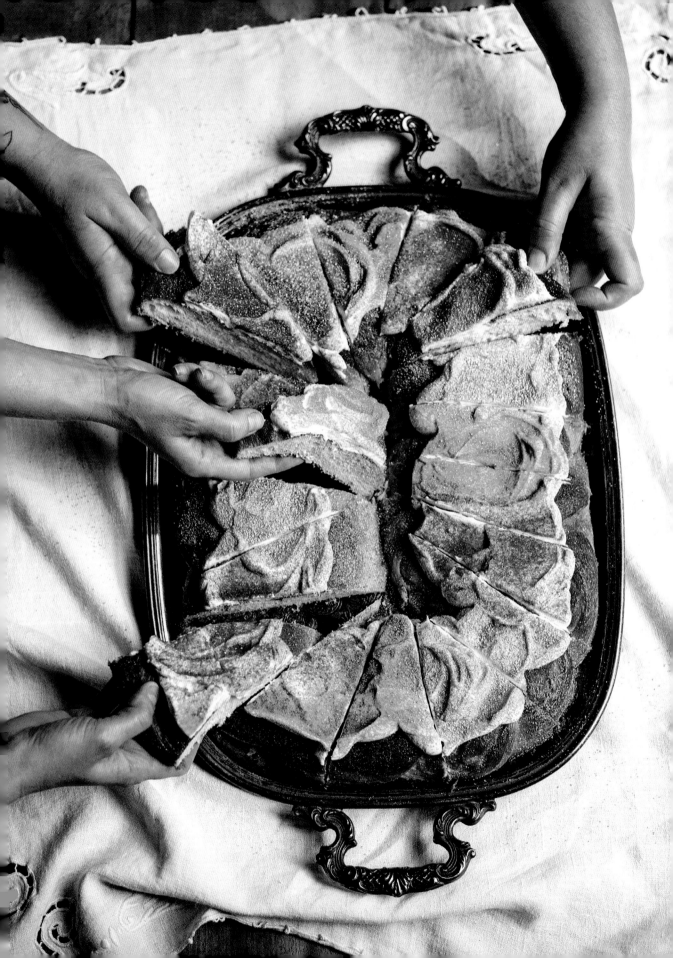

KING CAKE AS RITUAL

At gatherings on Epiphany, January 6, we mark the start of Carnival season. It's sacrilegious to participate in any Mardi Gras party or eat any king cake before Twelfth Night's Epiphany. Don't let your friends catch you slipping: It will ruin your reputation and give you bad Carnival karma. But once we've marked Epiphany, it's on, pecan!

We traditionally decorate king cake, the brioche-like braided cake or cinnamon roll, with bright sugars of purple, green, and gold that signify justice, faith, and power. The King of Rex, a Carnival krewe with mock pageantry, adorned balconies when entertaining a duke of Russia back in the late 1800s, and these colors were chosen to resemble a jeweled crown. New Orleans–style king cakes are iced with these colors, and the cake itself is thought to be a recipe from France. King cakes can be consumed after Epiphany, or the twelfth day of Christmas, which is when the baby Jesus was visited by the Three Wise Men. In modern times, a tiny plastic baby is hidden inside each cake, and whoever gets the baby in their slice is responsible for procuring the next king cake. In the past, the hidden surprises might have been coins, fèves, or nuts.

Oreilles de Cochon

MAKES 20 PIECES

These little fried-dough "pig ears" are fun to make, crispy, and delicious. If you are Cajun, you generally crave a little afternoon coffee and a sweet treat. Here's a decadent one topped with Poirier's cane syrup and toasted pecans. You can always sprinkle the fried dough with a little powdered sugar, too.

In a large bowl, whisk together the flour, baking powder, and salt for 1 minute. Make a well in the center of the mixture and pour in the eggs, melted butter, and milk and stir with a fork just until a ball starts to form. Knead the dough in the bowl for 1 minute. Separate the ball into 20 small pieces, each the size of a small meatball or Ping-Pong ball.

Prepare a tabletop fryer with oil and heat to 375°F (190°C). Alternatively, fill a large heavy-bottomed pot with 4 inches (10 cm) of oil and heat the oil over medium-high heat to 375°F (190°C). Cut out twenty 4-inch (10 cm) squares of parchment paper. Create a draining rack by placing a wire rack on top of a sheet pan.

On a clean, lightly floured surface, use a rolling pin to roll each ball into a circle about 4 inches (10 cm) in diameter. Place the first one on a square of parchment paper, place another square on top, and repeat to make a stack, ready to fry.

Place a dough circle, still on its parchment paper square, into the oil. Use tongs to quickly and carefully remove the paper. Place the tines of a long-handled fork in the center of the dough and then, thinking of a clock, twist the dough counterclockwise from 12 o'clock to 6 o'clock; the dough will twist into itself and look like a folded pig's ear. It will have a rustic appearance. Keep the fork in place until the pastry starts to turn brown, about 1 minute, then remove the fork, letting the pastry fall back into the oil. Flip the pastry and cook for

2 cups (250 g) all-purpose flour, plus more for dusting

1 tablespoon baking powder

1 teaspoon kosher salt

2 eggs

4 ounces (115 g) unsalted butter, melted and cooled

¼ cup (60 ml) whole milk

Canola oil, for frying

1 cup (240 ml) cane syrup, preferably Poirier's (see Resources, page 359)

¼ cup (60 g) chopped toasted pecans

1 minute more, until the pastry turns golden brown. Remove with
tongs and place on the prepared draining rack. Repeat with the
remaining dough circles.

In a small saucepan over low heat, gently warm the cane syrup. With
a small spoon, drizzle the cane syrup over the fried dough on the
draining rack, then sprinkle with the pecans. Eat immediately.

SIMPLICITY

—— ⸰⸱⸲⸳⸴⸵ ——

SIMPLICITY IS THE ULTIMATE SOPHISTICATION.
—*Leonardo da Vinci*

SPRING OFFERS THE LUCIDITY of light, bright foods that help our bodies reset after debauchery and feasting, and forty days of Lent. Lent is a solemn time in households across South Louisiana. The older generation fasts, giving up bread, rice, sweets, and other indulgences and abstaining from eating meat on Fridays. While this is an offering, we all must admit that giving up meat doesn't constitute much of a sacrifice in a region where seafood is plentiful and isn't considered meat.

Growing up on the bayou instilled minimalist values in me. We don't waste or overthink life but try to live a simple and sustainable existence. In spring we luxuriate in salads with fresh peas, beans, greens, strawberries, beets, and first-of-the-season tomatoes. We turn cabbage into filling salads, slaws, and ferments. We enjoy the time on the bayou when fish really start giving, and fill our freezers with meals for months. Fish-fry Fridays are celebrated in churches, schools, and homes across South Louisiana. Fish never tastes better than next to hush puppies and cabbage slaw or with a side of fresh peas stirred into rice.

The food we enjoy reflects recipes built on simplicity and comfort—simple if tethered to the supply chain, comforting with the cycle of the seasons. When we finally celebrate Easter, we are ready for shrimp season to commence and for farmers' markets to swell with produce, and we feel the warmth of summer creeping in.

Fresh Bean Salad with Tomatoes and Herbs

SERVES 8 AS A SIDE DISH

In spring I crave salads, and it's difficult to abstain from putting fresh peas and beans on everything I eat. Beans are versatile and can be used to deliver creamy flavors with herbs, oils, and vinegars. Treat this recipe as though making a salad with beans in place of greens.

Louisiana hothouse tomatoes first show themselves in spring at the market. Cherry tomatoes and heirloom tomatoes help round out this salad with a bit of acid. Find some great mixed cherry or heirloom tomatoes in your neck of the woods and the freshest peas and beans you can get your hands on. You can also shell your own beans.

In a small bowl, combine the shallots, vinegar, and honey. Let sit for 5 minutes.

Set the tomatoes on a plate or cutting board and season with the salt and pepper.

Place the beans in a large bowl. Add the shallot mixture and lemon juice, then gently fold everything together. Add the olive oil and gently mix again. Add the tomatoes and fold together.

Taste the salad: Does it need more salt and pepper? Adjust the seasoning as needed. Anoint the salad with the high-quality olive oil, then top the whole mess with the parsley, chives, and basil.

½ cup (100 g) thinly sliced shallots

2 tablespoons white balsamic vinegar, white wine vinegar, or apple cider vinegar

1 teaspoon honey

12 ounces (340 g) cherry tomatoes, cut in half, or other ripe tomatoes, cut into wedges

2 teaspoons kosher salt

½ teaspoon cracked black pepper

4 cups (600 g) raw mixed beans such as zipper peas, purple-hulled peas, pink eyes, and limas

1 tablespoon fresh lemon juice

¼ cup (60 ml) olive oil or canola oil

High-quality olive oil, for finishing

1 tablespoon finely chopped flat-leaf parsley leaves and stems

1 tablespoon finely chopped chives

Leaves from 2 sprigs basil, torn

Strawberries and Pickled Beets

SERVES 6

One of my favorite salads is a marriage of strawberries and beets, an unexpected but complementary pairing in salads, smoothies, and juices. Strawberries and beets are both sweet, so this salad is best paired with bitter greens, such as mizuna, arugula, and chicories. Lightly pickled beets add acid to this combination, and you can round it out with any number of herbs. I choose dill, which has a very short life span in South Louisiana in spring.

Preheat the oven to 450°F (230°C).

Make the roasted beets: In a small bowl, combine the sugar, salt, and lemon zest. Rub the lemon zest through the salt and sugar. Rub the beets with the olive oil, then roll them in the sugar mixture. Wrap the beets in aluminum foil and roast them on a sheet pan until a knife can easily be inserted, 40 to 60 minutes.

Remove the foil and let the beets cool slightly, then peel them.

Cut the beets into 1-inch (2.5 cm) pieces and place in a bowl. Add the vinegar and shallot to make a quick pickle, stirring a few times.

Assemble the salad: Place the strawberries and mizuna in a bowl and season with the salt and black pepper.

In a small bowl, combine the vinegar, cane syrup, and red pepper flakes. Pour onto the strawberries and mizuna and mix well.

Spread the strawberry mixture on a large platter and scatter the beets and shallots on top. Anoint the salad with the extra-virgin olive oil and more salt and pepper. Garnish with the parsley, dill sprigs, and candied pecans. Taste, adjust the seasoning if needed, and eat immediately.

FOR THE ROASTED BEETS

2 tablespoons raw sugar

2 tablespoons kosher salt

Zest of 1 lemon

½ pound (225 g) whole, raw, unpeeled beets, preferably smaller

2 tablespoons olive oil

2 tablespoons cane vinegar, preferably Steen's, or apple cider vinegar

2 tablespoons sliced shallot

FOR THE SALAD

1 pint (350 g) strawberries, hulled and quartered

¼ pound (115 g) mizuna or other bitter greens

2 teaspoons kosher salt, plus more as needed

½ teaspoon cracked black pepper, plus more as needed

2 tablespoons cane vinegar, preferably Steen's, or apple cider vinegar

1 tablespoon cane syrup or honey

Pinch of red pepper flakes

2 tablespoons extra-virgin olive oil

8 parsley sprigs, leaves picked and stems finely chopped

Dill sprigs, for garnish

¼ cup (30 g) Candied Pecans (page 349)

Fermented Cabbage

MAKES 3 CUPS (765 G)

Fermentation is one of the oldest forms of cooking and preserving. It's extremely easy; a lab setting is unnecessary. You can take temperatures, if you like, or you can build up intuition and trust yourself and make a countertop-fermented cabbage. It's easier than creating a sourdough starter or crème fraîche, which are both easy-to-do home ferments. I love this cabbage and carrot kraut with a simple dish of panfried fish cheeks over rice.

Start with a clean 1-quart (960 ml) mason jar and a weight that can be placed in the jar to hold the cabbage down. You can easily find these online (see Resources, page 359). For successful fermentation, the cabbage needs to be pressed down and stay in its own liquid. This will also keep mold from growing.

NOTE: *If you don't have a fermentation weight, use a smaller mason jar filled with water or rice as a weight.*

In a large bowl, mix together the cabbage, carrots, and salt. Massage the cabbage and carrots through your fingers, making sure they are evenly salted. Keep doing this until liquid starts to form. Let the mixture rest for 5 minutes, then massage again. The cabbage should release a good amount of liquid.

Place a little of the cabbage mixture in a sterilized widemouthed quart jar and firmly press or tamp down that layer. Repeat the layering little by little, pressing as much of the cabbage and carrots as you can into the jar. It should all fit. Once all the vegetables are transferred to the jar, give it another good press, then pour any liquid from the bowl into the jar. Insert a sterilized weight to press down on the vegetables during fermentation. You will leave this weight in the jar.

Cover the jar with cheesecloth or breathable cloth and secure it with a rubber band. Place the jar on a small plate and leave it on the counter.

1¼ pounds (570 g) cabbage, cut into rustic dice or sliced thinly, from about ½ large cabbage

1 cup (110 g) shredded carrots

2 tablespoons kosher salt

The cabbage will release more liquid and bubble. Firmly push down on the cabbage mixture every day, and taste it after a few days. The longer you leave it out to ferment, the tangier it gets. I leave my fermented cabbage out for at least 3 days and up to a week—that's if I can hold out that long before eating it. When the flavor is right for you, screw on the lid and place the jar in the fridge.

Dried Shrimp and Cabbage Salad

SERVES 8 AS A SIDE DISH

Cabbage is inexpensive and good for you. It's packed with so many nutrients, and can be added to soups, fermented, stuffed, stir-fried, grilled, or smothered. Cabbage can sit for a long time dressed; that means you can make this salad ahead of time and it will only get better. This quick-and-easy recipe incorporates dried shrimp, a delicacy on the bayou.

Some prep tips: Select a very sharp knife to finely slice the cabbage. Use larger carrots, as they are easier to work with, and shred them on the largest holes of a box grater. And a Microplane rasp grater will make short work of grating the garlic.

Place the cabbage and carrots in a large bowl. In a small bowl, combine the lemon juice, olive oil, pickled onions, sugar, red pepper flakes, lemon zest, and garlic.

An hour or so before serving, season the cabbage and carrots with the salt and black pepper. Add the lemon-and-oil mixture and toss with your hands to evenly coat the cabbage and carrots with the dressing.

Wait until you're about to serve the salad to add the parsley, green onions, peanuts, and shrimp. Taste and adjust the seasoning as needed.

4 cups (360 g) finely sliced cabbage

1 cup (110 g) shredded carrots

⅓ cup (80 ml) fresh lemon juice

¼ cup (60 ml) olive oil

¼ cup (60 g) Quick Pickled Yellow Onions (page 300)

2 tablespoons raw sugar

Pinch of red pepper flakes

Zest of 1 lemon

1 garlic clove, finely grated or finely chopped

2 teaspoons kosher salt

½ teaspoon cracked black pepper

¼ cup (15 g) finely chopped flat-leaf parsley

¼ cup (15 g) thinly sliced green onions, cut on a bias

2 tablespoons chopped dry-roasted peanuts

2 tablespoons chopped dried shrimp

Cabbage Slaw

SERVES 8 AS A SIDE DISH

I tasted this slaw for the first time at Danny's Fried Chicken (see page 309). It's a bitter, tangy, creamy concoction and a perfect complement to the fattiness of fried foods. Cabbage slaw is a crucial side with fried chicken, fried seafood, barbecue, and jambalaya. It is a necessity at a Friday fish fry for Lent.

For the best results, chop the cabbage into rustic pieces about 1 inch (2.5 cm) square (but don't split hairs on this), and shred the carrots on the largest holes of a box grater.

In a large bowl, combine the cabbage, carrots, and celery. In a small bowl, mix together the lemon juice, vinegar, sugar, red pepper flakes, and celery seeds. Add the mayonnaise and buttermilk, stir until combined, then pour the mayo mixture into the cabbage mixture and toss well to combine. Add the parsley and green onions and give the slaw a final toss. Finish with the salt and black pepper.

4 cups (360 g) chopped cabbage

2 cups (220 g) shredded carrots

¼ cup (25 g) finely sliced celery

2 tablespoons fresh lemon juice

2 tablespoons apple cider vinegar or Steen's cane vinegar

1 teaspoon raw sugar

Pinch of red pepper flakes

½ teaspoon celery seeds

1 cup (240 ml) homemade mayonnaise (page 338)

¼ cup (60 ml) whole-fat buttermilk

¼ cup (15 g) finely chopped flat-leaf parsley

¼ cup (15 g) finely chopped green onions

2 teaspoons kosher salt

½ teaspoon cracked black pepper

A SPRING HOLIDAY

On March 19, Saint Joseph's Day is celebrated in South Louisiana and in parts of Europe, including Spain, Switzerland, and Italy. Altars holding baked goods and food are erected in honor of Joseph, the stepfather of Jesus and husband of Mary. People from all over South Louisiana pilgrimage from altar to altar at churches, community centers, bakeries, restaurants, and homes.

The celebration and tradition were brought to South Louisiana by the Sicilian community that immigrated to Louisiana in the late 1800s. March 19 is also the date that New Orleans Mardi Gras Indians come out at night to parade in the streets, the two events coinciding, it is said, because the Mardi Gras Indians, a mystical secret society, historically felt safe to appear in public on this day celebrated by hardworking families from poverty-stricken neighborhoods, perhaps creating an understanding and commiserating in each other's resistance to hold on to light amid darkness and to commune as one.

Altars are constructed of rows of tables of different heights, traditionally three rows representing the Holy Trinity (Father, Son, and Holy Ghost as one, not onion, bell pepper, and celery). A statue of Joseph, a simple carpenter, stands at the center, and an abundance of food flanks him on all sides: arteries of fruits, vegetables, baked breads in various shapes, cookies, and cakes. The multitude of homemade offerings from kitchens of parishioners beat out from the heart of the installation. The altars are on display for a couple of days, and on March 19, Joseph is crowned and folks celebrate by consuming and sharing the bounty. Amid the solemn time of Lenten fasting comes a celebration of craftsmanship, abundance, and then feasting to honor a simple man etched in history. It's communion as high art and community.

Hush Puppies

MAKES 3 DOZEN HUSH PUPPIES

Hush puppies and fried fish are like peas and carrots—they go together. This batter is easy to tinker with and very forgiving, so you can make your own additions or just proceed in the minimalist fashion. I'm from a very "plain" school of thought, and I add only a touch of green onions rather than jalapeño and corn kernels to my hush puppies, but you can choose your own adventure. I eat my hush puppies with honey butter or Steen's butter.

¾ cup (95 g) all-purpose flour

¾ cup (120 g) fine cornmeal, preferably Bayou Cora Farms heirloom cornmeal

1 tablespoon raw sugar

1½ teaspoons baking powder

1¼ teaspoons kosher salt

Pinch of cayenne pepper

¾ cup (180 ml) whole-fat buttermilk

½ cup (40 g) minced green onions

2 tablespoons unsalted butter, melted

Canola oil or peanut oil, for frying

Soft butter and honey, for serving

In a medium bowl, whisk together the flour, cornmeal, sugar, baking powder, salt, and cayenne. Stir in the buttermilk, green onions, and melted butter. Let sit for an hour in the refrigerator.

Prepare a tabletop fryer with oil and heat to 350°F (180°C). Alternatively, fill a large heavy-bottomed pot with 4 inches (10 cm) of oil and heat the oil over medium-high heat to 350°F (180°C).

Working in batches and using a small scoop or tablespoon, drop the batter into the hot oil, forming 8 to 12 hush puppies per batch. (Pro tip: Hold the scoop close to the oil so it doesn't splatter at you when the batter drops in.) Fry, stirring to ensure even cooking, until golden brown, 4 to 5 minutes. Use a slotted spoon to pull a hush puppy out and split it open to make sure it's cooked in the center, then transfer all the hush puppies to a plate lined with paper towels to absorb excess oil. Repeat to fry the remaining batter or store the batter in an airtight container for a couple days.

Serve the hush puppies warm with soft butter and drizzled with honey.

FISHING

There's magic in fishing villages. I travel to them, seek them out, and feel romantic being near wharfs, boats, and industry. I'm not drawn to yachts or fancy leisure boats; I'm drawn to the boats that feed us, boats that symbolize a hard-earned living and a life on the water chasing seafood. I read menus at restaurants and ask questions about the seafood. When and where was it caught? I look for the words "sustainable" and "line caught" and I don't go for the fancier options but for the ones that are frugal, like the outstanding fried catfish at Porgy's Seafood in New Orleans, where chef Marcus Jacobs serves up Des Allemands catfish that are perfectly crispy. I want to taste a region's local oysters or prawns, its crabs, lobsters, or langoustines, the cockles, snails, and mussels. In Spain, I want the freshly oiled and vinegared sardines and the delicious salty anchovies. I seek out authenticity in a place through its food, its proximity to water, and the locals' willingness to use what the sea has to offer them and not settle for the unfortunate farm-raised, perfectly sized fish. And when I'm home on the bayou, I want to catch my own fish, or at least eat the fish procured by my family.

I am drawn to seafood because it is one of our last real wild foods. Unless you are a hunter, most of the food you eat on a regular basis will come from farms and be raised for consumption. One hopes to purchase food based on animal welfare and locality, but generally the meats we consume are raised on farms. Fish and seafood are different. Even farmed crawfish, now part of one of the most successful aquacultures in the United States, are living out their very natural patterns in rice fields—we aren't penning them in or changing their genetic makeup. Most of the shrimp, crabs, oysters, squid, and fish humans consume are wild. It is our duty to understand and protect seafood and our ability to fish for it.

For people like me and my family, fishing is life. It's wrapped up in meditation, necessity, and reverence. Being on the water is a divine act. Fishing is second nature to us and filled with the little things about our existence that we love, cherish, and fight to hold. It is both work and play. A day of fin fishing involves rituals and tiny celebrations, from the readying of the boat to the fresh-baked biscuits and coffee that prelude a fishing trip, the act of fishing, and then bringing back the catch, filleting, then frying a piece of freshly caught fish. Fin fishing, unlike crabbing, oystering, and shrimping, means patiently casting for fish one at a time.

A fishing day can last a long time if you're catching *and* if you're not catching. There is an outstanding will to succeed on the water even if we know the fish have outsmarted us. Sometimes I tell my dad it's time to give up, but he's usually willing to give it another six hours just in case. That's when I start rationing the drinking water. We either chase reds in the shallow water with our trolling motor or head to the old duck ponds for trout. Every fisherman has their spots, and some are very secretive about their favorites. Some of our fishing grounds are right behind the home my dad grew up in. The water and sky are filled with ducks, the levees little hills making the landscape.

We get excited when we start catching, and the boat buzzes. The large reds make hissing sounds when we reel them in, and their ruby scales and classic onyx markings glisten in the morning sunrise. Per the Louisiana Department of Wildlife and Fisheries, we can catch four reds and twenty-five trout. The limits are important so that we don't lose the redfish or trout population and wind up like Cape Cod—named after an industry that was all but destroyed during the height of the "cod wars."

When we hit our limit, we head home. My dad will meticulously clean his boat, put his reels back in order, offload the ice chest, and clean the fish. He puts the fish in a stainless-steel bowl filled with ice and delivers it to my mom, who is ready to pack them in ziplock bags for the freezer, after she's reserved a couple for the fryer. My dad is exhausted after a day of fishing, but he gives the fish table and himself a shower and then we sit down to supper prepared by my mom. Simple fried fish, a plate filled with memories made, and a communion with water. A rite.

SMOKING AT HOME

Most people brine or cure their fish before smoking it. A brine is a salt-and-sugar solution in water that the fish sits in for a couple hours or overnight. A cure is a dry salt-and-sugar mixture that is rubbed on the fish flesh and that the fish sits in overnight or longer. Brines can be seasoned with pepper and herbs to change the flavor of the fish, and cures can be laced with dill and spices. It is a simple process that adds layers of flavor.

If you own a smoker, use it to smoke fish and oysters and whatever you like. But you don't need a fancy smoker to put a bit of smoke flavor on fish or anything that can fit in a stovetop pan. If you want to make a stovetop smoker, here's how.

Preheat the oven to 350°F (180°C). Get a 4-inch-deep (10 cm) hotel pan or a heavy-bottomed pot that can hold a heatproof wire rack. Line the bottom of the pan or pot with a couple layers of aluminum foil. Add two handfuls of wood chips for smoking from a hardware store or online, then insert a wire rack. Place the pan over medium-high heat on your stove; the wood will start to smoke in about 8 minutes. Alternatively, you can use a pastry torch to prelight the wood chips.

Once the chips are smoking consistently, lower raw fish fillets onto the rack. Cover the pan with a sheet of foil, punch a few holes in it, and smoke the fish for about 10 minutes. Remove the fish from the smoker and finish in the oven for about 5 minutes, until cooked through.

NOTE: *Whenever you smoke something indoors, turn on the stove hood vent!*

Smoked Fish Dip

SERVES 8 AS A SNACK

One of the great things you can do with fish of all kinds is smoke it and make a dip to be eaten with crackers or crusty bread. You can also use it like chicken salad or tuna salad in a sandwich. If you are making fish dip for a party or gathering, it can be prepared up to five days in advance and will keep well in the refrigerator; it's tasty and convenient for a picnic or road trip, too.

This dip's texture is more rillette than pâté. I like a crumbly, rustic dip that needs to be spooned onto a piece of toast or a cracker. You can make it creamier by adding more mayo or sour cream. For best results, finely chop the celery and shallots to almost a mince.

NOTES: *You can get smoked fish online and at most grocery stores, or you can ask your fishmonger for a piece of fish that you can smoke yourself. Smoking is one of the oldest cooking techniques and is easy to do.*

Always check fish for bones. Before you put the fish in the food processor, press the fillets through your fingers to flake the flesh while searching for bones to remove.

Chop the smoked fish with a knife or in a food processor. If using a food processor, pulse, pulse, pulse until the fish is airy and finely chopped, not pasty and sticking together. I prefer my fish dip to be coarse and not too cohesive rather than smooth and creamy. Taste the fish to determine how salty it is; add or omit the salt to suit your preference.

Place the fish in a medium bowl and season with the cayenne and black pepper. In another medium bowl, using a wooden spoon, mix together the mayonnaise, lemon juice, and cream cheese until smooth. Add the fish to the mayonnaise mixture, fold together, then add the celery and shallots and stir until combined.

Garnish with the parsley and some pickled onions.

½ pound (225 g) smoked fish (see page 93)

Kosher salt, as needed

¼ teaspoon cayenne pepper, plus more as needed

Freshly ground black pepper

2 tablespoons homemade mayonnaise (page 338)

2 tablespoons fresh lemon juice

1 tablespoon cream cheese

½ cup (50 g) very finely chopped celery

½ cup (70 g) very finely chopped shallots

2 tablespoons finely chopped flat-leaf parsley, for garnish

Quick Pickled Red Onions (page 341), for garnish

Crab Egg and Sweet Pea Rice

SERVES 8 AS A SIDE DISH

On the bayou, we don't need a mysterious creature to see its shadow to know it's spring. We know it's spring when the sweet peas start coming in. This lovely dish is somewhere between fried rice and pilaf: Leftover rice is combined with shrimp or crab butter, crab eggs, and sweet peas. It's a simple dish; you should only taste the minimal ingredients. We serve this rice with fried stuffed crabs or fish collars at Mosquito Supper Club. You could easily make this an entrée by adding lump crabmeat or claw meat.

In a large sauté pan over medium-high heat, melt the shrimp butter. When the butter is foamy, add the shallot and cook for 1 minute. Add the lemon juice and water and stir constantly until a cohesive sauce forms, then simmer for 1 minute. Add the rice and stir for 2 minutes. Add the peas, salt, black pepper, and a touch of cayenne and stir for 2 minutes. Add the crab eggs, parsley, and green onion. Mix thoroughly and serve.

¼ cup (60 g) Shrimp Butter (page 339) or unsalted butter

1 tablespoon very finely chopped shallot

2 tablespoons fresh lemon juice

⅓ cup (80 ml) water

2 cups (400 g) leftover cooked rice, preferably Anson Mills Carolina Gold

1½ cups (220 g) fresh sweet peas

2 teaspoons kosher salt

¼ teaspoon cracked black pepper

Cayenne pepper

¼ cup (40 g) crab eggs

½ cup (30 g) finely chopped flat-leaf parsley

2 tablespoons finely chopped green onion

Fish Cheeks with Green Onion and Parsley

SERVES 4

When fishermen bring in fish and the fish heads are cut off and discarded, it means the delicate fish cheeks are thrown away, too. This is unfortunate because the head has so much flavor with its collars and cheeks, and these parts are excellent in fish stock. Please try to use the whole fish whenever you can (see Note). Fish cheeks, flaky and delicate, take a bit of precision to sear well and get onto a plate in one piece, but I have faith that you can easily prepare these at home. Serve with rice and Fermented Cabbage (page 80).

In a bowl, mix the flour, 1½ teaspoons of the salt, the black pepper, and the cayenne. Dry off the fish cheeks and pass them through the flour mixture; shake off the excess and place on a clean plate until you're ready to fry them.

Heat a large cast-iron pan (one with a lot of surface area) over medium heat for 2 minutes, then add the oil and heat for 1 minute, until a splash of water sizzles in the pan. Slowly add the fish cheeks, being careful not to crowd the pan. When the first side is browned and releases from the pan, flip the cheeks and brown the other side, 2 to 3 minutes per side (the fish is not ready to be flipped until it releases from the pan).

Ladle about ¼ cup (60 ml) of the stock into the pan and give it a little shake and stir to deglaze the pan, scraping up the delicious bits stuck to the bottom. Cook for 3 minutes. The fish is done when a paring knife slides through with no resistance and the internal temperature registers 145°F (63°C) on an instant-read thermometer.

Transfer the fish to a serving plate. Bring the liquid back to a boil and add the remaining ¼ cup (60 ml) stock, the remaining ½ teaspoon salt, and the green onion and parsley. Turn off the heat, add the butter, and swirl to incorporate. Add the lemon juice and swirl again. Spoon the pan sauce around the fish and serve.

¼ cup (30 g) all-purpose flour

2 teaspoons kosher salt

¼ teaspoon cracked black pepper

Pinch of cayenne pepper

1 pound (455 g) snapper or drum (or your local fish) cheeks

2 tablespoons olive oil or canola oil

½ cup (120 ml) chicken stock (page 348), seafood stock, or white wine, for deglazing

2 tablespoons finely chopped green onion

2 tablespoons finely chopped flat-leaf parsley

2 tablespoons unsalted butter, at room temperature

Squeeze of fresh lemon juice

NOTE: *Ask your fishmonger to break down a fish for you and to reserve the cheeks and collar as well as the head and backbone, because the whole fish has many meals to offer.*

Fried Fish Collars

MAKES 4 COLLARS

There is no snack I love better than fish collars. Ask your fishmonger for the collars of grouper, snapper, drum, or whatever fish is swimming in your local waters. The larger fish have meaty collars, and one collar paired with rice and slaw or a summer salad could make a hearty meal. The smaller ones are more snacky. I like to marinate the collars in a bit of buttermilk and hot sauce before frying, but for a simpler approach you can just dry the collars, season them, and press them into a pan with hot oil.

Place the fish collars in a bowl and cover them with the buttermilk. Add the hot sauce and ¼ teaspoon of the salt. Refrigerate overnight or for at least 6 hours.

Prepare a tabletop fryer with oil and heat to 350°F (180°C). Alternatively, fill a large heavy-bottomed pot with 4 inches (10 cm) of oil and heat the oil over medium-high heat to 350°F (180°C).

In a large bowl, season the flour with the remaining 2 teaspoons salt, the black pepper, and the cayenne. Dredge the fish collars in the seasoned flour.

Gently place the fish collars in the hot oil; fry large collars for 5 to 7 minutes on each side and fry smaller collars for 3 minutes on each side. The fish collar is done when a paring knife slides through with no resistance and the internal temperature registers 145°F (63°C) on an instant-read thermometer.

Serve with the lemon wedges.

4 (7- to 10-ounce/200 to 285 g) fish collars, scaled

2 cups (480 ml) whole-fat buttermilk

1 tablespoon hot sauce, preferably Original Louisiana Hot Sauce, plus more for serving

2¼ teaspoons kosher salt

Canola oil or peanut oil, for frying

2 cups (250 g) all-purpose flour

1 teaspoon cracked black pepper

½ teaspoon cayenne pepper

Lemon wedges, for serving

Filé Gumbo

SERVES 8 TO 12

We can trace the distinct origins of gumbo. Filé is made from the dried and ground leaves of sassafras, a tree indigenous to North America. It is an ingredient first used by American Indians. It was used medicinally as well as in cooking and to make root beer, too. Roux is one of the French mother sauces, and okra comes from West Africa.

You can make a gumbo with one or more—or none—of these. In South Louisiana, in the time before refrigeration, people would use filé to thicken gumbos when the okra ran out after the first frost. Once freezers became available, okra could be smothered while in season and frozen to use in gumbos until the following summer. Lots of people made gumbos by eliminating okra and just using filé, and other folks just use roux. You can choose your own adventure for gumbo as long as you understand the roots and the act of sharing. This is how we come to gumbo.

Filé gumbo with shrimp, yellow onions, and boiled eggs is what I ate growing up. The eggs help stretch the dish; this version has no okra and so it is quite thin until it is thickened with filé at the very end. Filé shouldn't be cooked; it has to be added like a garnish—and a little goes a long way.

NOTE: *If you come upon a sassafras tree, I encourage you to make your own filé by drying the leaves and grinding them. It is a fun project, and you will get to experience the umami flavors in the leaves—minty, sweet, and bitter. You can catch notes of root beer but also of thyme and savory.*

¼ cup (60 ml) canola oil

3 pounds (1.4 kg) yellow onions, finely diced

1 cup (100 g) finely diced celery

1 cup (145 g) finely diced green bell peppers

1 bay leaf

½ cup (90 g) diced fresh tomato

3 pounds (1.4 kg) peeled small shrimp

1 tablespoon kosher salt, plus more as needed

½ teaspoon cracked black pepper

¼ teaspoon cayenne pepper

2 tablespoons hot sauce, preferably Original Louisiana Hot Sauce

8 cups (1.9 L) shrimp stock (page 345), chicken stock (page 348), or water

1 to 2 tablespoons filé powder

8 to 12 hard-boiled eggs, peeled (optional)

Cooked rice, for serving

¼ cup (15 g) finely chopped flat-leaf parsley, for garnish

¼ cup (15 g) finely chopped green onions, for garnish

Warm a large heavy-bottomed soup pot or Dutch oven over medium heat for 2 minutes, then add the oil and heat for 30 seconds. Add the yellow onions to the pot and stir, stir, stir. This starts the very long process of browning the onions. Cook the onions for 1 hour, depending on how hot your stove runs, watching them closely and stirring every 3 to 5 minutes. If the onions start to stick too much, add a little bit of water or stock to loosen them, then stir to incorporate the browner onions and scrape up any stuck-on bits from the bottom of the pot. Stir, stir, stir until the onions are deeply caramelized and dark brown.

Add the celery, bell peppers, and bay leaf and stir. Reduce the heat to its lowest setting, cover, and let the vegetables smother together until very soft, with no bite remaining, about 30 minutes.

Add the tomato and stir to combine. Cover and smother for 30 minutes more, until the tomato has completely broken down.

Put the shrimp in a large bowl and season with 1 tablespoon of the salt, the black pepper, cayenne, and hot sauce. Stir the shrimp into the vegetables, cover, and smother for about 5 minutes. Add the stock and stir to combine. Raise the heat to medium to bring the liquid to a simmer, then reduce the heat so the gumbo is just barely at a simmer and cook, uncovered, for 45 minutes more.

Taste the gumbo: Does it need more salt or heat? Adjust as needed. Ladle the gumbo into serving bowls and top each with ½ teaspoon filé powder, a boiled egg (if desired), and a tablespoon or two of rice. Garnish with some parsley and green onions.

Gumbo keeps for 1 week in the refrigerator or 3 months in the freezer.

Bunny Carrot Cake

SERVES 12 TO 15

When I was a kid, every year for my birthday, which occasionally coincides with Easter, my mother would make me a yellow Duncan Hines cake in the shape of a bunny and top it with Hershey's cocoa frosting and sprinkles (the round ones, not the long ones). I love this cake, but as I've gotten older, my fondness for carrot cake has grown stronger. The solution is to turn carrot cake into a bunny shape and frost it with a simple cream cheese frosting that combines the best of buttercream and cream cheese but reduces the sugar.

The first carrot cake I ever made was from the pages of *Martha Stewart Living*. I later followed the *Joy of Cooking* recipe, too, and loved how moist the cake stayed because of the oil. Those two cakes are the inspiration for this one and for my love of carrot cake.

Make the cake: Preheat the oven to 375°F (190°C). Grease and flour two 8-inch (20 cm) round cake pans.

In a large bowl, sift together the flour, pecans, baking powder, cinnamon, salt, and a tad of nutmeg.

In the bowl of a stand mixer fitted with the whisk attachment or in a large bowl using a handheld mixer, cream together the raw sugar and eggs on high speed until light and fluffy, 5 to 7 minutes. Scrape down the sides of the bowl and add the oil. Mix until combined. Add the sour cream and vanilla, then mix until just combined. Add the carrots and ginger, then mix until just combined. Remove the bowl from the mixer, add the flour mixture, and fold together with a silicone spatula.

In a coffee cup or small bowl, stir together the boiling water and baking soda, then gently fold into the cake batter. →

FOR THE CAKE

3 cups (280 g) all-purpose flour or Crema pastry flour from Carolina Ground (see Resources, page 359), plus more for the pans

1 cup (120 g) pecans, finely ground

2 teaspoons baking powder

1½ teaspoons ground cinnamon

1 teaspoon kosher salt

Freshly grated nutmeg

2 cups (400 g) raw sugar

3 eggs, at room temperature

1 cup (240 ml) canola oil

½ cup (120 ml) sour cream

1 tablespoon pure vanilla extract

1 pound (455 g) grated carrots (use the largest holes of a box grater)

1½ tablespoons grated fresh ginger

2 teaspoons boiling water

2 teaspoons baking soda

FOR THE CREAM CHEESE FROSTING

1 pound (455 g) cream cheese, at room temperature

4 ounces (115 g) unsalted butter, at room temperature

→

Divide the batter between the prepared pans and bake for 35 to 40 minutes, until the cake springs back and a knife inserted in the center comes out clean. Allow the cakes to cool, then remove from the pans. Once cool, use one of the cakes to cut out two bunny ears and a bow tie. Transfer the cake pieces to a sheet pan or cutting board for decorating (but no need to arrange them carefully—you can frost each piece individually before assembling the bunny).

Make the frosting: In the bowl of a stand mixer fitted with the whisk attachment or in a large bowl using a handheld mixer, mix together the cream cheese and butter until combined. Sift in powdered sugar, ½ cup (50 g) at a time. Divide the frosting evenly between two small bowls. Add the orange zest, lemon zest, grated ginger, and a pinch of nutmeg to one bowl of frosting. Let both frostings rest in the refrigerator for 1 hour.

When the cake is cool, bring out the bowl of frosting with the zest and allow it to warm up for 5 to 10 minutes. If it is not spreadable, give it a spin in the mixer with the paddle attachment. Frost the round cake, ears, and bow tie with a crumb coat, a thin layer of frosting that functions like a paint primer to ready the cake for the final coat of frosting that makes the showstopping finished product. Transfer the cakes to the refrigerator for 1 hour. Remove the cakes and the bowl of plain frosting and assemble the bunny face by placing the ears above the round and the bow tie below (see photo on page 108). Then, using an offset spatula, spread the plain frosting on the bunny cake as a finishing coat. To get a shiny, even finish, wipe down your spatula between coats and heat up the blade of the spatula in a bowl of hot water, but be sure to dry the warm blade thoroughly before you use it.

To finish the cake, create your own bunny face with sprinkles, candies, edible flowers, or herbs. This should be a fun activity; if you have kids, invite them to join in.

Carrot cake gets better with time. Store it, covered, in the refrigerator for up to 1 week; cut slices and let them warm up slightly to loosen up the crumb before serving.

1 cup (100 g) powdered sugar

Zest of 1 orange

Zest of 1 lemon

1 tablespoon grated fresh ginger

Freshly grated nutmeg

Sprinkles, candies, edible flowers, or herbs, for decorating

Strawberry Poke Cake

MAKES ONE 9 BY 13-INCH (23 BY 33 CM) CAKE

I love an icebox cake, and this strawberry poke cake is always on rotation at my family's Easter celebrations. My mom makes it with Duncan Hines white cake mix and strawberry Jell-O. I've given it a bit of a glow-up with white cake made from scratch and a natural alternative to Jell-O, Simply Delish natural strawberry gelatin.

Make the cake: Preheat the oven to 350°F (180°C). Grease and flour a 9 by 13-inch (23 by 33 cm) glass baking dish.

In the bowl of a stand mixer fitted with the whisk attachment or in a large bowl using a handheld mixer, cream together the butter and the lard on medium speed for 1 minute. Scrape down the bowl, add the superfine sugar, and whisk, starting on low speed and gradually moving to high speed, for 5 to 7 minutes, stopping occasionally to scrape down the sides and bottom of the bowl and to clean off the whisk. The mixture will be fluffy.

In another bowl, sift or whisk together the flour, baking powder, salt, and baking soda.

In a small bowl, stir together the buttermilk and vanilla.

Scrape down the mixer bowl really well. With the mixer on low speed, add 1 egg white and let it combine for about 15 seconds, then scrape the bowl. Working in the same way, add the remaining 3 egg whites one at a time until they are all incorporated. (You can place the egg whites in the same small bowl and pour in a little at a time; they naturally stay somewhat separated.) Give the bowl another good scrape, then whip the mixture on high speed for 30 seconds. It will get light and fluffy; do not overwhip or it will start to separate. →

FOR THE CAKE

2¾ cups (360 g) cake flour, plus more for dusting

4 ounces (115 g) unsalted butter, at room temperature, cut into 1-tablespoon pieces

4 ounces (115 g) leaf lard, at room temperature

1½ cups (300 g) superfine sugar (or raw sugar run through a food processor to make it finer)

1 tablespoon baking powder

1 teaspoon kosher salt

½ teaspoon baking soda

1 cup (240 ml) whole-fat buttermilk, at room temperature

1 tablespoon pure vanilla extract

4 egg whites, at room temperature

1 cup (240 ml) hot water

1 small package strawberry gelatin, preferably Simply Delish

½ cup (120 ml) cold water

2 cups (290 g) whole strawberries, for decorating

→

Scrape down the bowl, add one-third of the flour mixture, and mix on low speed just until incorporated, a couple seconds. Add half of the buttermilk mixture, mix until incorporated, and scrape the bowl down. Add another one-third of the flour mixture and mix just until combined. Add the remaining buttermilk mixture and mix just until combined, then add the remaining flour mixture and mix just until combined. Take the bowl off of the mixer and, using a silicone spatula, gently fold in any remaining bits of dry ingredients; you do not want to overmix. The batter should be fluffy and thick, not liquid or runny.

Using the silicone spatula, spoon the batter into the prepared baking dish. Bake on the center of the middle rack, making sure the dish isn't shoved to one side or the back of the oven. After 20 minutes, rotate the cake and bake until the cake springs back when pressed, about 20 minutes. (Depending on how hot your oven runs, it could cook in less time or a bit more.) Transfer the dish to a wire rack, then run a butter knife along the inside edge of the dish to ensure the cake doesn't stick to the sides. Let the cake cool in the glass dish.

Once the cake is completely cool, use a chopstick or similar utensil to poke holes in the cake, about 8 rows of 10 holes each, with some going all the way through and others going down three-quarters of the way through. This will create a marbling effect.

In a small bowl, pour the hot water onto the dry gelatin. When the powder is completely dissolved, stir in the cold water, mix thoroughly, and pour the warm gelatin over the cake. Cover with plastic wrap and set in the refrigerator.

Make the bouillie: In a medium heavy-bottomed pot, heat the milk over medium heat, stirring often so it doesn't scorch on the bottom, until it comes to a boil and gets foamy; you want the foam to start its climb up the pot but not boil over.

Meanwhile, in a medium bowl using a handheld mixer or a whisk, whisk the egg yolks until frothy, slightly thickened, and pale in color.

FOR THE BOUILLIE (CUSTARD)

3 cups (720 ml) whole milk

4 egg yolks

1½ cups (300 g) superfine sugar

½ cup (65 g) cornstarch

½ teaspoon kosher salt

4 ounces (115 g) unsalted butter, cut into 4 pieces and chilled

2 tablespoons pure vanilla extract, or 1 vanilla bean, split lengthwise and seeds scraped out

FOR THE WHIPPED CREAM

1 cup (240 ml) heavy cream

¼ cup (25 g) powdered sugar, sifted

Pinch of kosher salt

Add the superfine sugar and mix well. Add the cornstarch and mix well.

While whisking continuously, slowly pour ¼ cup (60 ml) of the hot milk into the egg mixture and whisk until incorporated to temper the egg (this prevents the egg from scrambling when you add it to the hot pan later). Repeat three times, whisking in ¼ cup (60 ml) of the hot milk each time.

Bring the remaining milk in the pot to a rolling boil over medium-high heat. As soon as it reaches a rolling boil and starts to creep up the pot, add the tempered egg mixture to the pot and continue to cook, whisking continuously, for 5 minutes, until the bouillie is thick. (A handheld mixer is handy here.) Remove the pot from the heat, add the salt, and, while whisking continuously, add the butter one piece at a time and whisk until fully incorporated, then stir in the vanilla until incorporated. Transfer the bouillie to a medium bowl and refrigerate until completely chilled, at least 4 hours and preferably overnight.

Once the bouillie is cold, prepare the whipped cream: Pour the cream into a mixing bowl and chill it in the freezer for about 10 minutes, then add the powdered sugar and salt. Using a stand mixer fitted with the whisk attachment or a handheld mixer, whip the cream, starting on low speed and gradually moving to high speed, until stiff peaks form, about 5 minutes.

To assemble the cake, remove the bouillie from the refrigerator, transfer it to the bowl of a stand mixer fitted with the whisk attachment, and whisk on medium speed until smooth, about 1 minute. Use a silicone spatula to gently fold the whipped cream into the bouillie until thoroughly incorporated. Spread the bouillie cream on top of the cake.

Refrigerate the cake for at least 30 minutes, then decorate the top with strawberries. Serve right away.

WARMTH

———— ·ı·ᷟıı ————

Bayou Shrimp Salad in the Style of Nice *121*

Nanny's Shrimp Boulettes *123*

Creole Tomato Dressing with Boiled Shrimp *126*

Pickled Shrimp *131*

Shrimp and Watermelon Salad *132*

Shrimp Rolls *135*

Fresh Okra, Shrimp, Rice, and Benne *136*

Crab Boil with Potatoes and Corn *145*

Jumbo Lump Crab Salad with Shallot Vinaigrette *146*

Decadent Crab Rolls *149*

Panfried Soft-Shell Crab *150*

Red Crab Stew *155*

Summer Seafood Gumbo *157*

Blackberry Sweet Tarts *160*

Buttermilk Ice Cream *164*

SUMMER ON THE BAYOU celebrates the bounty of the sea and moving slow with your friends and family to make it through heat waves and temperature spikes. Shoes are optional and clothes get lighter. It's also about eating well.

Inland shrimp and blue crabs peak during the heat. When it's time to toss a cast net off a dock and pull up some crab traps, life is about to get delicious. If the crabs and shrimp aren't enough, you can walk the bayou side and pick blackberries and mulberries. Gardens and farmers' markets brim with tomatoes, eggplants, cucumbers, peppers, okra, and melons.

There is no better time to make simply executed meals with minimal ingredients than in summer. Late-afternoon shrimp and crab boils are for lingering over seafood plucked from the waters hours before. Quick panfried soft-shell crab pairs with a cucumber and tomato salad. Shrimp salad is beautiful with snap beans and potatoes. Chilling the wine, beer, and tea is as important—and routine—as picking up the mail.

Summer means slow and simple meals with unfussy ingredients that don't need much to accentuate their forms: shrimp tossed in dressing and tucked away in rolls; a boiled crab claw dipped in drawn butter. An herby shrimp and watermelon salad with the precise amount of spice to make you sweat and cool you down but not weigh you down. We also make room for the occasional weekly gumbo because things aren't quite right without leftover gumbo in the icebox.

Bayou Shrimp Salad in the Style of Nice

SERVES 8

Nice, France, is a coastal town much like towns on the Gulf Coast in the sense that it sits on the sea and is blessed with an array of seafood from its waters. All the ingredients in a Niçoise salad can be found on the counters and in the refrigerators of any good bayou Cajun home in summer. When the temperature is in the high nineties, we want the stove to be on as little as possible, and we want to eat light meals. So why not put the tomatoes and green beans from our summer gardens, the potatoes that we got from our friend up the bayou, local eggs, and leftover boiled shrimp all together on a platter and feast?

The key to this salad is to cook each part separately, dress and season each part separately, then assemble the parts and eat as one. The recipe calls for boiled shrimp, hoping you have leftovers in the fridge. If you don't, you can quickly boil some. Serve this salad with a side of olives and some crusty bread, perhaps a couple cheeses, and wine.

Wash and dry the green beans. Then top them, tail them, and snap them (remove the very top and bottom and break them in half). If the beans are large, I would slice them lengthwise also. If they are small, you can leave them whole.

Bring a large pot of salted water to a boil over high heat. Fill a large bowl with ice and water. Carefully add the beans to the boiling water and blanch for 30 seconds, then immediately transfer them to the bowl of ice water. (Keep the hot water in the pot; you'll use it later.) Line a sheet pan with a clean dish towel, then remove the beans from the ice water and set them on the towel to drain.

In a small bowl, mix the beans with 1 tablespoon of the shallot, ½ teaspoon salt, a turn of pepper, and 2 tablespoons of the vinegar. Let sit for about 15 minutes, then add 2 tablespoons of the olive oil and toss. →

6 ounces (170 g) fresh green beans

Kosher salt

2 tablespoons finely minced shallot or whites of a green onion

Cracked black pepper

3 tablespoons red wine vinegar

5 tablespoons (75 ml) olive oil, plus more for serving

2 pounds (910 g) small red potatoes

6 eggs, at room temperature

12 ounces (340 g) cherry tomatoes (about 2½ cups), cut in half, or 1 pound (455 g) ripe tomatoes, cut into wedges

1½ pounds (680 g) peeled boiled medium-to-large shrimp (see page 340)

1 lemon, for squeezing

Leaves from 6 parsley sprigs, for garnish

Return the bean blanching water to a boil and cook the potatoes until a fork can easily pierce them, about 10 minutes. Use a slotted spoon to remove the potatoes (keep the water boiling) and set them aside on a tray to cool completely. Cut the cooled potatoes into bite-size pieces and place them in a small bowl with 1 tablespoon olive oil, 1 teaspoon vinegar, ½ teaspoon salt, and a touch of pepper.

Gently lower the eggs into the pot of boiling water. Immediately set a timer for 7 minutes, and refresh the bowl of ice water, if needed. Remove the eggs promptly at 7 minutes and plunge them into the ice bath to cool completely. Then peel them and cut in half lengthwise with a sharp knife. Sprinkle on a little salt and pepper and set aside.

In a medium bowl, sprinkle the tomatoes with a bit of salt and pepper, then pour 1 tablespoon olive oil and 1 teaspoon vinegar over them.

In a large bowl, combine the shrimp, the remaining 1 tablespoon shallot, 1 teaspoon vinegar, and 1 tablespoon olive oil. Season with salt and pepper and mix with tongs.

Arrange the ingredients on a large platter so everyone can serve themselves what they like. Top the whole platter with another drizzle of olive oil and a generous squeeze of lemon juice. Season with salt and pepper and garnish with the parsley leaves. Serve immediately.

Nanny's Shrimp Boulettes

SERVES 8 AS A SNACK

There are many different versions of seafood balled up in some manner and fried: croquettes, beignets, boulettes, fritters, and other likenesses. All around the world, people like to fry little bits of food, dip them in sauces, and consume. Boulettes are usually a way of using up odds and ends; this recipe is from my late nanny, my godmother. It binds simply with potatoes.

NOTES: *It is essential to dry the shrimp and potatoes really well. If you don't, the batter will not fry up but will steam instead and not hold together precisely how you want it. I dry my shrimp with a clean dish towel or paper towels. You could also place the shrimp in a single layer on a towel and leave them uncovered in the refrigerator overnight to dry them a bit more.*

This recipe should be made only with a meat grinder: either an old-fashioned hand-crank one or an attachment to your KitchenAid mixer. Avoid using a food processor; you won't get the right texture.

Dry the shrimp with a clean dish towel or paper towels. You want the shrimp to be as dry as possible.

In a large bowl, combine the potato, bell pepper, celery, green onion, parsley, salt, black pepper, cayenne, and hot sauce. Add the shrimp. Toss to distribute the ingredients evenly. Using an old-fashioned meat grinder or a KitchenAid attachment, grind the mixture together. It's ready when you do not see any chunks of vegetables; the boulette mixture should be a homogenous paste.

Prepare a tabletop fryer with oil and heat to 375°F (190°C). Alternatively, fill a large heavy-bottomed pot with 4 inches (10 cm) of oil and heat the oil over medium-high heat to 375°F (190°C). →

1¼ pounds (570 g) peeled and deveined small or medium shrimp

1 cup (170 g) grated russet potato, squeezed in a towel like a tourniquet to remove all moisture

¼ cup (35 g) coarsely chopped green bell pepper

¼ cup (25 g) coarsely chopped celery

2 tablespoons coarsely chopped green onion

2 tablespoons coarsely chopped flat-leaf parsley

1½ teaspoons kosher salt, plus more as needed

⅛ teaspoon cracked black pepper, plus more as needed

⅛ teaspoon cayenne pepper, plus more as needed

1 tablespoon plus 1 teaspoon hot sauce, preferably Original Louisiana Hot Sauce, plus more as needed

Peanut oil, for frying

There are many schools of thought as to shaping the boulettes; you can use two spoons or a small (#100) cookie scoop to form a ball of the boulette mix no bigger than the diameter of a quarter. Or you can use a fork and the finished boulette will look organic and more like a pakora. Either way, carefully drop the mixture into the hot oil. Fry a tester boulette for about 6 minutes, stirring it around occasionally until evenly golden brown on the outside. Transfer the boulette to paper towels or a brown paper bag to absorb excess oil and let it cool. Taste the boulette: Does the mix need more salt? More pepper or more heat? If so, add more salt, black pepper, cayenne, or hot sauce to your liking—I like boulettes to have a slightly vinegary taste, and hot sauce gives them that flavor. There is no one perfect formula. You have to taste your mix every time.

Once you've adjusted your mix, drop about 15 balls at a time into the hot oil and fry until golden brown, about 6 minutes. Transfer the boulettes to paper towels or a brown paper bag to drain briefly, then serve them immediately, letting them cool only long enough that they don't burn your mouth.

NOTE: *The boulette mix will keep, covered, in the refrigerator for a couple of days. The salt may make the mix sweat and look a little watery, but it will still be fine to fry. If making it ahead of time, add the salt right before frying.*

Creole Tomato Dressing with Boiled Shrimp

SERVES 8 AS A SNACK

The French and my Cajun French dad eat many things with aioli, and down the bayou we think mayonnaise is a great condiment for shrimp, cucumbers, fried seafood, boiled seafood, and just about anything else. When I was growing up, we always had the store-bought variety in the icebox, so I was astonished later on in life when I learned how simple it was to make mayonnaise from scratch. Creole tomato dressing is an easy condiment made with a mayonnaise base that can be used as a dip or dressing on salads. It pairs perfectly with boiled shrimp; add a side of celery sticks and some Ritz or saltine crackers and you have a proper snack during the summer months.

1 very ripe small tomato, cut in half

2 cups (400 g) homemade mayonnaise (page 338)

1½ teaspoons cracked black pepper

2 garlic cloves

1 teaspoon kosher salt

1½ pounds (680 g) boiled large shrimp (see page 340)

Thinly sliced green onion, for garnish

Squeeze the tomato to remove any excess liquid, and discard (or drink!) the liquid. Place the tomato, mayonnaise, pepper, garlic, and salt in a food processor and pulse until completely combined and smooth. Taste and adjust the seasoning.

Garnish the dressing with green onion and serve alongside the boiled shrimp, for dipping.

Store extra dressing in an airtight container in the refrigerator for up to 1 week.

Pickled Shrimp

SERVES 8

I learned how to prepare pickled shrimp from the highly decorated New Orleans chef Susan Spicer, and she learned it from a cook of hers. I made it for the first time out of the pages of her cookbook for a party my brother was attending. He needed to bring a dish and asked if I could make one. I remember I cut the shrimp into bite-size pieces, and I think he almost passed out. I'm sure the guests loved it all the same.

Pickled shrimp is a Low Country dish and not Cajun, but you see this kind of preparation anywhere seafood is prevalent. It is simply shrimp mixed with oil, acid, and herbs, like the classic Sicilian preparation of raw fish. It keeps for a while in the refrigerator and is perfect for picnics and snacking during summer. You can use leftover boiled shrimp for this preparation or quickly parcook shrimp; you don't want to use overcooked shrimp or the acid will make them mushy.

In a large bowl, mix together the olive oil, lemon juice, lime juice, grapefruit juice, sugar, Dijon mustard, garlic, salt, black pepper, bay leaves, and red pepper flakes. Mix in the shrimp. Refrigerate for 15 minutes to 1 hour, then serve, garnished with parsley stems, pickled mustard seeds, and pickled red onions. Serve with a baguette or toast.

1 cup (240 ml) olive oil

3 tablespoons fresh lemon juice

2 tablespoons fresh lime juice

2 tablespoons fresh grapefruit juice

2 tablespoons raw sugar

2 teaspoons Dijon mustard

2 garlic cloves, minced

2 tablespoons kosher salt

½ teaspoon cracked black pepper

2 bay leaves

Pinch of red pepper flakes

1½ pounds (680 g) peeled boiled medium-to-large shrimp (see page 340)

1 tablespoon finely chopped parsley

Pickled Mustard Seeds (page 341)

Quick Pickled Red Onions (page 341)

Baguette or toast, for serving

Shrimp and Watermelon Salad

SERVES 8

What a perfect combination for summer: fresh herbs and in-season shrimp and watermelon. I've served this salad in many different forms at many different restaurants in my career. I've also made it on our beach vacations and during summer, when the heat is unbearable and light fare is in order. People love the sweet, cold watermelon, fresh basil and mint, and delicious shrimp dressed with a garlicky lime vinaigrette. Here's a version I distilled from the original—a salad I learned in the Napa Valley from chef Kelly McCown. I love its Vietnamese flavors, which I am accustomed to in New Orleans— we are lucky to have a thriving Vietnamese population.

Make the vinaigrette: Place the lime juice, oil, fish sauce, jalapeño, sugar, garlic, and salt in a blender and blend until combined. The vinaigrette will need to be stirred again right before use.

Assemble the salad: In a large bowl, toss the shrimp and watermelon with the vinaigrette, then season with salt and pepper. Transfer the mixture to a platter and top with the basil, mint, jalapeño rings, and peanuts and serve.

FOR THE VINAIGRETTE

½ cup (120 ml) fresh lime juice

⅓ cup (80 ml) peanut oil

¼ cup (60 ml) fish sauce

1 jalapeño or 3 Thai bird chiles, stems removed

2 tablespoons raw sugar

2 tablespoons chopped garlic

1 teaspoon kosher salt

FOR THE SALAD

1½ pounds (680 g) peeled boiled medium-to-large shrimp (see page 340)

4 cups (600 g) cubed and seeded watermelon

1 teaspoon kosher salt or Maldon coarse salt

¼ teaspoon cracked black pepper

¼ cup (15 g) torn fresh basil

¼ cup (15 g) torn fresh mint

1 jalapeño or Thai bird chile, thinly sliced into rings

¼ cup (40 g) chopped toasted peanuts

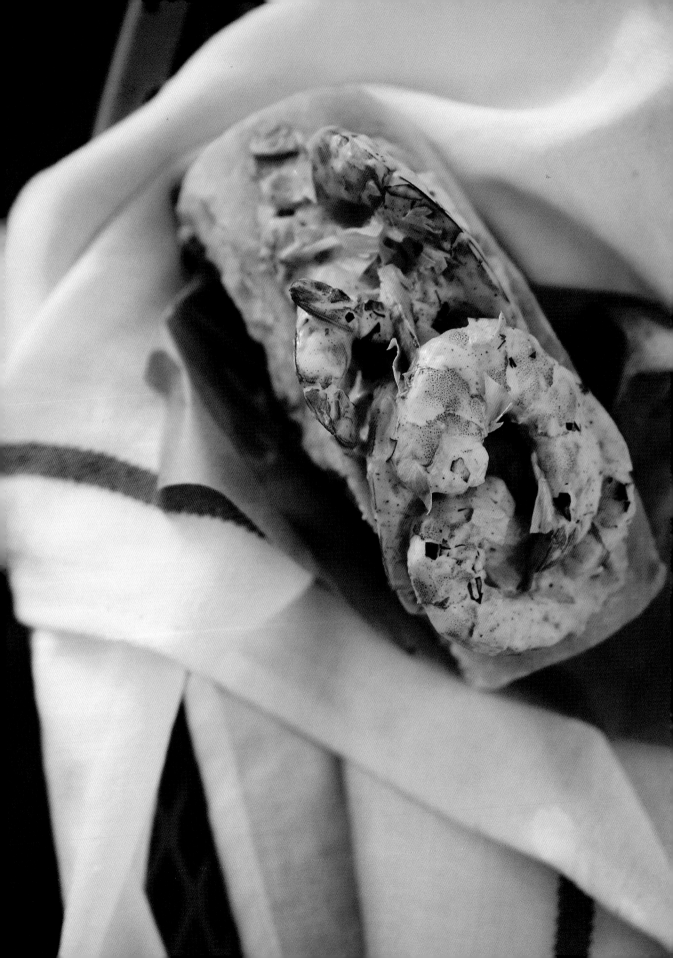

Shrimp Rolls

SERVES 8

Summer is about easy meals put together with little effort and shared with friends. Shrimp rolls are perfect for a gathering, whether as an appetizer or the entrée. You don't need much to make them. Use a soft white roll or the bread you would use for a lobster roll; Texas toast works well, too. A shrimp roll and a bag of potato chips with a glass of natural white wine is high cuisine in my neck of the woods.

Put the mayonnaise in a medium bowl and stir it a little to smooth it out. Mix in the buttermilk and mustard. Add the shrimp, celery, parsley, green onion, and lemon zest, then season with the hot sauce, salt, cayenne, paprika, and a tad of black pepper. Mix everything together. Taste the shrimp and adjust the seasoning.

Heat a large skillet over medium-high heat for 1 minute. Working in batches, spread soft butter on the rolls and place them cut-side down in the pan; toast for 1 to 2 minutes. Repeat until all the rolls are toasted, then fill them with the shrimp mixture and serve immediately.

½ cup (100 g) homemade mayonnaise (page 338)

2 tablespoons whole-fat buttermilk

1 teaspoon Dijon mustard

1½ pounds (680 g) peeled boiled medium shrimp (see page 340)

¾ cup (70 g) finely sliced celery hearts with leaves

2 tablespoons finely chopped flat-leaf parsley

2 tablespoons thinly sliced green onion

Zest of 1 lemon

1 teaspoon hot sauce, preferably Original Louisiana Hot Sauce

1 teaspoon kosher salt

¼ teaspoon cayenne pepper

¼ teaspoon paprika

Cracked black pepper

4 ounces (115 g) unsalted butter, at room temperature, for buttering the rolls

8 large rolls (split-top hot dog buns are perfect)

Fresh Okra, Shrimp, Rice, and Benne

SERVES 8

Add this dish to your repertoire for when the heat is so oppressive that eating a heavy meal seems like bad medicine. The flip side of hot weather is that the farmers' market is brimming with great fresh produce. Or you may be growing most of this recipe's ingredients in your own backyard.

This dish starts the same way most Cajun dishes do: with yellow onions, bell peppers, and celery cooked down until their flavors marry. It's then mixed gently with fresh okra and served with nutty rice, if you like. I like to include a medium-size ripe tomato too soft for salad but perfect for smothering. I pull it apart with my hands and add its flesh and juices to the pot. I started using rice from Anson Mills at Mosquito Supper Club because we can trace its identity and know it's grown naturally. Its roots tell a story we want to share. This dish is a fresh alternative to a heartier stew or étouffée.

Warm a large heavy-bottomed sauté pan over medium-high heat for 2 minutes, then pour in the oil. Add the yellow onions, stir, reduce the heat to medium-low, and cook until they are translucent and just starting to turn golden brown, about 20 minutes. Add the tomato, bell pepper, celery, bay leaf, and thyme. Reduce the heat to its lowest setting and cook, covered, until the celery and bell pepper have lost their bite and the tomato has begun to fall apart and smother, about 40 minutes.

In a medium bowl, combine the shrimp with the salt, black pepper, cayenne, and hot sauce.

Move the vegetables in the pan over to one side, turn the heat up to medium-high, and add the shrimp and garlic. Cook the shrimp for 2 minutes on one side, then flip and cook for 2 minutes on the other. Then stir everything in the pan together, add the stock, reduce the

2 tablespoons canola oil or olive oil

2 cups (250 g) finely diced yellow onions

1 cup (180 g) torn tomato pieces

½ cup (75 g) finely diced green bell pepper

½ cup (50 g) finely diced celery

1 bay leaf

4 thyme sprigs

1½ pounds (680 g) peeled medium-to-large shrimp (reserve the heads for stock; see page 345)

1 tablespoon kosher salt, plus more as needed

½ teaspoon cracked black pepper

⅛ teaspoon cayenne pepper

1 tablespoon plus 1 teaspoon hot sauce, preferably Original Louisiana Hot Sauce

1 tablespoon finely chopped garlic

1 to 1½ cups (240 to 360 ml) shrimp stock (page 345), chicken stock (page 348), or water

¼ cup (30 g) benne seeds, preferably from Anson Mills

heat to medium, and cook for 4 minutes, letting everything marry while some of the stock cooks off.

Warm a cast-iron skillet over medium heat for 1 minute, then add the benne seeds and cook until they are fragrant, 3 to 4 minutes. Move the pan frequently, shaking the seeds up a lot. Transfer the seeds to a small bowl.

Anoint the rice with the butter and a touch of salt, stir to combine, and divide among individual bowls. Scoop the shrimp and vegetables over the rice. Top with the okra, parsley, green onions, and crunchy toasted benne seeds.

3 cups (600 g) cooked rice, preferably Anson Mills Carolina Gold, kept warm

1 tablespoon unsalted butter

16 small okra pods (114 g), thinly shaved

2 tablespoons finely chopped flat-leaf parsley

¼ cup (15 g) finely chopped green onions

WATER GIVES, WATER TAKES

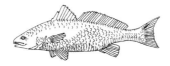

As seen from space, Earth is a water planet. The amount of land is small compared to the magnitude of water lapping its shores, and the vast majority of that water is salt water. The small amount of fresh water available to us is our lifeline, quenching our thirst, nourishing our plants, sustaining our fields, and keeping the natural world in balance. Water is indispensable, holding the livelihood and traditions of generations of fishermen. Fresh water, brackish water, and salt water are three defining factors that control South Louisiana's fishing food chain. Everywhere I look I see water.

Though located on the shores of the Gulf of Mexico, Cajun country shares only some of the common cultural bonds of the South. We are our own island. The Mississippi River drains from thirty-two states and two Canadian provinces, carrying snow and rain down to the Gulf, depositing sediment along the way. That sediment forms the Delta region, on which American Indians and a whole network of immigrants settled, including the group that would become known as Cajuns. This environmental Eden evolved into estuaries, marshes, swamps, basins, brackish waters, and freshwater and saltwater habitats. From these habitats comes a cornucopia of seafood.

Humans tried to tame one of the greatest rivers in the world—an engineering project that changed the course of the river so that the port city of New Orleans could thrive. Levees provided for more human habitation, and diversions helped the city grow, but diversion also robbed the Delta region of much-needed sediment to build land. Because of the oil fields and hurricanes, humans are losing. On Louisiana's coast, our relationship with water is fundamental but complicated: We crave it and fear it.

We are now seeing hurricane seasons unlike in the past. The coast is battered every year by stronger storms that organize themselves and draw power from the warm waters of the Gulf astonishingly quickly. In twenty-four hours, a Category 1 storm can turn into a monster Category 5, drifting hauntingly in the waters south of the Mississippi River, then taking its pick of the communities in its path. The former barrier islands that protected communities and coastline have been ravished by salt water and subsidence.

Besides hurricanes, salt water has been encroaching on South Louisiana's shoreline and making its way up man-made canals and bayous, inundating swamps and marshes, altering the landscape. One day we find brackish fish and the next day a freshwater variety. One day brown shrimp and the next only white. Oyster beds flourishing with perfect salinity and then not a mollusk to harvest.

Although Cajun and bayou cuisines have been shaped by the traditions of American Indians, Acadians, Africans, Europeans, and many more who settled here, there is something unique about the cuisines of South Louisiana—perhaps because of our complicated relationship with water, perhaps because of our expansive cuisine developing rapidly over the past three hundred years with influences from so many places, both high cuisine and peasant cooking, or perhaps because of the resiliency of the people who have lived along the edge.

We are living the mistakes of the past and trying to survive the present moment, wondering what our future is and how we can preserve what's left of South Louisiana. If the water rises and the people are gone, then the story of a tiny fishing community pushing out seafood for the country becomes a fiction, due to the impossibility of living sustainably off what was once one of the nation's greatest fisheries.

Cajuns are once again on the verge of massive displacement. The Acadians saw it when the British expelled them from the Canadian Maritimes; American Indians saw it from the colonization of the North American territories; and enslaved Africans experienced it as they were torn from their homes. These dispersions created the foodways we know; now they are in peril. We struggle against nature to preserve more than three hundred years of change and culture.

Water is bittersweet. We ultimately cannot control it. With all these factors, Cajuns still live along the bayou. We celebrate living here, and we rise through the hardships and survive them. We look for those tiny miracles, those tiny celebrations that keep us joyous and bound to this place. Our food, our lives, and our memories depend on them.

Crab Boil with Potatoes and Corn

SERVES 8

Boiled crabs create a slow eating experience where the food demands work; no one can fly through the peeling of crabs, which requires patience but is well worth the effort. You'll want to round out the meal with potatoes, corn, lemon aioli, and bay-scented drawn butter.

Place a strainer insert in a 10-gallon (38 L) stockpot and fill halfway with water. Add the onions, celery, lemons, bay leaves, cayenne, peppercorns, mustard seeds, and coriander seeds. Bring the water to a boil over high heat, then reduce the heat to low and simmer until the vegetables are soft and the stock has developed a delicious vegetal, lemon-scented, spicy aroma, about 1½ hours.

Raise the heat to medium-high and return the stock to a rolling boil. While it's heating, rinse off the crabs with cold water from a hose. You can do this in a large strainer; we use what's called a bushel, which holds a lot of crabs or shrimp at one time.

Add the crabs to the stock and use tongs to immediately press all the crabs under the liquid. Cover the pot and let the stock come back to a rolling boil. Once it does, cook the crabs for 15 minutes.

Turn off the heat, add the salt to the pot, and let the crabs soak for 15 to 30 minutes. Taste a crab by peeling one and trying the meat; if you think it needs more seasoning, add more salt and spices. Remove the strainer insert and let the crabs drain, then place them on trays for eating or on a table covered with newspaper.

Replace the strainer in the pot and bring the stock back to a boil. Add the potatoes and boil until they can be pierced with a fork, about 10 minutes, then strain and place them on the table. Replace the strainer once again and boil the corn for 5 minutes. Strain and set on the table alongside the crabs. Serve with the aioli, drawn butter, and crackers.

10 pounds (4.5 kg) yellow onions, peeled and halved

3 bunches celery (about 24 stalks), cut into 4-inch (10 cm) pieces

24 lemons (about 6 pounds/ 2.7 kg), cut in half

24 bay leaves

½ cup (45 g) cayenne pepper

½ cup (70 g) whole black peppercorns

½ cup (55 g) mustard seeds

½ cup (43 g) coriander seeds

48 live medium-to-large blue crabs

2 cups (280 g) kosher salt, plus more as needed

24 red potatoes

8 to 12 ears corn, shucked and broken in half

Lemon Aioli (page 338), for serving

Drawn Butter with Lemon and Bay (page 339), for serving

Ritz crackers and saltines, for serving

Jumbo Lump Crab Salad with Shallot Vinaigrette

SERVES 1 OR 2

Let's face it: There never was a Cajun who set out to make a jumbo lump crab salad in South Louisiana. Cajuns sit down to large piles of crabs to peel. The succulent meat usually never gets past that table, but occasionally the extras get made into crab patties and crab cakes, sometimes crab-stuffed shrimp or stuffed crab. If you have some extra crab or can get your hands on a tub of jumbo lump crab, then this is another perfect summer dish that requires no cooking, just assembling.

This salad graces restaurant menus all over New Orleans and South Louisiana. You must be careful with crab; almost everything overpowers it. This salad calls for a simple broken shallot vinaigrette, basil, and crab eggs to reinforce the richness of crab as a whole.

Make the vinaigrette: In a small bowl, whisk together the vinegar and honey until the honey has dissolved. Add the olive oil, shallot, salt, peppercorns, and red pepper flakes and whisk together vigorously.

Assemble the salad: On a platter, arrange the lettuce, crabmeat, and tomato wedges and season with the salt and black pepper. Spoon the vinaigrette over the lettuce and tomatoes. Crumble the crab eggs (if using) over the salad, then anoint the whole thing with lemon juice. Garnish with the croutons, basil, parsley, and green onion.

FOR THE BROKEN SHALLOT VINAIGRETTE

2 tablespoons apple cider vinegar

1 tablespoon honey

¼ cup (60 ml) olive oil or canola oil

2 tablespoons finely diced shallot

¼ teaspoon kosher salt

Pinch of fine black peppercorns

Pinch of red pepper flakes

FOR THE SALAD

1 small butter lettuce, halved

¼ pound (115 g) jumbo lump crabmeat

1 ripe tomato, cut into wedges

2 teaspoons kosher salt

½ teaspoon cracked black pepper

2 tablespoons (20 g) crab eggs (optional)

Juice from ½ lemon

½ cup (40 g) croutons

Leaves from 4 or 5 basil sprigs, for garnish

1 teaspoon finely chopped flat-leaf parsley, for garnish

1 teaspoon finely chopped green onion, for garnish

Decadent Crab Rolls

SERVES 6

Is there anything more decadent than a crab roll? A lobster roll is indulgent, sure, but lobster is easier to peel than crab. You really need to take your time and know your way around a crab; you need to slide nimble fingers into tiny crevices of cartilage to extract all the meat, then you must go through the crabmeat again to make sure you've picked out all the shells. I heard a rumor that one fancy restaurant would use a blue light to see if any shell had been left behind. I assure you that we don't do that on the bayou; we use our intuition and a lifetime of skill that kids develop from a very young age. The only thing that could make these crab rolls better is if you have female crabs and are able to mix in crab eggs for even more rich goodness.

Like shrimp rolls, crab rolls are a great appetizer or lunch sandwich. Make these on a special occasion in the summer when crabs are abundant and temperatures high.

1 pound (455 g) jumbo lump crabmeat

2 tablespoons (20 g) crab eggs (optional)

1 tablespoon fresh lemon juice, plus more as needed

½ teaspoon kosher salt, plus more as needed

Cracked black pepper

Cayenne pepper

½ cup (120 ml) Drawn Butter with Lemon and Bay (page 339)

6 soft rolls or split-top hot dog buns

4 ounces (115 g) unsalted butter, at room temperature, for buttering the rolls

Working over a medium bowl, gently pick through the crabmeat without breaking apart the crab too much. Remove any shells, then mix together the crab and the crab eggs, if using. Stir in the lemon juice, salt, a tad of black pepper, and a touch of cayenne. Taste the crab and adjust the seasoning. Add the drawn butter.

Heat a large skillet over medium-high heat for 1 minute. Working in batches, spread the rolls with the butter, place the rolls cut-side down on the skillet, and toast for 1 to 2 minutes. Repeat until all the rolls are toasted, then fill them with the crabmeat mixture. Top with a tad more salt and enjoy.

Panfried Soft-Shell Crab

SERVES 4

Soft-shell crabs are a delicacy. At one time, they were a sign of the warmer spring weather, but in Louisiana and along much of the coast, the water these days stays steadily warm and soft-shell crabs have become available for more of the year, a constant reminder of rising global temperatures. Warm temperatures may be great for crabs, but they're not great for our own natural cycles. As esteemed New Orleans chef Frank Brigtsen declared, "Let it be known I'm serving soft-shell crabs in February."

The best thing to do with soft-shell crabs is to clean them and get them in a pan as soon as possible, no marinating or fussy stuff. When panfrying soft-shell crabs, be careful standing near the pan, as the crabs will pop as they release water.

NOTE: *Soft-shell crabs are cleaned while they are still alive, and this is no task for the faint of heart. You can sometimes buy them already cleaned and frozen; these are good but a bit more watery when frying.*

2 cups (250 g) all-purpose flour, plus more for dusting

1½ teaspoons kosher salt, plus more as needed

½ teaspoon cracked black pepper

½ teaspoon mustard powder

Cayenne pepper

4 medium-to-large soft-shell crabs (¼ pound/ 115 g each), cleaned (see opposite page)

½ cup (120 ml) canola oil or peanut oil

Hot sauce, preferably Original Louisiana Hot Sauce, for serving

Lemon wedges, for serving

In a medium bowl, whisk together the flour, salt, black pepper, mustard powder, and a tad of cayenne. Dredge the crabs in the flour mixture, being sure to get every crevice coated with flour, then place them on a floured sheet pan or large platter.

Warm a large cast-iron pan at least 10 inches (4 cm) in diameter over medium heat, then add the oil (it should cover the bottom of the pan) and heat for 2 minutes. Check the readiness of the oil by dropping a drop of water in the pan; it should hiss.

Carefully place 2 crabs in the hot oil one at a time, quickly and with control, so that you don't get splattered with popping oil. Lay each crab down in the pan starting from the end of the crab that's closest to you, then gently set the rest of the crab down moving away from you, toward the back of the stove. This way, any popping oil will mostly direct toward the back of the stove. Once the crabs are in the pan, step away from the oil; it will hiss and whistle, pop, and crack. Let the oil quiet down; this will signal that the moisture is being cooked away and the crabs should be almost done.

Cook medium-size crabs until golden brown, 2½ minutes on each side; allow a little longer, 3 to 5 minutes a side, for busters. Transfer the crabs to paper towels or brown paper bags to absorb excess oil. Repeat to fry the remaining crabs.

Salt the tops again and serve with hot sauce and a squeeze of lemon.

HOW TO CLEAN A SOFT-SHELL CRAB

First remove the gills (the parts that look soft and feathery on the bottom of the crab) by cutting them off with scissors or a sharp knife. Then cut off the flap (the part that determines the sex of the crab) located in the middle of the bottom of the crab: The male has a slender pointy shape and the female has more of a fan shape. Finally, remove the tiny sac that would make the crab taste sandy. The "sand sack" is normally the size of a dime and light pink in color; you'll have to feel inside the crab to find it. Once the crab is clean, you can cut it in half, if you'd like, or fry it whole.

Red Crab Stew

SERVES 8

Eating crab stew means getting your hands dirty. The roux and crab will form a sweet-savory sauce, delivering comfort in each bite. The rice under it will have so much flavor. The stew will linger with the taste of the sea, and so will the meal as you pick each crab and eat until all the sweet meat is devoured.

Unlike a Cajun brown stew, this stew is on the red side, and some would say the Creole side, because it contains tomato. The tomato gives it a clean acidic flavor.

If you want to make crab butter or if you have some in your freezer, then use it for the roux. Otherwise, make your roux with butter, oil, lard, or any other fat. For the liquid, chicken or seafood stock is great, but water will do just fine, too.

Crab stew is perfect with crusty bread. In Chauvin, it's served over cooked rice with a side of something pickled and a crisp green salad.

NOTE: *Ask your fishmonger or seafood purveyor for fresh cleaned crabs. A cleaned crab has been broken down with the top shell, gills, and back flap removed. If you know a crabber who can sell you crabs off the boat, even better. It's best to use small or medium cleaned crabs, but if you only have boiled ones, they will work, too—just use less salt and spices in the recipe and adjust as needed at the very end.*

4 ounces (115 g) unsalted butter

½ cup (65 g) all-purpose flour

2½ pounds (1.1 kg) yellow onions, finely diced

1 tablespoon plus 2 teaspoons kosher salt, plus more for the roux

2 garlic cloves, finely diced

½ cup (75 g) finely diced green bell pepper

½ cup (50 g) finely diced celery

1 large ripe tomato, coarsely diced

3 pounds (1.4 kg) small or medium cleaned crabs (about 12; see Note)

1 teaspoon cracked black pepper

¼ teaspoon cayenne pepper

¼ cup (60 ml) hot sauce, preferably Original Louisiana Hot Sauce, plus more as needed

1 bay leaf

1 quart (960 ml) unsalted chicken stock (page 348) or water

Lemon wedges, for serving (optional)

Cooked rice, for serving

¼ cup (15 g) finely chopped flat-leaf parsley, for garnish

¼ cup (15 g) finely chopped green onions, for garnish

To make the roux, warm a large heavy-bottomed soup pot, 8-quart (7.5 L) skillet, or Dutch oven over medium heat for 2 minutes, then put the butter in the pan. When it melts a little, stir in the flour and cook, stirring continuously with a wooden spoon, until the roux is a little darker than café au lait, closer to the color of peanut butter—10 to 15 minutes, depending on how hot your stove runs and how well your pan conducts heat. When making a roux, you need to commit to it. Don't walk away; focus on stirring your roux. Put on an audiobook or, better yet, meditate and stir, listening for the roux's cadence: In the beginning it bubbles and hisses, then it quiets down and the bubbles become smaller as the moisture cooks out and the roux browns. It's a lovely symphony of sound and scent for the senses.

Gently add the yellow onions and a dash of salt and stir to combine. (Be careful to avoid splattering the roux when adding the onions— this is when folks sometimes burn themselves.) Cook, stirring occasionally, until the onions are soft and translucent, about 15 minutes.

Add the garlic and stir, giving the garlic a couple minutes to release its aroma. Stir in the bell pepper, celery, and tomato. Reduce the heat to low, cover, and let the vegetables smother together until very soft, with no bite remaining, 20 to 25 minutes, stirring halfway through to ensure even cooking.

Meanwhile, put the crabs in a medium bowl and season with the salt, black pepper, cayenne, hot sauce, and bay leaf. Using tongs, toss the crabs to coat them evenly. Set aside at room temperature to marinate while the vegetables cook.

Once the vegetables have no more crunch to them, add the crabs, stir, and smother everything together for 5 minutes. Add the stock and stir. Bring the liquid to a boil, uncovered, over medium-high heat, then reduce the heat to maintain a simmer for about 1 hour, so that the flavors marry. You want to reduce the stew's liquid by a quarter or half, depending on how thick you want your stew.

Taste the stew: Does it need more salt or black pepper? Add some. Does it need more heat? Add cayenne. Does it need acid? If so, add hot sauce or a squeeze of lemon.

Serve the stew over rice and garnished with the parsley and green onions. Expect to use your hands to pick through the crab to get to the sweet crabmeat.

Summer Seafood Gumbo

SERVES 8 TO 10

Summer gumbo should be spicy so you sweat and become one with the temperature outside. When I taught a gumbo class at the New Orleans Center for Creative Arts, I made a simple gumbo three ways: a shrimp okra gumbo, a shrimp okra gumbo with a roux, and a shrimp gumbo with filé. Each slightly different, each a practice in gumbo styles. We tasted and tasted, each person selecting their favorite and explaining what they liked about it and why. The students noticed the subtle differences in each version and how the dish could change with the addition of thickeners, okra, filé, and roux—a voyage from Africa and France to South Louisiana. At the end we mixed all the gumbos together, and I said, "This is New Orleans and South Louisiana."

This gumbo is a brothy seafood stew using both okra and roux. The combination of roux and crabs makes magic, and you can certainly sprinkle a little filé on top.

NOTES: *This gumbo is made with smothered okra. Okra takes some time to smother correctly. You will need 12 hours just to prepare the okra before you start the gumbo.*

Gumbo is always better the next day. If you're having a dinner party, cook the gumbo the night before. Place the gumbo in a heatproof container and chill it in the sink by surrounding it with ice; refrigerate once chilled. The next day, pull the gumbo out several hours in advance of serving it. Let it come almost to room temperature, then transfer it to a pot and slowly *bring it up to a simmer. If you blast your gumbo at high temperatures to reheat it, you'll destroy the flavor nuances you worked hard to create.*

Warm a large heavy-bottomed soup pot or Dutch oven over medium heat for 1 minute, then add the oil and heat for about 20 seconds. Stir in the flour and cook, stirring continuously, until your roux is

---

1 cup (240 ml) canola oil

1 cup (125 g) all-purpose flour

4 pounds (1.8 kg) yellow onions, finely diced

1 cup (240 g) Smothered Okra (page 344)

3 bay leaves

2½ cups (250 g) finely diced celery

1½ cups (220 g) finely diced green bell peppers

1 ripe tomato

6 small gumbo crabs (1½ pounds/680 g), cleaned and cracked in half

2 tablespoons kosher salt

1 teaspoon cracked black pepper

¼ teaspoon cayenne pepper

2 tablespoons hot sauce, preferably Original Louisiana Hot Sauce

4 pounds (1.8 kg) small shrimp, peeled and deveined

2 quarts (1.9 L) shrimp stock (page 345) or chicken stock (page 348), warmed

Cooked rice, for serving

¼ cup (15 g) finely chopped flat-leaf parsley, for garnish

¼ cup (15 g) finely chopped green onions, for garnish

the color of peanut butter, 20 to 30 minutes. Gently add the yellow onions and cook, stirring occasionally, until the mixture is brown and caramelized, about 40 minutes.

Add the smothered okra and the bay leaves and stir. Reduce the heat to its lowest setting, cover, and let the vegetables smother together for about 10 minutes. Add the celery, bell peppers, and tomato and stir to combine. Cover and smother until the tomato has completely broken down and the celery and bell peppers are very soft, with no bite remaining, about 20 minutes.

Put the crabs in a large bowl and season with 1 tablespoon of the salt, ½ teaspoon of the black pepper, the cayenne, and 1 tablespoon of the hot sauce. Add the crabs to the pot with the vegetables and simmer, uncovered, for 10 minutes.

Put the shrimp in a large bowl and season with the remaining 1 tablespoon salt, ½ teaspoon black pepper, and 1 tablespoon hot sauce. Add the shrimp to the vegetables and simmer, uncovered, for about 8 minutes.

Add the stock to the gumbo and let it simmer and steep for about 1 hour. The liquid may shake a bit and tiny bubbles may rise from the bottom of the pot to the surface, but you do not want your gumbo to boil.

Taste the gumbo and adjust the seasoning. Serve the gumbo over rice, garnished with the parsley and green onions.

Blackberry Sweet Tarts

MAKES FOUR 5-INCH (13 CM) TARTS

You can't have tasty berries without consistently hot weather, and so I'll sweat a little because nothing beats cooked wild berries in a sweet tart dough. This dough bakes more like a cakey sugar cookie than a traditional piecrust, turning golden brown with a crunchy exterior and a soft, forgiving center. The lightly sweetened berries nestle into the sweet dough and become one with it while baking.

NOTE: *For optimal success, move very quickly, as the heat from your hands will inevitably warm up the soft dough and you want it to stay as cold as possible. I use a pizza cutter and an offset spatula or dough scraper as well as a rolling pin to make these tarts. I also roll the piecrust first and stick the shells in the freezer, then I roll the lattice pieces and stick them in the freezer. It's easier to form a lattice or even cheat a lattice with a crosshatch when the pieces are slightly chilled, even if only for 5 minutes.*

Make the filling: In a large bowl, combine the berries, raw sugar, and lemon juice. Let macerate for 1 hour or more so the berries release their juice. Strain out the juice and combine the berries with the tapioca starch and salt.

Make the dough: In a food processor, combine the flour, superfine sugar, baking powder, and salt, then hold down the pulse button for about 10 seconds to combine. Add the butter and hold down the pulse button for another 20 seconds to cut it into the flour. Add the eggs, evaporated milk, and vanilla and process until the dough comes together and forms a ball, about 20 seconds.

Remove the dough from the food processor, divide into four 5-ounce (140 g) pieces and one 8-ounce (225 g) piece, and form each piece into a disk. The 5-ounce (140 g) pieces will become the bottom crusts and the 8-ounce (225 g) piece will be used to make the lattice

FOR THE FILLING

3 cups (420 g) blackberries

½ cup (100 g) raw sugar

2 tablespoons fresh lemon juice

¼ cup (30 g) tapioca starch or cornstarch

¼ teaspoon kosher salt

FOR THE DOUGH

2½ cups (315 g) all-purpose flour, plus more for dusting

1 cup (195 g) superfine sugar

1 teaspoon baking powder

½ teaspoon kosher salt

4 ounces (115 g) unsalted butter, cut into cubes and chilled

2 eggs

2 tablespoons evaporated milk

1 teaspoon pure vanilla extract

1 egg yolk

1 tablespoon whole milk

2 tablespoons coarse raw sugar

Buttermilk Ice Cream (page 164) or whipped cream (see page 113), for serving tops. Place them in a bowl, cover with a clean dish towel, and set in the refrigerator to chill for about 5 minutes.

Preheat the oven to 375°F (190°C).

Assemble the tarts: Working quickly, place one 5-ounce (140 g) disk on a clean, lightly floured surface or between sheets of parchment paper. Roll out the disk to fit your individual tart pans, about 6 inches (15 cm) in diameter. The dough will be very soft and a bit sticky, and you will need to work fast—but it's very forgiving, and you can press it back together if it tears or cracks. Roll out the remaining smaller disks and press them into the tart pans. Divide the berry mixture evenly among the shells.

Roll out the 8-ounce (225 g) disk into a 5 by 16-inch (13 by 41 cm) rectangle with a long side closest to you. Cut thirty-two ½-inch (1.3 cm) strips. Set the strips on a cookie sheet and freeze for 5 minutes. Arrange the chilled strips over the filled shells in a crisscross pattern by placing 4 strips vertically across each tart first and then 4 strips horizontally; no need to weave the strips. After you're finished with the top strips, use your thumbs and forefingers to seal the outer edges by quickly pinching together the edges of the bottom crusts and the lattice and then slightly folding the edges over. It will not look perfect, but this is a rustic dough.

In a small bowl, whisk together the egg yolk and milk to make an egg wash. Brush the tart dough with the egg wash and sprinkle with the coarse sugar. Bake for about 25 minutes, until the fruit filling bubbles over and the crust is golden brown. Serve with the ice cream or whipped cream.

Buttermilk Ice Cream

MAKES 1 QUART (960 ML)

Buttermilk ice cream is the ice cream we spin the most at Mosquito Supper Club. I think it is my favorite ice cream ever. I'm a very simple woman, so a nice scoop of vanilla usually does it for me. But when given a choice between buttermilk and vanilla, I must choose buttermilk. You will need an ice cream maker for this recipe and two days for chilling and freezing the ice cream, so plan ahead. Serve with pie or cookies or just as a simple scoop.

NOTE: *After cooling the custard overnight and adding the buttermilk, you can let the mixture sit for a couple days in the refrigerator to develop more tang.*

6 egg yolks

1 cup (200 g) granulated or superfine sugar

1¼ cups (300 ml) heavy cream

1¼ teaspoons kosher salt

1¼ cups (300 ml) whole-fat buttermilk

In the bowl of a stand mixer fitted with the whisk attachment on medium speed, or in a large bowl using a spoon and elbow grease, whisk the egg yolks until light and frothy, about 6 minutes. Add the sugar and stir or whisk until the mixture thickens.

In a medium heavy-bottomed saucepan, warm the cream over low heat until it just starts to simmer. While stirring or whisking continuously, slowly drizzle ¼ cup (60 ml) of the warm cream into the egg mixture and whisk until incorporated to temper the eggs (this prevents the egg from scrambling when you add it to the hot pan). Then slowly pour the egg mixture into the cream mixture, stirring constantly so that it doesn't stick or scorch on the bottom.

Add the salt to the pan. Increase the heat to medium and cook, stirring continuously, until the custard comes to a simmer and coats the back of a spoon, 5 to 6 minutes. (If you draw a line with your finger through the custard on the back of the spoon, the edges of the line should not bleed back together.) I never take a temperature here, but if you wish to, the custard should register 180°F (82°C) on an instant-read thermometer.

Cool the custard overnight in an airtight container. The next day, stir in the buttermilk until thoroughly combined (see Note). Transfer the mixture to an ice cream maker and churn according to the manufacturer's instructions, then place the ice cream in the freezer overnight to set. It will keep for about 2 weeks in the freezer.

GRACE

——— •·›·‹‹ ———

RESOURCEFUL HOME COOKS THRIVE in making something out of nothing; they can "gather honey from a weed." This isn't an idea exclusive to Cajun cooks; peasant cuisines around the world evolved out of necessity. Frugality helped build Cajun culinary traditions. Bayou cuisine is grounded in yellow onions, bell peppers, celery, rice, potatoes, eggs, salt pork, a plethora of seafood, parsley, and green onions. It is grounded in a bit of grace and ingenuity.

Thrifty cooks can pull together a meal with minimal ingredients and passed-down cooking techniques. Across the globe, families roast chickens, pull the meat and pair it with rice to stretch it, then use the bones to make a stock for many meals to come. My grandmother used oyster water and salt pork to make a soup to feed many kids. To truly be able to make something out of nothing depends on having great ingredients as well. Then you're just nudging them onto a plate. With time-honored techniques, we can push ingredients to release layers of flavor. We can learn to be frugal and eat sustainably in the places we are rooted.

The recipes in this chapter are uncomplicated and thrifty. They are not meat-heavy but are side dishes or light main dishes. The ingredients represent the end of high summer and the hope of fall, a time when refrigerators are spilling over with squash, corn, and eggplant. Perhaps you can make use of a fruit from a nearby tree or the last push of tomatoes from your garden. Frugal meals are the ones I crave, celebrate, and want to eat over and over.

7UP Biscuits

MAKES 12 LARGE BISCUITS

Forget what you know about biscuits and proceed with eyes wide open. This recipe most likely came from the side of a box but has become a family favorite. The original recipe calls for Pioneer baking mix, but you can make your own mix to avoid food additives whose names you can't pronounce. These are the biscuits I have every time I go to my parents' house in Chauvin, the biscuits I eat with blackberry or muscadine jelly before fishing with my dad or having coffee with my mom. They are good the next day warmed up in the toaster, too.

I like to use lard or butter for these biscuits, but they can be made properly with any fat, including duck fat if you have some on hand, or Crisco, if you must.

NOTES: *These are rustic biscuits that come together quickly. Have your ingredients ready to go so your butter melts in the oven while you are putting the dough together. Cut the biscuits with a well-floured knife, bench scraper, or biscuit cutter, methodically placing the tool back in the flour before you make another cut. Move the biscuits quickly to the baking pan and then to the oven. I like to nestle my biscuits together so they help each other rise by leaning and climbing on one another in the oven.*

2 ounces (60 g) cold unsalted butter, cut into small pieces

3¼ cups (405 g) all-purpose flour, plus more for dusting

1 tablespoon baking powder

1 tablespoon raw sugar

2 teaspoons kosher salt

2 ounces (60 g) lard or unsalted butter, chilled

1 cup (240 ml) 7UP

¾ cup (180 ml) heavy cream

Butter and Muscadine Preserves (recipe follows), for serving

Preheat the oven to 425°F (220°C). If your oven runs hot, go for 375° to 400°F (190° to 200°C).

Place the butter in a 9-inch (23 cm) square baking pan and set in the oven so the butter melts. Set a timer for 3 to 5 minutes so you don't forget. Remove once it has melted.

In a large bowl, whisk together the flour, baking powder, sugar, and salt. (You can sift these together, but it's not necessary.) Add the cold fat (not the melted butter) and cut it in with your fingers until it resembles coarse, pebbly meal. →

Make a well in the center of the mixture and add the 7UP and cream. Mix together with a fork just until the dough comes together. The mixture will be very sticky.

Turn the dough out onto a clean, lightly floured surface and shape it into a craggy rectangle with the short ends at left and right. Fold the left side of the rectangle over to meet the right side, then fold the right side over to meet the left. Press the dough (no need to roll it) into a rough 8 by 13-inch (20 by 33 cm) rectangle about 1 inch (2.5 cm) thick.

Using a floured sharp knife or bench scraper, cut the rectangle into four equal parts, flouring the knife each time you make a cut. Divide each part into three biscuits to yield 12 biscuits. I like my biscuits 2 inches (5 cm) wide. Place the biscuits snugly in the pan with the melted butter.

Bake immediately for 20 minutes, rotating the pan after 10 minutes. The biscuits are done when the tops are golden brown and their internal temperature registers 200°F (95°C) on an instant-read thermometer. Remove from the oven, place a clean kitchen towel over the dish, and let the biscuits rest for 5 minutes. Serve warm with butter and preserves.

MUSCADINE PRESERVES

MAKES ABOUT 3 CUPS (840 G)

I used to make deranged amounts of jam—so much that I couldn't give it all away. I would buy enough strawberries to fill a 10-gallon (38 L) ice chest and make jam like the world was ending or I was on deadline with my nonexistent jam company. Now I am more realistic. I make enough for my immediate family for quick eating, because I even stopped canning my jam. I simply put it in a clean jar and place it in the refrigerator; we eat it and then it's gone. If we have extra, we freeze it and later spread it between layers of cake or fold it into frosting. If you'd like to can your preserves, sterilize your jars and lids

1 gallon (about 6 pounds/ 2.7 kg) muscadine grapes, washed

2 cups (400 g) plus 2 tablespoons raw sugar

1 (1.75-ounce/50 g) package Sure-Jell powdered pectin

in rapidly boiling water for 10 minutes beforehand, then follow hot-water-canning techniques by boiling the filled jars for 10 minutes.

NOTE: *Jelly rises in the pan when it's cooking; it starts creeping up like boiled milk—then before you know it, it's all over your stove. So when I encourage you to use an 8- to 10-quart (7.5 to 9.4 L) pot, I'm not kidding. Also, jelly is hot like molten lava, so be really careful when processing it.*

With a paring knife, score each grape with a small slit and place in a large bowl. Add 1 cup (200 g) of the sugar and mix into the grapes with your hands, squeezing the grapes to release the pulp and juice from the skin. Let macerate at room temperature for 1 hour, mashing with a large cooking spoon every once in a while.

Place two small plates in the freezer for a jell test later on.

Transfer the muscadines to a heavy-bottomed 8- to 10-quart (7.5 to 9.4 L) pot, bring to a boil over medium heat, then reduce the heat to medium-low and simmer for about 45 minutes, skimming off any foam that rises to the surface. Strain the fruit through a strainer, pressing against the sides with a wooden spoon until all the juice is released; you'll have about 6 cups (1.4 L) of juice. Discard the solids. Pour the juice back into the pot, bring to a rapid boil, and cook for 5 minutes.

Meanwhile, in a small bowl, mix the 2 tablespoons sugar and 2 tablespoons of the pectin. Add to the boiling juice, return to a boil, and cook for 1 minute. Be careful of the hot liquid now, and watch out for the rising jelly. Stir in the remaining 1 cup (200 g) sugar and rapidly boil for 1 minute, again watching for the rising jelly. Turn off the heat. Spoon a teaspoon of jelly onto a freezer plate, let set for 30 to 45 seconds, then check for doneness: If it sets on the plate, your jelly is perfect. If it runs, boil it a bit more and test with the second freezer plate.

When the jelly is done, ladle it into clean jars and cool, then cover with lids and store in the refrigerator for up to 3 months.

Milk-Soaked Fried Eggplant

SERVES 8 AS A SNACK

This recipe is a quick and shockingly tasty way to treat eggplants. I learned about soaking eggplants in milk from Andalusian recipes that serve the vegetable with cane syrup. The technique is simple, and it completely alters the eggplant: The milk helps temper the raw eggplant bitterness that makes your mouth pucker and adds a creaminess that turns the center of the eggplant custardy. If you can't wait overnight for the full soaking, at least give the eggplants a couple hours to bathe in the milk. With so much Spanish influence in South Louisiana, it makes sense to prepare eggplant in this style as a continuous reminder of our shared history.

1 pound (455 g) globe eggplants

4 cups (960 ml) whole milk

Canola oil or olive oil, for frying

3 cups (375 g) all-purpose flour, plus more for dusting

2 to 3 teaspoons coarse sea salt, for sprinkling

¼ cup (60 ml) cane syrup, preferably Poirier's (see Resources, page 359), for serving

Slice the eggplants into rounds ½ inch (1.3 cm) thick and place in a large container. Cover with the milk, put a plate or something heavy on top of the slices to keep them submerged, and let soak overnight in the refrigerator.

The next day, prepare a tabletop fryer with oil and heat to 350°F (180°C). Alternatively, fill a large heavy-bottomed pot with 4 inches (10 cm) of oil and heat the oil over medium-high heat to 350°F (180°C).

Remove the eggplant from the milk and pour the milk into a shallow bowl. Place the flour in a separate shallow bowl.

Dredge the eggplant first in the flour, then in the milk, and then again in the flour. This is known as double-battering. Set the dredged eggplant slices on a lightly floured platter until you have 6 to 8 to fry. Once a batch goes into the fryer you can start dredging the next batch.

When the oil is hot, fry the slices in batches until golden brown, about 4 minutes per side. Use a slotted spoon to transfer the eggplant to a paper towel–lined tray to absorb excess oil. Let cool for a minute or two, then enjoy sprinkled with sea salt and drizzled with cane syrup.

Fried Potato Sandwiches

MAKES 2 SANDWICHES

There is nothing wrong with white bread and fried potatoes. If you grew up in my household, fried potato sandwiches were a solid meal. Maybe my mom made them because she had run out of everything in the cupboards and my parents were waiting on a check to feed hungry kids, or maybe she made them because we loved to eat them. Either way, this is a simple sandwich that will fill you up.

Place the potato wedges in a bowl and run cold water over them while you heat the oil. Agitate the potatoes a bit in the water by swishing them around; this removes some of the extra starch.

In a sauté pan over medium-high heat, add ¼ inch (6 mm) of oil and heat for about 5 minutes until an instant-read thermometer registers 350°F (180°C). If you don't have a thermometer, carefully place a drop of water in the oil; if the oil pops and sizzles, it is ready.

When the oil is hot, pat the potatoes dry and, working in batches, carefully place slices in the pan. Put in only a few pieces at a time so that the oil temperature stays between 325°F (170°C) and 350°F (180°C). Cook the potatoes until golden brown on both sides, 2 to 3 minutes on each side.

Transfer the potatoes to a paper towel–lined plate or brown paper bag to absorb excess oil. Sprinkle with salt and pepper, then flip over and season on the other side. Let cool for a couple minutes.

Meanwhile, toast the bread. Heat a large cast-iron skillet over medium-high heat. Butter both sides of the bread, then place in the skillet for 2 to 3 minutes on each side. Slather one side of the toasts with mayonnaise, then load the potatoes on 2 slices and top each sandwich with the remaining toast. Serve ketchup alongside for dipping, if desired—just like my siblings and I did as kids.

1 (12-ounce) russet potato (340 g), peeled and cut into flat ½-inch (1.3 cm) wedges

Canola oil, for frying

Pinch of kosher salt

Pinch of cracked black pepper

2 tablespoons unsalted butter, at room temperature

4 slices white bread, such as Texas toast

2 tablespoons homemade mayonnaise (page 338)

Ketchup, for dipping (optional)

A DAY IN AUGUST

August on the bayou means the heat index is above 100, thunder acts passive-aggressive, and rain comes and goes. The humidity is thick. As soon as you walk outside, your clothes stick to you. In the words of Maurice Sendak, we are all cooking pots.

Into this heat and steam, my brother, Leslie, and his wife, Kate, had a new baby. This precious addition to our already large family mesmerized us all, and so their home became holy ground for gatherings in New Orleans. Week after week, I would cross the Mississippi River to catch up on life, see what was growing in their garden, eat meals, hold the baby, and deliver hearty home-cooked lasagnas, gumbos, pastas, and soups to the new parents. Many meals are shared in their cottage kitchen, most made with ingredients foraged from the bayous of South Louisiana and Leslie's garden and cooked by myself or my mother.

Leslie has muscadine vine trellises on fences that surround his oversized city lot. He knows which muscadines are the best; in his opinion, it's the sweetest, darkest muscadines that are almost matte. I think ripeness lies in the eye of the beholder, and my dad and I both love the tart ones, too. Sometimes we eat enough to make our bellies sour. It takes us a while to pick all the grapes, but a possum family can eat every single one in an evening, so you must act swiftly when the muscadines are ready. Maybe that's how muscadines got their nickname: possum grapes. If the muscadines make it past Labor Day, then the grapes are at peak sweetness. That's when I bring them home to macerate and make muscadine preserves and muscadine dumplings.

Leslie trades a few gallons of muscadines for a couple gallons of okra from a musician friend. He picks grapes while my mom and I prep the okra and chat about life. She washes the pods and dries them with a towel, and I cut them into small pieces so we can smother them, discarding the hard okra that have grown too large. She craves a shrimp okra gumbo, and with the shrimp season opening in August, we are in luck. She has just put away a mess of fresh shrimp in the

freezer after my cousin went shrimping days before. In less than thirty minutes, we wash and chop the okra, locate a heavy-bottomed pot in the kitchen, and start smothering the okra on the electric stove.

My mom has only cooked on gas ranges and basically thinks cooking anything on an electric stove is impossible. Standing at the stove, she asks me, "What do we use to get rid of the slime?" I say, "A tomato, Mom," looking at her with questions across my face. This is a tip she taught me many years ago. I have cut and smothered okra with my mom, aunts, and grandmother since I could see above the table. So I am taken aback by this query, and it makes my heart ache. My parents are growing older gracefully. They are in their seventies, humble and active, but my mother has lost two sisters, a brother, a brother-in-law, best friends, and so many other people close to her in recent years.

But for now my parents are healthy, and we are fortunate to have food grown by friends and fished by cousins. So I try not to worry and I cook with my mother while I can. While smothering okra, my mom also makes fried shrimp po'boys from my cousin's freshly caught shrimp. I dress mine with lettuce, pickles, mustard, mayonnaise, a fresh tomato seasoned with salt and black pepper, and a few healthy shakes of hot sauce. The po'boy is so good; I savor each bite, a luxury and presence to crave.

Shaved Persimmons and Greens

SERVES 8

The name Plaquemine was derived from the native *piakemine*, which means "persimmons." The eastern United States was once abundant in persimmon trees, and in Louisiana they were introduced about the time citrus was planted by missionaries from Japan. But constant hurricanes have depleted the persimmon population and threatened orchards in the city of Plaquemine.

In late summer and early fall, we have a couple weeks of persimmon season. We always take the opportunity to use the fruit in a salad or make a cake so we can savor their brief appearance. This salad puts persimmons front and center. Use Fuyu persimmons here; they are nonastringent and delicious. Wait until you are just able to press the persimmon flesh; you don't want it too soft or you won't be able to slice it. The persimmon will be deliciously sweet and pairs well with bitter greens, such as mizuna or arugula, and a slightly sweet vinegar dressing.

NOTE: *Fuyu persimmons are the variety you can eat raw. The Hachiya variety is very bitter and astringent, and you must wait until they are ripe and very soft in order to use them in baked goods or other cooking applications. A ripe Hachiya persimmon will feel like a very ripe tomato, and you can simply scoop out its flesh and bake it into a cake or freeze for another time.*

2 Fuyu persimmons (about ½ pound/225 g)

3 tablespoons finely diced shallot

¼ cup (60 ml) cane vinegar or apple cider vinegar

1 teaspoon cane syrup

1 pound (455 g) mizuna or arugula

3 tablespoons canola oil or olive oil

1 teaspoon kosher salt

Cracked black pepper

½ cup (60 g) Candied Pecans (page 349)

2 ounces (60 g) Parmesan, shaved, for garnish

Cut the persimmons in half and place them flat-side down on a cutting board. Slice them slightly thinner than ¼ inch (6 mm).

In a small bowl, whisk together the shallot, vinegar, and cane syrup.

Place the mizuna in a large bowl. Drizzle the oil over the greens, then add the vinegar mixture. Gently toss with your hands or salad tongs and season with the salt and a touch of pepper. Arrange the persimmons and candied pecans on top, garnish with Parmesan, and serve.

Mirliton Slaw

SERVES 8

Mirliton is a squash or gourd by the name of *chayote* in Spanish. It made its way to New Orleans from the Spanish when the city was a French colony, but it was the Creole French from Haiti who probably dubbed it *mirliton* when they immigrated to New Orleans. It has a hint of cucumber flavor and grows well in Louisiana's subtropical climate.

Mirliton acts like a green papaya, and you can slice it easily for salad. This is a great time to use a mandoline, if you have one. If not, use a sharp knife and take your time breaking down the mirliton, squaring it off and slicing it.

Place the mirlitons in a colander. Sprinkle them with 1 teaspoon of the salt and mix with your hands. Let sit for 20 to 30 minutes to release water.

In a small bowl, combine the yellow onion with the remaining ¼ teaspoon salt, 1 teaspoon of the vinegar, and the sugar.

Transfer the mirlitons to a medium bowl. Squeeze the lemon juice on top and season with the black pepper. Add the onion mixture, tabasco pepper, garlic, oil, cane syrup, 1 tablespoon of the green onion, and the remaining 1 tablespoon vinegar. Using your hands or tongs, toss together gently so you don't break the mirlitons.

Taste and adjust the seasoning. Garnish with the parsley and the remaining 1 tablespoon green onion and serve.

1 pound (455 g) mirlitons (about 2), seeded and thinly sliced about 4 inches long by ⅛ inch wide (10 cm by 3 mm)

1¼ teaspoons kosher salt

¼ cup (35 g) thinly sliced yellow onion

1 tablespoon plus 1 teaspoon cane vinegar or apple cider vinegar

⅛ teaspoon raw sugar

Juice from ½ lemon

¼ teaspoon freshly ground black pepper

1 fresh tabasco or Criolla Sella pepper, Thai bird chile, or jalapeño, seeds removed

1 garlic clove, finely chopped

2 tablespoons olive oil or canola oil

1 teaspoon cane syrup or honey

2 tablespoons thinly sliced green onion

1 tablespoon finely chopped flat-leaf parsley

Corn and Squash Salad with Peaches

SERVES 8

When you're at the farmers' market and staring down a barrel of yellow squash, don't let your spirits fall. This salad is the answer. It combines three unlikely subjects—corn, squash, and peaches—for a delicious summer salad that won't weigh you down. This crisp salad pairs well with crab, fish, shrimp, chicken, and other proteins. It's also effective on its own. The corn gets special treatment with a bit of open-flame cooking, which (bonus) warms your house with the smell of popcorn. Use whatever herbs you have on hand to top the salad. I love dill and mint, but you could include rosemary, thyme, or tarragon or go in a different direction with cilantro and lime. At any rate, this recipe will make your summer squash sing.

NOTE: *A trick for cutting corn kernels off the cob is to stand your corn up in the center hole of a Bundt pan, then use a sharp knife to slice off the kernels so they fall into the pan. After the kernels are off, run the dull side of the knife up and down the cob to release all the milky liquid. Don't let a drop get away.*

Shuck the corn and place on an open gas flame, turning frequently every 30 seconds until the kernels char just slightly, about 7 minutes. Alternatively, you can place the corn in a low broiler setting for 15 minutes, turning every 5 minutes, or char the corn in a cast-iron pan over medium-high heat, turning frequently, for about 10 minutes. Let the ears cool, then cut the kernels into a bowl (see Note).

Add the squash and peach to the corn and toss to combine. Add the vinegar, lemon juice, olive oil, kosher salt, and pepper and gently combine. Top with the parsley, dill, and mint and toss gently one more time. Serve with a sprinkle of coarse salt on top.

1½ to 2 pounds (750 g) ears corn (about 3), to yield about 1¾ cups (255 g) kernels

1 yellow crookneck squash, cut on a bias into 1-inch (2.5 cm) pieces, to yield 2½ cups (about 10 ounces/285 g)

1 peach, halved and thinly sliced

2 tablespoons white balsamic vinegar or apple cider vinegar

2 tablespoons fresh lemon juice

2 tablespoons olive oil

1¼ teaspoons kosher salt

¼ teaspoon freshly ground black pepper

1 tablespoon finely chopped flat-leaf parsley

1 tablespoon finely chopped dill

1 tablespoon finely chopped mint

Maldon or other coarse salt, for garnishing

Corn Maque Choux

SERVES 8 AS A SIDE DISH

Closely related to succotash, a native dish cooked with corn and beans, maque choux is one of the oldest dishes in Louisiana's culinary history. It is an amalgamation of so many different food cultures of the Americas; this version will have you smother the corn and other vegetables. It can be prepared with salt pork or bacon or made vegetarian. I like maque choux as an accompaniment to a nice piece of panfried redfish, but it can serve as a side dish to anything or even be a main dish.

NOTE: *If you ever roast corn on the barbecue pit or over a grill fire and have leftovers, use it to take maque choux to a new level.*

Warm a heavy-bottomed 5-quart (5 L) Dutch oven or skillet over medium heat for 2 minutes, then add 2 tablespoons of the butter. When the butter melts, add the yellow onions and cook over medium-low heat, stirring occasionally, until translucent, soft, golden, and lightly caramelized, about 20 minutes.

Stir in the bell pepper and cayenne pepper, cover, reduce the heat to low, and cook until the peppers are softened, about 10 minutes. Add the garlic, stir, and cook until fragrant, about 2 minutes. Stir in the tomato, cover, and cook until the tomato is stewy and completely broken down, about 8 minutes.

Meanwhile, cut the kernels off the corncobs (see Note on opposite page). Add the corn, cream, salt, black pepper, and the remaining 1 tablespoon butter to the smothered mixture. Stir, cover, and smother together for about 15 minutes to let the flavors marry.

Taste and adjust the seasoning. Garnish with the green onions and parsley and serve.

3 tablespoons unsalted butter

1 pound (455 g) yellow onions, finely diced

¾ cup (110 g) finely diced green bell pepper

½ small fresh cayenne or other hot pepper, seeded and finely chopped

3 garlic cloves, finely chopped

1 ripe tomato, cut into ½-inch (1.3 cm) cubes

8 ears corn, shucked

2 tablespoons heavy cream

1 teaspoon kosher salt, plus more as needed

½ teaspoon cracked black pepper, plus more as needed

⅓ cup (20 g) finely chopped green onions

2 tablespoons finely chopped flat-leaf parsley

Corn, Salt Pork, and Tomatoes

SERVES 8 AS A SIDE DISH

My dad used to take a can of corn and a can of tomatoes, cook them together, and eat it over rice while trawling on a shrimp boat. It was an entrée for tired fishermen who didn't have much time to put a meal together. When my mom was in a pinch, she would make this for him at home and add some smothered onions. A bit of salt pork improves the recipe. And yes, this can be your dinner, but I think it works best as a side dish.

NOTE: *If using bacon instead of salt pork, you may want to drain off some of the bacon fat so the dish isn't too oily.*

Warm a heavy-bottomed 5-quart (5 L) pot or skillet over medium heat, then add the oil and heat for 30 seconds. Add the salt pork and cook, turning as needed to brown it on all sides, about 8 minutes. Add the onions and cook until translucent and lightly golden, about 20 minutes.

Add the corn, salt, black pepper, and cayenne, reduce the heat to low, cover the pot, and let the onions and corn smother together for about 15 minutes. Remove the lid and tear the tomato apart above the pot, letting the pieces and juices drop in. Cover the pot and smother the tomato with the corn for 25 minutes.

Taste the dish: Does it need more salt? Add it. More heat? Stir in some more black pepper and a touch of cayenne. Add the butter, stir again, and serve with hot sauce, if you like.

2 tablespoons canola oil

¾ cup (115 g) salt pork or bacon (see Note), cut into small cubes

2 cups (250 g) finely diced yellow onions

6 to 8 ears corn, shucked and kernels cut off, or 3 (15.25 ounce/432 g) cans corn, to yield about 1 quart (620 g) kernels

1 teaspoon kosher salt, plus more as needed

¼ teaspoon cracked black pepper, plus more as needed

Pinch of cayenne pepper, plus more as needed

1 large ripe tomato

2 tablespoons unsalted butter

Hot sauce, preferably Original Louisiana Hot Sauce (optional)

Shrimp-Stuffed Mirlitons

SERVES 6 TO 8

Mirliton, like many vegetables in South Louisiana, is a perfect vessel for stuffing. Cajuns, Creoles, and folks across the globe have long stuffed vegetables as a way of stretching foods. I've been to my Italian friends' homes and they do this, too, stuffing zucchini with Italian sausage and covering it in cheese, as one example. Around the world and on the bayou, folks cook small amounts of seafood and meat and stretch them with other ingredients to satiate large families.

Most Cajuns boil their mirliton first, but I believe that adds too much water to the flesh of the gourd. It's thus best to bake it instead. If you can't find mirliton, this recipe will work with any gourd, such as larger yellow squash or zucchini.

NOTE: *Buy shrimp already peeled or buy more shrimp than you need and peel enough to make ½ pound (225 g). The quantity will vary based on the size of the shrimp.*

Preheat the oven to 350°F (180°C). Line a sheet pan with parchment paper.

Cut the mirlitons in half and scoop out the seeds. Coat the insides with 3 tablespoons of the butter and season with 1 teaspoon of the salt. Place them on the prepared sheet pan cut-side up and bake until the pulp is soft and can be pierced with a fork, but not so long that the mirlitons lose their shape, about 45 minutes.

Set the sheet pan on a wire rack until the mirlitons are cool enough to handle. Using a spoon, scoop out some of the mirliton pulp, leaving ¼ inch (6 mm) along the skin so the squash can still stand up. (It's okay if a mirliton tears or isn't perfect; once they are stuffed you will nestle them together in a pan so that they stay upright.) Roughly chop the scooped pulp and transfer to a large bowl. Set aside. →

6 mirlitons (about 12 ounces/340 g each)

2 ounces (60 g) unsalted butter, at room temperature

2 teaspoons kosher salt

¼ cup (60 ml) olive oil or canola oil

1 pound (455 g) yellow onions, finely diced

3 thyme sprigs

1 bay leaf

½ cup (120 ml) shrimp stock (page 345), plus more as needed

¼ cup (35 g) finely diced green bell pepper

¼ cup (25 g) finely diced celery

6 garlic cloves, finely chopped

2 green onions, finely chopped, plus more for garnish (optional)

½ pound (225 g) peeled small shrimp (see Note)

¼ teaspoon cracked black pepper

⅛ teaspoon cayenne pepper

1 teaspoon hot sauce, preferably Original Louisiana Hot Sauce

1 cup (45 g) coarse breadcrumbs, made from good bread

1 cup (100 g) grated Parmesan

2 tablespoons finely chopped flat-leaf parsley

Warm a large heavy-bottomed skillet over medium heat, then add the olive oil and heat for 2 minutes. Add the yellow onions, thyme, and bay leaf. Stir to coat the onions evenly with the oil, and cook until they are translucent, caramelizing, and taking on a golden hue, 20 minutes. Stir in a little of the stock to deglaze the bottom of the pan if the onions are sticking.

Add the bell pepper, celery, garlic, and green onions and cook over medium-low heat until the bell pepper and celery have lost their bite, 20 to 30 minutes.

Add the shrimp to the bowl with the reserved mirliton pulp and stir in the black pepper, cayenne, hot sauce, and remaining 1 teaspoon salt. Add this mixture to the skillet of vegetables, increase the heat to medium-high, and stir in the remaining 1 tablespoon butter and the stock. Cook, stirring frequently, until the shrimp turn pink and the liquid from the mirlitons and stock has evaporated, about 5 minutes. There will be some residual moisture but no liquid visibly bubbling or sitting on the bottom of the pan when you stir. You will have about 4 cups (960 g) of filling.

Fill the mirliton shells with about ⅓ cup (80 g) stuffing each (depending on the size of your mirlitons), then top with a liberal amount of breadcrumbs, Parmesan, and parsley. Snuggle together the stuffed squash in one or two 12 by 17-inch (30 by 43 cm) casserole dishes and bake for 45 minutes, or until the breadcrumbs are golden brown. Let cool slightly, garnish with green onion, if desired, and serve.

Camille's Mirliton and Okra Succotash

SERVES 8

Succotash is an American Indian dish featuring the three sisters: corn, beans, and squash. This version of succotash by Camille Cook, chef de cuisine at Mosquito Supper Club, features corn, mirliton, lima beans, and okra, all available as summer and late-summer produce. The key is to cook each element alone, then mix them together.

In a small saucepan, bring the stock and lima beans to a simmer over medium heat, then reduce the heat to low and cook until they are tender. Check for doneness after 20 minutes. If the beans are still crunchy, keep simmering until they are al dente. Drain the beans and set aside.

Warm a large cast-iron or enameled cast-iron skillet over medium heat, then add 2 tablespoons of the oil and heat for 2 minutes. When the oil is shimmering, carefully add some okra in a single layer, working in batches so as not to crowd the pan. Stir to coat with the oil, then season with ½ teaspoon of the salt. Sear in the skillet until golden, 2 to 3 minutes, then flip the okra and cook for 2 minutes more. Transfer to a bowl. Repeat with the remaining okra.

Warm the remaining 2 tablespoons oil in the pan. When it's shimmering, add the mirliton and stir to coat. Sprinkle ½ teaspoon salt on the mirliton and cook, stirring occasionally, until it begins to brown, about 8 minutes total or 4 minutes on each side. Add the garlic and stir until aromatic, about 1 minute. Add the corn kernels and stir again.

Add the lima beans, butter, hot sauce, pepper, and the remaining ½ teaspoon salt and stir to incorporate. When hot, add the okra to the pot and stir gently to avoid breaking the okra. Taste and adjust the seasoning, and serve.

2 cups (480 ml) chicken stock (page 348)

2 cups (340 g) fresh baby lima beans

¼ cup (60 ml) canola oil

6 cups (930 g) fresh okra, cut on a bias, or if tiny, halved lengthwise

1½ teaspoons kosher salt, plus more as needed

4 cups (about 500 g) mirliton (from about 2 large), peeled, seeded, and cut into ½-inch (1.3 cm) cubes

3 garlic cloves, finely chopped

3 ears corn, shucked and kernels cut off to yield 2 cups (290 g; see Note on page 186)

2 tablespoons unsalted butter

1 tablespoon hot sauce, preferably Original Louisiana Hot Sauce

¼ teaspoon cracked black pepper

White Bean, Andouille, and Greens Soup

SERVES 8 TO 12

I normally want white beans, andouille, and greens separate on a plate lunch. But I've fallen in love with this simple soup that combines these three favorite South Louisiana ingredients in a one-pot meal. This recipe mirrors a Sicilian soup; you can make it with any sausage, but andouille is best. Enjoy with Corn Bread (page 301) or Hush Puppies (page 89).

NOTE: *To prepare the beans, place 1 cup (180 g) dry beans in a bowl, cover with 2 cups (480 ml) water, and let soak overnight. The next day, in a large pot, bring to a boil 2 quarts (1.9 L) of water salted to taste like the sea. Add the beans and cook for 15 minutes. Check the beans for doneness; you want them to be al dente. Strain, then let cool until the recipe calls for them.*

Warm a heavy-bottomed 12-quart (11 L) pot over medium heat for 2 minutes, then add the oil and andouille and cook until browned, about 10 minutes. Add the onions and cook until translucent and golden brown, about 20 minutes. If the onions are sticking to the pot, add a splash of the stock to deglaze the pot and scrape up any bits stuck to the bottom. Add the garlic and cook until fragrant, 2 minutes.

In a small bowl, season the tomatoes with the salt, black pepper, and cayenne and add them to the pot. Add the stock, thyme, hot sauce, bay leaf, and a touch of allspice. Bring to a simmer, stirring occasionally, then reduce the heat to maintain a low simmer until the tomatoes soften and break down, about 30 minutes. You can press the tomatoes against the side of the pot with a spoon to break them apart. Add the white beans and cook for 15 minutes more.

To serve, place a handful of greens in individual bowls and ladle hot soup on top. For any leftovers, store the greens and soup separately so the greens stay vibrant. The soup keeps for 1 week in the refrigerator.

2 tablespoons canola oil

1 pound (455 g) andouille, cut into ¼-inch (6 mm) rounds or bite-size pieces

2 pounds (910 g) yellow onions, finely diced

3 quarts (2.8 L) chicken stock (page 348), at room temperature

8 garlic cloves, finely diced

2 large ripe tomatoes, cored and cut in half

1 tablespoon kosher salt

1 teaspoon cracked black pepper

Pinch of cayenne pepper

1 tablespoon chopped fresh thyme, or a few sprigs tied with twine

1 tablespoon hot sauce, preferably Original Louisiana Hot Sauce

1 bay leaf

Ground allspice

1 cup (180 g) cooked navy beans or great northern beans (see Note)

1 pound (455 g) greens: kale, Swiss chard, or collards, with stems removed and leaves roughly chopped

Persimmon Cake

SERVES 8

My time spent cooking in Napa opened my eyes to the different ways I could use the fruits and vegetables that we harvest seasonally in South Louisiana. I learned to make this persimmon pudding cake filled with dried fruits and nuts that is so moist it barely holds together. There the cakes were baked individually in a water bath; this recipe is made in a Bundt pan but could also be made in a classic cake pan. The water bath is optional.

This cake has a hint of fall spice and a happy surprise: brandy-soaked raisins. You can omit the raisins, but I wouldn't.

NOTE: *For persimmon puree, deseed 2 or 3 ripe persimmons and put them in a blender. No need to cook the persimmons first.*

At least 1 hour before making the cake, soak the raisins in a bowl with the brandy. You can soak them longer; you can't oversoak them.

Preheat the oven to 350°F (180°C). Grease a Bundt pan, then coat it with the 2 tablespoons sugar.

In a food processor, pulse the pecans to the texture of almond flour, stopping before they turn into a nut butter.

In the bowl of a stand mixer fitted with the whisk attachment or in a large bowl using a handheld mixer, beat the eggs and the remaining 1¼ cups (250 g) sugar for 5 minutes on high speed until light and fluffy.

In a blender, blend to combine the persimmon puree, butter, and lemon juice. Strain the raisins and reserve for later; add the brandy soaking liquid to the blender and blend again. →

½ cup (95 g) golden raisins

3 tablespoons brandy

1¼ cups (250 g) raw sugar, plus 2 tablespoons for coating the pan

½ cup (60 g) pecans

2 eggs, at room temperature

1¼ cups (265 g) persimmon puree (see Note)

4 ounces (115 g) unsalted butter, melted

1 tablespoon fresh lemon juice

1¼ cups (155 g) all-purpose flour

1 teaspoon ground cinnamon

¼ teaspoon kosher salt

2 tablespoons water

2 teaspoons baking soda

In a bowl, sift together the all-purpose flour, pecan flour, cinnamon, and salt. Now you are ready to assemble the cake batter.

To the bowl of eggs and sugar add one-third of the flour mixture and whisk until combined, then add half of the persimmon mixture and mix until combined. Add another third of the flour mixture, then the remaining half of the persimmon mixture, and finally the last third of the flour mixture, beating well after each addition.

Let the batter sit while you heat the water in a small pan over medium heat or in a bowl in the microwave. Add the baking soda to the hot water, mix together, and stir into the cake batter. Using a silicone spatula, gently fold in the reserved raisins. Scrape the batter into the prepared Bundt pan.

Bake for 45 minutes, or until a cake tester inserted in the center comes out clean. Let the cake cool in the pan for about 5 minutes, then turn it out onto a platter. Let cool completely and serve.

Satsuma Sorbet with Condensed Milk and Benne

MAKES 1 QUART (890 G)

Nothing beats a Sno-ball in a South Louisiana summer, but I can't give you a recipe for one because you'd need the patented machine that hails from Louisiana. Sorbet is the closest you can get to standing in line at Hansen's Sno-ball stand. Satsuma sorbet gets the royal treatment with condensed milk and benne seeds in this refreshing dessert. Keep in mind that this recipe requires an ice cream maker and there is alcohol in the mixture, which keeps the ice from freezing too hard.

NOTE: *Freezing satsuma juice when the fruit is in season and making sorbet throughout the year is a pro move.*

3½ cups (840 ml) satsuma juice (see Note)

½ cup (100 g) granulated sugar

2 tablespoons honey

¼ teaspoon kosher salt

2 tablespoons orange liqueur

Zest and juice of 1 lemon

1 cup (240 ml) condensed milk, for finishing

2 tablespoons benne seeds, preferably from Anson Mills, for finishing

In a small saucepan over low heat, warm ½ cup (120 ml) of the satsuma juice and stir in the sugar, honey, and salt until dissolved. Let cool. Add the mixture to a blender with the remaining 3 cups (720 ml) satsuma juice, the orange liqueur, and the lemon zest and juice. Blend until combined.

Strain the mixture through a fine-mesh strainer into a bowl, then transfer the mixture to an ice cream maker and churn according to the manufacturer's directions. We churn it until slushy, then freeze overnight. Sorbet will keep in the freezer for 2 weeks; if it gets too icy, you can melt it and re-spin it.

To serve, remove the sorbet from the freezer about 15 minutes in advance so it's easier to scoop. Top each large scoop of the sorbet with 1 to 2 tablespoons of the condensed milk and a scattering of the benne seeds.

TRADITION

—— ·'·‚'‚ ——

TRADITIONS IN SOUTH LOUISIANA easily integrate into the fabric of everyday life. In fall, when temperatures start breaking and nature is alive, a little bayou road can become a parade of heritage on display, with sugarcane trucks and folks pulling duck blinds. The air is littered with sugarcane leaves, roseaus, palmettos, and excitement as South Louisiana prepares for autumn. We dip into real lore like gathering for boucheries. Fall brings savory treasures, hearty stews, prized game meats, and the joy of fresh-dropped pecans baked into warm cake.

Hunting, a ritual older than recorded time, is part of every culture around the globe. Acadians settling in the New World, aided by American Indians, learned to hunt for survival. Down on the bayou, hunting season starts in balmy September with alligator season, quickly followed by duck, turkey, quail, deer, and rabbit seasons. Cajuns stock their freezers with game as they do with seafood. The freezer is a promise of future duck gumbos and duck fricassees, rabbit and dumplings, and fried quail. Turkeys are put away for holiday tables. Hunters spend their time in the field from October through January in a dance as important as breathing for them.

In late October and early November, when temperatures drop, families carrying on the art of boucherie set a date for the festivities. It's a whole-hog affair with all hands on deck to butcher the animal and make cracklins, boudin, sausages, hog's head cheese, salt pork, and stews. Fall also delivers sweetness with pecan and sugar harvests to make our cakes and pastries possible.

Cracklins

MAKES 2 POUNDS (910 G)

Go to any respectable gas station in Louisiana and you can get a brown paper bag of cracklins. If they are hot, you'll want to stop what you're doing and eat them—I mean pull over on the side of the road. Hopefully you have some cane syrup handy in your glove box because that is the perfect accompaniment.

Cracklins are a religion in Louisiana and a huge part of the boucherie day. Everyone wants to know when the cracklins are done. They are the first snack from a boucherie. The skin off the back of the hog is cut into pieces, blanched, and fried in hot oil. This double-fry method is used in any restaurant that serves fresh French fries—you must fry them and then fry them again; it works wonders on cracklins, too.

Canola oil or peanut oil, for frying

2 pounds (910 g) pork fatback or belly, cut into 1½-inch (3.8 cm) cubes

Coarse finishing salt, such as Maldon

Cane syrup, preferably Poirier's or Steen's (see Resources, page 359), for dipping

Prepare a tabletop fryer with oil and heat to 225°F (105°C). Alternatively, fill a large heavy-bottomed pot with 4 inches (10 cm) of oil and heat the oil over medium-high heat to 225°F (105°C). Set a wire rack over a sheet pan.

Add 1 pound (455 g) of the pork to the hot oil, stir, and fry until a brilliant golden brown, about 15 minutes. Use a slotted spoon or spider to transfer the cracklins to the wire rack and let them cool completely. Repeat with the remaining 1 pound (455 g) pork.

When you are ready to serve the cracklins, line a sheet pan with paper towels or brown paper bags and heat the oil to 400°F (200°C). Carefully place the cracklins in the hot oil; I use a spider for this. You can cook all the cracklins at this point, frying until their skins crack and start looking like Funyuns. If your oil smokes or is too hot, bring it down to 375°F (190°C). You never want your oil to smoke. Use the spider to transfer the cracklins to the prepared pan. Let cool slightly, then place in a bowl and toss with coarse salt. Serve with Poirier's cane syrup, if you're lucky, or simply Steen's cane syrup. Eat immediately.

BOUCHERIES, EXPLAINED

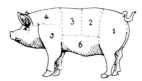

Even with the invention of freezers and the prevalence of butcher shops, meat markets, and big-box grocery stores on the bayou, some families still gather in fall for a boucherie. They raise their own hogs and then get together for a communal slaughtering.

My entire life, I've heard stories about boucheries from my dad. He grew up near his extended family in houses scattered across a couple acres. With no fences, they lived on a large plot of land sandwiched between Bayou Petit Caillou and Lake Boudreaux with shared cisterns, gardens, and duties of raising hogs, cows, and chickens and running a small butcher shop. Every year when the weather cooled around November and the hog was fat enough, family and friends got together to slaughter the pig and process the meat.

My dad remembers being so scared of seeing the hog slaughtered that he stayed home to wait until that part was done. He also remembers waking at five a.m. when he was older to see the men slit the hog's throat and drink the blood to thank it for another boucherie. They did not shoot the hog, as is often done today, but preferred this method for collecting the blood for making blood sausage.

During a boucherie, large sheets of plywood are placed over sawhorses for production. As soon as the hog's blood is collected and salt whisked in to congeal it, the hog is moved to the wooden table to be cleaned and prepped. Number 3 galvanized tubs of boiling water are readied over wood fires, and the water is poured over the pig to clean it. Oyster sacks are placed over the pig, and more boiling water is poured over to steam the hog's skin and ready it for scraping off its wiry fur. Only after the pig is thoroughly cleaned can the butchering begin.

My dad's uncles, Oris, Walter, and Julian, would work to separate the quarters. Once separate, parts of the hog are moved to large pans, and the skin is readied for cracklins. The production of boudin, smoked sausage, and hog's head cheese begins, as well as making backbone stew, salting pig parts, and pickling. My dad remembers the production of the day and everyone working, helping each other, and having a good time. A boucherie is like a little festival; people come from up and down the bayou to lend a hand and enjoy the day together.

Cajun music plays live or on the radio, and there's a good amount of locally brewed beer iced down in pirogues and galvanized tubs, too. The majority of the day is taken up with work, but it's done in unison. My dad says that as soon as he could smell the cracklins being pulled from the oil, he would run back and get a little paper bag full of them. That was his favorite part; he remembers how fresh they were.

At a boucherie, the prepared food is separated and divided for each family. When my dad was young, no one had a freezer bigger than a microwave, so sausage was smoked and hung for the cold months, hog's head cheese put in the refrigerator, cracklins mostly consumed within a week, pig feet pickled, and other pig parts salted. And, of course, as at any family gathering, there was cake to share: banana, pineapple, and pecan.

Torchbearers carry on this tradition today. Louisiana chef John Folse holds an annual boucherie festival to teach chefs and people from the community the traditional techniques of breaking down and preparing every bit of a hog. The boucherie is part of the motion of a year, a communal event that serves as nourishment for months to come and a social gathering of craft and workmanship.

Hog's Head Cheese

MAKES 11 POUNDS (5 KG)

Hog's head cheese is a Cajun creation that is somewhere between a rillette and a pâté. It doesn't have the smooth consistency of pâté and, although rustic, it is not prepared in the typical way rillettes are, with fat. It is its own animal and a delicious one. It has been nice to see it in the resurgence of butchery in Louisiana.

When I was young, we got hog's head cheese from the deli, and it was sliced for sandwiches and always wrapped in white paper with freezer tape. It's not easy to make a small recipe of hog's head cheese— after all, you are using a hog's head. However, you can have the butcher split the hog's head in half, which still yields more than ten pounds. You'll want to make this recipe with a friend, and you'll want to be prepared to put some away for the year. You can freeze it or store it in jars to give to friends.

Hog's head cheese takes about 5 hours to make, and needs to rest overnight to jell up before serving.

NOTES: *The exact amount of water you need will depend on the size of the hog's head and the pot; you want the water to cover the head. For easy removal, bundle your whole spices and thyme in cheesecloth.*

Wash the hog's head and feet thoroughly. Break down the pork butt into 2-inch (5 cm) pieces. Place the pork in a large pot over two burners. Add the yellow onions, celery, bell peppers, cayenne, paprika, bay leaves, hot sauce, and salt. Place the peppercorns, mustard seeds, coriander seeds, and thyme in a cheesecloth, tie it closed, and add it to the pot. Pour in enough water to completely cover the head, 1 to 1½ gallons (3.8 to 5.7 L); if there is an ear sticking up, that's okay. Bring to a boil, which should take about 20 minutes, then maintain a rolling simmer for 3 to 4 hours, using tongs and a large stirring spoon to flip the head over after the first and second hours, until the meat is tender and can easily be pulled away from the bone and shredded. If

½ hog's head (about 11 pounds/5 kg)

2 hog's feet (about 1½ pounds/680 g), split in half by a butcher

2 pounds (910 g) pork butt or shoulder

4 cups (500 g) finely diced yellow onions

2 cups (200 g) finely diced celery

2 cups (290 g) finely diced green bell peppers

1 tablespoon cayenne pepper

1 tablespoon paprika

5 bay leaves

1 cup (240 ml) hot sauce, preferably Original Louisiana Hot Sauce

½ cup (120 g) kosher salt

⅓ cup (45 g) whole black peppercorns

⅓ cup (65 g) whole mustard seeds

⅓ cup (20 g) whole coriander seeds

1 bunch thyme (8 to 12 sprigs)

FOR SERVING

Coarse Creole mustard, cornichons, crackers, toast points, French bread, or baguette

Chopped flat-leaf parsley and green onion

Quick Pickled Red Blackberries (page 342)

the pot begins to lose too much liquid, then put on the cover halfway through.

Turn off the heat. Use tongs and a slotted spoon to transfer the head and pork butt to a sheet pan to cool. Once they are cool enough to handle, pick the meat off the head and the fat from the bones. Discard the fat, the hog's eye, bones, and any too-sinewy pieces. Chop the meat into roughly ½-inch (1.3 cm) cubes.

Strain the liquid in the pot through a medium strainer, discarding the solids and the cheesecloth bundle. Return the liquid and meat to the pot and bring it back to a boil over medium-high heat, then reduce the heat to maintain a simmer and reduce the liquid by half, 20 to 30 minutes.

Line two beautiful terrine pans or loaf pans with parchment paper or plastic wrap. Ladle the mixture into the pans and square it off so that it is flat on top. Refrigerate the terrines to set overnight or up to 24 hours.

When you're ready to serve, turn the molds out onto a cutting board and slice the head cheese into bread-size slices. Serve with the mustard, cornichons, crackers, and toast points or bread. I also like to crown the cheese with a bit of parsley and green onion and have some pickled red blackberries on the side.

Boudin

I remember being young in my mom's kitchen with my aunts making boudin. We had a hand-crank meat grinder attached to my mom's 1980s pale blue kitchen countertop and big stainless-steel bowls filled with boudin mix. We watched as the ground meat was stuffed into casings. Boudin is synonymous with Cajun country. Most of our sausages derive from German and French roots, but our boudin is different. It is made from cooked pork shoulder and livers, onion, bell pepper, celery, and spices with rice. Most sausages are made with raw meat and are aged or smoked. But once boudin is cased, you can poach it and eat it immediately, as here, or you can smoke it (see Notes).

If you are lucky enough to be driving through South Louisiana, you will find boudin at any well-respected gas station; near Lafayette, Scott, and Youngsville you will reach the boudin epicenter.

NOTES: *If you don't want to encase boudin the traditional way, you can skip the casing step and make boudin balls or boudin patties (see Variations).*

You can smoke your boudin, too. Follow your smoker's instructions and smoke gently for 10 to 15 minutes. Since the ingredients in the sausage are already cooked, you don't have to worry about it reaching an internal temperature—you are just adding a smoky flavor to the boudin.

---

4 pounds (1.8 kg) pork shoulder, cut into 1-inch (2.5 cm) cubes

¼ pound (115 g) pork liver, cut into 4 pieces

¼ cup (35 g) kosher salt

2 tablespoons freshly ground black pepper

½ teaspoon cayenne pepper

¼ cup (60 ml) hot sauce, preferably Original Louisiana Hot Sauce

¼ cup (60 ml) canola oil

1 cup (125 g) diced yellow onion

¼ cup (35 g) diced green bell pepper

¼ cup (25 g) diced celery

2 tablespoons diced jalapeño

5 cups (770 g) cooked rice

¼ cup (15 g) chopped flat-leaf parsley

¼ cup (15 g) chopped green onions

4 feet (121 cm) sausage casings (buy the smallest length possible online or at a butcher shop), cleaned (see page 225)

Place the pork shoulder and liver in a large bowl and season with the salt, black pepper, cayenne, and hot sauce. Allow to sit for at least 2 hours or overnight in the refrigerator.

Warm a large heavy-bottomed pot over medium heat, then add the oil and heat for 30 seconds. Add the yellow onion and cook, stirring, over medium-high heat for 5 minutes, then reduce the heat to medium-low and cook until translucent and without bite, about

20 minutes. Stir in the bell pepper, celery, and jalapeño and cook until the vegetables have lost their bite, about 20 minutes.

Put the marinated meat in the pot and add water to cover the mixture by about 2 inches (5 cm); it'll be about 8 to 10 cups (1.9 to 2.4 L). Slowly bring the meat mixture, uncovered, to a gentle simmer and cook, adjusting the heat as needed to maintain a consistent low simmer, until the meat is tender and can be easily pulled apart with a fork, about 1½ hours. A diffuser can help with maintaining temperature (see page 19).

When the mixture is tender, strain the contents into a large bowl and reserve the liquid. Let cool, then hand-chop the meat into roughly ½-inch (1.3 cm) pieces. The chopping will be easy; you can do it with a bench scraper. Having a cutting board with grooves for catching the juices also helps. Alternatively, use an old-fashioned hand crank or the grinder attachment for a KitchenAid mixer. You don't need anything fancy—you aren't starting a boudin shop, just making boudin for your family.

Add the rice, parsley, green onions, and 1 cup (240 ml) of the reserved liquid to the meat mixture. If the mixture seems dry, add a little more reserved liquid, keeping in mind the rice will absorb some liquid. Use your hands to thoroughly mix the rice, greens, and meat together. Taste your mixture. Does it need more salt, black pepper, or cayenne? How about parsley or green onion? Adjust as needed.

At this point, you can make boudin balls or boudin patties (see Variations), you can reserve some boudin to stuff in a chicken to bake (see page 234), or you can stuff the boudin into casings. To stuff the casings, have ready the cleaned casings, a large sheet pan with damp dish towels or a little moisture on it so the casings don't stick, a grinder or a grinder attachment for a mixer, and a stuffing tool (such as a KitchenAid attachment for stuffing sausage into casings). Begin by tying off one end of the casing and placing the open end on the feeder tube, sliding almost all of the casing onto the attachment. Feed the boudin mixture through the top opening of the grinder attachment and use a silicone spatula to help push the stuffing down; the mixture will start filling the casing. Let it fill to 12 inches (30 cm), then twist the sausage two or three times to create a seal. Continue feeding, pushing, and twisting until you've used your desired amount of boudin mix. Once all the boudin is cased, let it rest for about 15 minutes at room temperature.

Fill a pot large enough to hold the boudin with water and bring to a boil. Reduce the heat to maintain a simmer and gently poach your boudin for about 10 minutes. Now it's ready to eat—perhaps as I do, like a hot dog with Creole mustard and white bread. Boudin can be kept in the refrigerator for 1 week or in the freezer for about 3 months.

VARIATIONS

Boudin Balls or Boudin Patties

To form the boudin mixture into balls or patties, flour a small measuring cup, fill it with the boudin mixture, then knock the mix out of the cup, form it into a ball or patty, and flour it again. I don't use a scale; I just eyeball the amount. Once all the balls or patties are formed and floured liberally on all sides, fry them in a lightly oiled cast-iron skillet until golden brown, about 3 minutes per side.

Jarred Boudin

If you don't have time to case the boudin or make patties, here is an easy, delicious way to store, cook, and serve boudin. Fill Weck jars with the boudin mix, seal, and store in the refrigerator. When it's time to serve, let the jars come to room temperature. Fill a skillet or wide-bottomed pot with 1 inch (2.5 cm) water, place the sealed jars in the water, bring to a simmer, and heat for about 10 minutes. Carefully remove the jars and let cool, then carefully remove the lid and serve the mix with toast points, Creole mustard, and pickles. This is a great way to serve boudin at a party.

Pork Backbone Stew

SERVES 8 TO 10

During the boucherie, backbone stew is cooked to feed the hardworking families who are butchering, cooking, frying, singing, and dancing. All the elements of Cajun cooking are in backbone stew and, coupled with frugality and sustainability, are easily adaptable for home cooking. Backbone stew is made with a dark roux, delicious pork backbones, and all the lovely ingredients you've come to expect from Cajun cooking: onions, bell peppers, celery, a bit of cayenne, hot sauce for heat, and rice to serve it over. This recipe sticks to your bones and is best made when the temperature has dropped.

NOTE: *Use a wide, heavy-bottomed pot for this. It makes preparing a roux and cooking down the onions an easier task. A dark roux is best accomplished with a pinch-hitter friend and a cold beer. Tap your friend to stir before your elbow gets tendinitis.*

Wash the backbones really well, dry them really well, then season the backbones and pork shoulder with the vinegar, salt, black pepper, cayenne, and hot sauce, rubbing the seasoning into the meat. Set aside at room temperature while you make a roux.

Warm a deep, heavy-bottomed 10-quart (9.4 L) pot over medium heat for 1 to 2 minutes. Add the flour and oil and cook, stirring continuously with a wooden spoon and reducing the heat to low when the flour starts to change color and begins to smoke slightly. Don't walk away—focus on stirring your roux. When the roux is the color of dark chocolate, 45 minutes to 1 hour, carefully add the yellow onions, stirring to coat them thoroughly with the roux. Increase the heat to medium and cook, stirring every 5 minutes, until they turn a deep, dark caramelized color, another 45 minutes to 1 hour. Be careful of the sticking on the bottom of the pot; a little sticking is good if you scrape it up quickly. Add the bell peppers, celery, garlic, tabasco peppers, and bay leaves and cook, stirring often so the

3 pounds (1.4 kg) pork backbones or necks

2 pounds (910 g) pork shoulder, cut into 2-inch (5 cm) cubes

¼ cup (60 ml) apple cider vinegar or Steen's cane vinegar

2 tablespoons kosher salt

2 tablespoons cracked black pepper

2 teaspoons cayenne pepper

1 cup (240 ml) hot sauce, preferably Original Louisiana Hot Sauce

3 cups (375 g) all-purpose flour

2½ cups (600 ml) canola oil

4½ pounds (2 kg) yellow onions, finely diced

2 cups (290 g) finely diced green bell peppers

1 cup (100 g) finely diced celery

¼ cup (35 g) finely chopped garlic

2 fresh tabasco or Criollo Sella peppers, or jalapeños, finely chopped

3 bay leaves

2 quarts (1.9 L) pork stock (page 346)

Cooked rice, for serving

¼ cup (15 g) finely chopped flat-leaf parsley

¼ cup (15 g) finely chopped green onions

vegetables don't stick and the precious roux doesn't burn, until
the vegetables soften and have lost their bite, 20 to 30 minutes.
Reduce the heat if necessary.

Move all the vegetables to one side of the pot. With the heat on
medium, add the backbones and quickly give each side a sear, then
transfer to a platter and do the same with the pork shoulder. Place all
the pork back into the pot, reduce the heat to its lowest setting, and
cover the pot. Let smother for 1 hour and 45 minutes, stirring often
to keep things from sticking to the bottom of the pot.

Just before the meat mixture finishes cooking, warm the stock in a
pot over medium heat, then add it to the stew 1 quart (960 ml) at a
time. Bring the pork and stock to a simmer after adding each quart.
Simmer for another 1 hour and 45 minutes. You're making a stovetop
braise and you don't want to boil the pork, so keep the heat as low as
possible and make sure you are barely simmering the liquid and it is
not at a rolling boil. Check to see if the pork is starting to come apart.
Once it is tender and braised, the stew is ready. Your stock will have
reduced a bit.

Serve the stew over rice and top with the parsley and green onions.

Smoked Sausage

MAKES SIX 6-INCH (15 CM) LINKS

Learn to make a simple smoked sausage and build on the recipe as your skills advance. Traditionally, most people do not cook down their vegetables to make sausage, but I cook the vegetables to bring out the different levels of sweet and vegetal flavor that I prefer.

I have a simple electric home smoker for smoking foods, but it is easy to build a stovetop one if you have a hood above your stove or windows in your kitchen. I prefer the electric smoker because it will hold a specific temperature consistently. But a traditional smoker is great, too, if you have time to build a fire and spend the day tending it; it's a meditative practice to use with this recipe.

In a large bowl, combine the ground pork, 2 tablespoons of the lard, the diced fatback, salt, black pepper, paprika, and cayenne and let sit in the refrigerator.

Warm a small heavy-bottomed Dutch oven over medium heat. Add the remaining 2 tablespoons lard, the yellow onion, and the bay leaf. Sweat the onion until translucent, with no bite remaining, about 20 minutes. Add the bell pepper and celery and cook until they have lost their bite, about 20 minutes. Cool completely. Discard the bay leaf.

Remove the bowl of pork from the refrigerator and let it come to room temperature. Add the cooled vegetables, parsley, and green onion and combine thoroughly; this is best done with your hands. Remove a meatball-size amount and sear it in a pan so you can taste the mixture. Adjust the salt and spice levels, if needed.

At this point, you can form the mixture into patties and fry them or use it as you would ground meat. If you would like to stuff your sausage into casings and smoke it, proceed with the recipe.

1 pound (455 g) pork shoulder or pork butt, ground through a large die

4 tablespoons (60 g) lard

2 tablespoons diced fatback, from the pork butt

2 teaspoons kosher salt, plus more as needed

1 teaspoon freshly ground black pepper, plus more as needed

1 teaspoon smoked paprika

¼ teaspoon cayenne pepper

¼ cup (35g) finely chopped yellow onion

1 bay leaf

2 tablespoons finely chopped green bell pepper

2 tablespoons finely chopped celery

2 tablespoons finely chopped flat-leaf parsley

2 tablespoons finely chopped green onion

4 feet (121 cm) sausage casings (buy the smallest length possible online or at a butcher shop)

Prepare the casings by soaking them in cold water, rinsing, then draining. Traditionally you could rinse the casings by running hose water through them. Dry with a towel and slightly wring the casings, then get your supplies ready to stuff the casings.

There are specific appliances you can buy to grind and stuff sausage; I use the stuffing attachment for my KitchenAid mixer. If you're making a small amount, the attachment is sufficient. After the attachment is in place, begin by tying off one end of the casing and placing the open end on the feeder tube. Feed the filling mixture through the top opening of the grinder and use the plunger to push the meat through to start filling the casing. Let it fill to about 6 inches (15 cm), then twist the casing two or three times to create a semi-seal. Continue feeding, pushing, and twisting until all the sausage is cased.

Prepare a smoker to a temperature of 140°F (60°C). Use nice wood for smoking sausages, like pecan, apple, cherry, or hickory; these are easily found at hardware stores. Smoke the sausages for 1 hour, increase the temperature to 160°F (71°C), and smoke for 1 hour more. You want the internal temperature to reach 160°F (71°C), but no higher, or your sausage will dry out.

Smoked sausages keep for about 1 week in the refrigerator or 4 to 6 months in the freezer.

TOTALLY STUFFED

I grew up eating smoked sausage at home; my mom uses it in red beans and gumbos and every so often in jambalaya. Smoked sausage is a mix of minced pork, vegetables, and spices. Andouille, by contrast, is a chunkier sausage made with pork and offal. Both are smoked, but andouille is double-smoked. The andouille that has become synonymous with Cajun and Creole cooking is a distant cousin to the sausages that Germans make. The recipe has evolved over years in South Louisiana, making it a one-of-a-kind regional sausage. Both smoked sausage and andouille give dishes a singular flavor. Andouille is a bit sharper and spicier, while smoked sausage is typically mellower.

South Louisiana has an "andouille trail" through small bayou towns that is great for snacking while driving. You can meander along the Mississippi River up and down the bayous and eat sausages and meats from tiny family-owned operations. Sometimes you come upon a shack where folks are smoking meat, and other times you'll see a larger operation like Wayne Jacobs, who sells online and has a famed reputation. During the holidays, if you make your way to La Bon Boucon, in Vacherie, you can order a very large sausage called maudlin that is essentially a big andouille. This loaf-size sausage is perfect for slicing off and sautéing a lunch-meat portion to put between two pieces of white bread.

In West Louisiana and the towns close to Lafayette, you find folks who still make ponce or chaudin, a sausage stuffing mix placed inside a hog's stomach and then sewn back up and cooked, usually steamed or slowly cooked and ladled with liquid for many hours. The lining of the stomach becomes taut during cooking, making ponce easy to slice and eat like a cured, smoked sausage. It's a delicacy that is slowly disappearing from Cajun cooking as we lose our skilled older generations and evolve into a world that has little time for artful, lengthy cooking projects. Luckily, ponce is an art form still found in people's homes and many family-owned butcher shops in prairie Cajun country: the Superette or Mowata Store in Eunice, Paul's Meat Market or Teet's in Ville Platte, the Best Stop in Scott, Nonc Kev's in

Rayne, Rhea's Specialty Meat in Basile, and Mel's Grocery in Mamou, to name a handful. In New Orleans and the neighboring parishes, you can find chaurice, similar to chorizo, with influences in Spanish cooking but its own Cajun and Creole flair. The renowned Leah Chase swore by using chaurice for her gumbo.

You don't see as much blood pudding and boudin noir on restaurant menus these days, but when I can find it, I love to have it with pears and potatoes. Cajuns mostly stick to making boudin, the cooked-rice variety (spicy or mild links). Some parishes even have boudin drive-throughs, situated next to the drive-through daiquiri shop.

At butcher shops during the holidays, you can also pick up turducken, Louisiana's popular turkey stuffed with both a duck and a chicken. Although Paul Prudhomme claimed it as his own and trademarked the name, turducken was "created" by Junior and Sammy Hebert in Maurice, Louisiana, according to record. In 1984, the Heberts say, they granted a farmer's wish to have all three fowls cooked one inside another. But a home cook is probably the first to have actually made a yet-to-be-named turducken in Louisiana, or elsewhere, long before the Hebert brothers or Paul Prudhomme made the dish famous. Old cookbooks around the world record how the act of stuffing birds into one another was popular for as long as we know. In the 1800s, French gastronomist Alexandre-Balthazar-Laurent Grimod de la Reynière used seventeen birds—bustard, chicken, duck, garden warbler, goose, guinea fowl, lapwing, lark, ortolan bunting, partridge, pheasant, plover, quail, teal, thrush, turkey, and woodcock—stuffed together to create a roast without equal. If you want something a bit more accessible, there's the popular Boudin-Stuffed Chicken (page 234), much simpler than the seventeen-bird affair, and for which people go quite mad.

Deer Tamales

MAKES 32 TAMALES

This recipe was created by chef Anne Churchill, my recipe tester for this book and an essential team member of Mosquito Supper Club. Her tamales are always perfect and so she incorporated her skills into this Cajun version.

Tamales are one of the oldest recorded foods in history, dating back to 8000 BCE. The name derives from the Aztecs and means "steamed corn." They are a simple, delicious, nutritious food that stores well in the freezer. But they can be a chore to fold, so make these as a group project.

I grew up eating Mickey Brown's deer tamales; people from all over South Louisiana bring their deer to Mr. Brown and he turns it into tamales. On the bayou, we are lucky that almost every household has a hunter and so deer meat is readily available to expand our pantry or the contents of the chest freezer. We pack our freezers full of ground venison and corn in husks for quick, easy treats anytime.

Lay the corn husks flat in a large heatproof bowl or casserole. Pour boiling water over the husks and use a plate to submerge them. Let soak until ready to use.

Make the masa mix: Put the 10 ounces (285 g) lard in the bowl of a stand mixer fitted with the paddle attachment. Whip on medium speed until light and fluffy, about 3 minutes. In a separate bowl (keep dry and wet ingredients separate), combine the masa with the salt, baking powder, sweet paprika, and mustard powder.

In a medium pot, boil 2 cups (480 ml) of the stock and pour it over the masa mix, using a fork to incorporate it until a smooth paste forms. Gradually add the masa mix 1 cup (240 ml) at a time to the lard with the mixer on low speed. At first, you'll see it kind of broken apart as the lard incorporates. By the time all the dry ingredients are incorporated, it'll look more like a cookie dough. Gently pour

½ bag dried corn husks (about ½ pound/225 g; see Resources, page 359)

FOR THE MASA MIX

10 ounces (285 g) lard

3½ cups (325 g) masa

1½ tablespoons kosher salt

1½ teaspoons baking powder

1 teaspoon sweet paprika

1 teaspoon mustard powder

3 cups (720 ml) chicken stock (page 348) or water, plus ½ cup (120 ml) as needed

FOR THE FILLING

1 pound (455 g) deer meat, ground or in small chunks

1 pound (455 g) pork shoulder, ground or in small chunks

1 tablespoon kosher salt

2 teaspoons chili powder

1½ teaspoons smoked paprika

1 teaspoon ground cumin

1 teaspoon ground coriander

½ teaspoon freshly ground black pepper

Pinch of cayenne pepper

2 tablespoons lard or bacon grease

in the remaining 1 cup (240 ml) stock and beat until thoroughly incorporated. Cover the mixer bowl and place in the fridge. Leave the mixer out.

Make the filling: In a medium mixing bowl, thoroughly mix the deer, pork, salt, chili powder, smoked paprika, cumin, coriander, black pepper, and cayenne.

Heat a cast-iron skillet over medium-high heat for 2 minutes, then add the 2 tablespoons lard. When it has melted, stir in the meat mixture. Mash up any big bits, let the mixture cook untouched until the meat starts to brown, then stir. After 10 to 15 minutes, move the meat to the side of the pan. Place the garlic in the middle of the pan and give it a stir. When it starts to sizzle, add the jalapeño and oregano. Stir in the ground oats. Cook over low heat for 5 minutes more while the oats absorb the excess fat. Let cool.

Assemble the tamales: Remove the masa from the refrigerator and rewhip in the stand mixer using the paddle attachment. If it feels too crumbly, add up to ½ cup (120 ml) more stock until the masa feels like sugar cookie dough.

Drain the soaked husks and select 32 of the biggest, nicest ones. If you do not have 32 large husks, use smaller, overlapping pieces to make enough. Set a small bowl of water to the side to wet your fingers. Use an ice cream scoop to portion out the masa. Lay out 6 husks and scoop 1 masa ball into each husk. Wet your fingers and press each masa ball into a 4-inch (10 cm) square. Then scoop 2 tablespoons of the meat filling into each dough square. Now think of each husk as a compass: Bring the east and west husk edges together and give the husk a gentle squeeze, rolling it a bit to seal it and form a cigar-shaped tamale. Tuck the south bottom part under the north and place on a sheet pan seam-side down. Continue until you have completed all 32 tamales.

Place the tamales in a bamboo steamer, in a perforated pan on top of another pan, or in a colander inside a big pot. Fill the lower pot with just enough water so that it doesn't come in contact with the

2 tablespoons finely chopped garlic

1 tablespoon seeded and finely diced jalapeño

1 teaspoon dried oregano or 1 tablespoon fresh

½ cup (45 g) oats, ground in a food processor, food mill, or spice grinder

steamer. Cover. Bring to a boil over high heat, then reduce the heat so the water stays at a hearty simmer and cook the tamales for 1½ hours, checking periodically to make sure the water level does not get low. If it does, add more water and bring back to a simmer.

Test the tamales for doneness by removing one from the steamer and letting it cool slightly. Tamales are super soft when freshly steamed but firm up as they cool. Make sure the masa has lost its raw taste and fluffed up a bit. If the tamales are not done, let them cook for 20 minutes more and taste again. Cooking times vary depending on how crowded the tamales are in the vessel.

To reheat, use the same steaming process to re-steam the tamales until they are warmed through, about 20 minutes once the water is boiling. Tamales keep for 1 week in the refrigerator or 3 months in the freezer.

Boudin-Stuffed Chicken

SERVES 4 TO 6

In fall, butcher shops around Louisiana are flooded with orders for boudin-stuffed chicken. A holiday just isn't complete without one, and friends and family ship them around the world to loved ones craving this delicious treat. You can make one yourself just as well. It's not as easy as ordering online but much more satisfying when you pull your hard work out of the oven and enjoy it for dinner.

This recipe uses a spatchcocked chicken that is then deboned. If you have a butcher who can sell you a deboned chicken, you are in luck; start with a deboned chicken. If not, follow the deboning method in this recipe; it is quite easy but takes a bit of patience and practice. Serve with your favorite salad and pickles.

NOTE: *You will need a meat thermometer, preferably one with a probe of some kind, and a very sharp deboning knife, paring knife, or utility knife. Also have on hand some dish towels to clean up, dry the chicken, and keep your space tidy.*

3- to 4-pound (1.4 to 1.8 kg) spatchcocked chicken, preferably air chilled

2 tablespoons canola oil

1½ tablespoons kosher salt

1½ teaspoons cracked black pepper

¼ teaspoon cayenne pepper

1 pound (455 g) Boudin (page 217), casings removed

Place the spatchcocked chicken skin-side down on a cutting board. The bird should be laid so you can see the breastbone with the balls of the feet facing you. Working on one side at a time with a sharp knife, gently scrape the flesh off the ribs in small motions, running along the ribs. It helps to hold on to the bone and let gravity assist you. The meat will begin to fall away. This is a slow process; take your time.

Next, slowly begin to peel the meat from the breastbones with the same motion. Using the tip of the knife, snip away the tendons surrounding the wing bones and free the meat from the bone, leaving the skin attached. Now do the same on the other side.

Scrape the meat off the wishbone located between the breast and neck of the bird, then slowly finish removing the rib cage along the sternum until the bone is completely separated from the meat. →

Place the chicken on a platter or sheet pan. Rub the chicken on both sides with the oil. In a small bowl, mix together the salt, black pepper, and cayenne. Sprinkle the spice mix all over the chicken, then rub it in. Place the chicken in the fridge, skin-side up and uncovered, ideally for 24 hours, to dry cure. If you don't have the time, let it cure for as long as you are able.

When ready to cook, preheat the oven to 350°F (180°C). Remove the chicken and boudin from the fridge and bring to room temperature.

Place the chicken skin-side down on the cutting board. Spread the boudin in the middle of the chicken and form it into a football shape. Fold the chicken around the boudin, swaddling the boudin. Using skewers or sewing, fasten the bird back together where the spine used to be. Flip the bird over and mold it to its original shape. You may truss or use another skewer or a toothpick to attach the legs together, but it's not necessary. Place in a roasting pan or on a sheet pan and bake for 45 to 55 minutes, until the internal temperature in the middle of the chicken reaches 150°F (65°C).

The bird will continue to cook when removed from the oven; check it again after 5 to 10 minutes, when the internal temperature should register 165°F (75°C). Let the chicken rest for at least 20 minutes before serving. Eating it the day of baking is best for moisture content, as with most baked chicken.

Duck and Mushroom Fricassee

SERVES 6

A Cajun fricassee has a bit more color than a French one because we brown the meat heavily. Oyster mushrooms grow in the backwoods in South Louisiana, so it's easy for us to collect a basket of them to use in a fricassee. Most Louisianians have ducks in their chest freezers destined for all kinds of entrées, but this fricassee will be just as good with duck legs from the grocer.

In a large bowl, combine the duck legs with the hot sauce, salt, black pepper, and cayenne. Let marinate together for a couple hours or overnight in the refrigerator.

Remove the duck legs from the refrigerator and let them come to room temperature. Fill a medium bowl with the flour. Pass each duck leg through the flour and gently shake to remove the excess. Place the duck legs on a sheet pan.

Warm a large Dutch oven over medium-high heat for a couple minutes, then add ¼ cup (60 ml) of the duck fat. Working in batches if needed, carefully place the floured duck legs in the hot fat, reduce the heat to medium, and fry until golden, about 4 minutes on each side. Use tongs to transfer the seared duck legs to the sheet pan and repeat the steps with any that didn't fit in the first round. Pour out all but roughly 2 tablespoons of the fat and discard.

Stir in the wine to deglaze the pot, scraping up any bits stuck to the bottom; pour out any liquid and reserve. Add the remaining ¼ cup (60 ml) duck fat to the pot and let it warm for a minute. Add the yellow onions and cook over medium-low heat until they are translucent and soft, about 30 minutes.

Return the duck to the pot, add the celery, garlic, bay leaf, thyme, and stock, and mix well. Bring to a simmer over high heat, cover the

2½ pounds (1.2 kg) duck legs (about 6), skin and fat removed

1 tablespoon hot sauce, preferably Original Louisiana Hot Sauce

1 tablespoon kosher salt

1 teaspoon cracked black pepper

1 teaspoon cayenne pepper

2 cups (250 g) all-purpose flour

½ cup (120 ml) rendered duck fat or canola oil

1½ cups (360 ml) dry white wine or sherry, or stock

3 pounds (1.4 kg) yellow onions, finely diced

1 cup (100 g) finely diced celery

1 tablespoon finely chopped garlic

1 bay leaf

6 thyme sprigs

2 cups (480 ml) chicken stock or duck stock (page 348), plus more as needed

3½ ounces (100 g) diced oyster mushrooms or white mushrooms

¼ cup (60 ml) heavy cream

1 tablespoon unsalted butter

Cooked rice or mashed potatoes, for serving

¼ cup (15 g) finely chopped flat-leaf parsley, for garnish

¼ cup (15 g) finely chopped green onions, for garnish

pot and reduce the heat to its lowest setting, and cook, letting the duck smother, for 2 hours. The duck should be falling off the bone. If not, cook it for 20 to 30 minutes more.

Trying not to disturb the duck legs, so they stay whole, stir in the mushrooms, cook for about 2 minutes, then stir in the cream and butter. If you want more sauce or a thinner consistency, add a little more stock. Taste and adjust the seasoning.

Serve over rice or mashed potatoes, garnished with the parsley and green onions.

Duck and Andouille Gumbo

SERVES 8 TO 10

In recent years duck has become widely available in grocery stores, from whole ducks to breasts and legs and even duck fat. If duck isn't in your rotation as a home cook, it should be. Duck breasts are easy to render and cook fast. Duck legs are versatile and can be braised, stewed, or used in a gumbo. You can also confit duck legs, and they'll last for a month submerged in fat. Pull the meat for salads or stir-fries or serve the legs whole with beans or lentils. Made with a dark roux, this gumbo layers flavor on top of flavor with onions, andouille, and poultry.

NOTES: *You do not have to make your own andouille; you can get it from many sources online (see Resources, page 359) or around Louisiana. I always look for a butcher who can identify the farmer. When I can trace my meat to a family, I know the hog was well cared for.*

If you have a chance to grind your duck fat, it will melt and render more quickly.

In a large bowl, season the duck legs with the hot sauce, salt, black pepper, and cayenne. Let come to room temperature.

Warm a large heavy-bottomed skillet or Dutch oven over medium heat for 2 minutes, then add the duck fat and let sizzle and fry for 5 minutes. Reduce the heat to medium-low and let the fat start melting into a clear oil. Once the fat is rendered, after 20 to 30 minutes, remove it from the pot and reserve for making the roux.

Place the skillet over medium-high heat, add the andouille, and sear for about 2 minutes on each side; remove and reserve in a bowl. Working in batches, add the duck legs to the same skillet and sear on all sides, about 4 minutes per side; you may need to reduce the heat a bit after the meat contacts the pan. Transfer the duck to a platter and

5 to 6 pounds (2.3 to 2.7 kg) duck legs, skin and fat removed and reserved

2 tablespoons hot sauce, preferably Original Louisiana Hot Sauce

1½ tablespoons kosher salt

½ teaspoon cracked black pepper

½ teaspoon cayenne pepper

1 pound (455 g) andouille sausage, cut into 1-inch (2.5 cm) rounds and the rounds halved

2 quarts (1.9 L) chicken stock or duck stock (page 348)

1 cup (125 g) all-purpose flour

3 pounds (1.4 kg) yellow onions, finely diced

1½ cups (220 g) finely diced green bell pepper

1 cup (100 g) finely diced celery

1 bay leaf

¼ cup (15 g) finely chopped flat-leaf parsley, for garnish

¼ cup (15 g) finely chopped green onions, for garnish

Cooked rice, pickles, and potato salad, for serving

reserve for later. Pour in 2 cups (480 ml) of the stock to deglaze the pan, scrape up any bits stuck to the bottom, then pour this liquid into the bowl with the sausage. Wipe down the pan and prepare to make your roux.

Warm the same skillet over medium-low heat for 1 to 2 minutes, then add 1 cup (240 ml) of the rendered duck fat and the flour. Cook, gently stirring continuously with a wooden spoon and reducing the heat to low when the flour starts to change color and smoke slightly. Don't walk away—focus on stirring your roux. When the roux is the color of dark chocolate, about 45 minutes, carefully add the yellow onions and cook over medium heat, stirring about every 5 minutes, for 45 minutes more. Do not let the onions burn or you will ruin all your hard work on the roux. Be careful of sticking on the bottom of the pan; a little sticking is good if you scrape it up quickly. Keep deglazing the pan with a bit of water, a tablespoon at a time, if the onions start to stick too much. The onions will darken and caramelize and shrink to less than half the size you started with.

Add the duck legs, bell pepper, celery, and bay leaf to the pan. Cover and cook on the lowest setting for 2 hours, smothering the duck so it releases all its juices. After 2 hours, stir in the remaining 6 cups (1.4 L) stock, add the andouille and the liquid you gathered from first deglazing the pan, and bring to a simmer. Let simmer, uncovered, for 30 minutes. You want to see bubbles slowly rising from the bottom to the top, not a constant boil. At this point you're letting all the flavors marry.

If you'd like, you can pull the meat off the duck legs and return it to the pan, but it's not necessary.

Garnish the gumbo with the parsley and green onions. Serve with rice, pickles, and potato salad. Gumbo keeps for 1 week in the refrigerator (it's always better the next day) or up to 3 months in the freezer.

Rabbit and Dumplings

SERVES 6 TO 8

Rabbit and dumplings is essentially a rabbit stew, but instead of serving the stew over rice as Cajuns mostly do, you make dumplings and cook them in the stew. It is a variation on chicken and dumplings and a favorite throughout the South. Serving protein in a stew with dumplings is reminiscent of a fricot, a staple dish of traditional Acadian life throughout the Canadian Maritimes. One of the biggest differences between traditional Cajun ingredients and the original fricot is carrots. Cajuns don't cook with a lot of carrots, but they are present here; it's a recipe that showcases our roots but is a crowd-pleaser, too.

Make the stew: Place the rabbit in a bowl with the hot sauce, salt, black pepper, and cayenne. Let marinate for an hour at room temperature.

Warm a large heavy-bottomed Dutch oven over medium-high heat, then add the ¼ cup (60 ml) oil and heat for 2 minutes. Add the yellow onions and cook for about 5 minutes, then reduce the heat to medium and cook, stirring occasionally, until the onions are limp and translucent and have a golden hue, about 20 minutes. Reduce the heat if the onions are getting too brown.

Meanwhile, place the flour in a large bowl and dredge the rabbit in the flour.

Move the onions to one side of the pot, increase the heat to medium, and add the remaining 2 tablespoons oil. Place the rabbit in the oil and lightly sear for about 4 minutes on each side until evenly browned (this locks in the seasoning). Since this is a rustic cooking technique, I like to put the onions on top of the rabbit while searing it. Alternatively, you can remove the onions from the pot, sear the

FOR THE STEW

3-pound (1.4 kg) whole rabbit

2 tablespoons hot sauce, preferably Original Louisiana Hot Sauce

2 tablespoons kosher salt

1 teaspoon cracked black pepper

¼ teaspoon cayenne pepper

¼ cup (60 ml) plus 2 tablespoons canola oil

2 pounds (910 g) yellow onions, finely diced

½ cup (65 g) all-purpose flour

4 to 6 cups (960 to 1,440 ml) chicken stock (page 348)

2 cups (200 g) finely diced celery

2 cups (280 g) finely diced carrots

1 bay leaf

FOR THE DUMPLINGS

1½ cups (190 g) all-purpose flour

1½ teaspoons baking powder

1½ teaspoons kosher salt

1 tablespoon unsalted butter, cut into small cubes and chilled

2 eggs

½ cup (120 ml) whole milk

→

rabbit, then replace the onions. If needed, add a splash of the stock to deglaze the pot and scrape up any bits stuck to the bottom. Then add the celery, carrots, and bay leaf. Give the whole pot a big stir then reduce the heat to its lowest setting, cover, and smother for 45 minutes, stirring halfway through the cooking time. If the rabbit meat hasn't started to pull away from the bone, cook the stew for about 15 minutes more. Use a slotted spoon to transfer the rabbit meat and bones to a plate or pan to cool.

Make the dumplings: In a medium bowl, whisk together 1 cup (125 g) of the flour, the baking powder, and the salt.

Just like cutting butter in for biscuits, smudge the butter into the flour mixture with your fingers, mixing it in as evenly as possible.

Make a well in the flour mixture and add the eggs and milk. Start to bring everything together by stirring gently with a fork to make a shaggy dough. Don't overmix or the gluten will develop and make your dumplings tough. Incorporate everything together, then sprinkle the dough with the remaining ½ cup (65 g) flour to keep the top from forming a crust and help the batter slide off the spoon or cookie scoop. You're looking for a semi-wet, slightly loose and jiggly dough, just a bit thicker than pancake batter, so you'll end up with light, fluffy dumplings.

Add enough of the stock to the soup pot to have 4 inches (10 cm) of liquid. Bring to a boil over medium heat and maintain the boil.

Working in batches, use two tablespoons (or a #100 cookie scoop) to drop the dumpling batter into the boiling liquid, forming 8 to 10 tablespoon-size dumplings per batch (more than 10 will crowd most pots). Keep the liquid boiling and cook the dumplings for 4 minutes on one side and 2 to 3 minutes on the other. Use a slotted spoon to pull out a dumpling and split it open to make sure it's cooked in the center, then transfer the cooked dumplings to a clean plate. Add more stock if necessary to have 4 inches (10 cm) of liquid in the pot and cook a second batch. Make as many dumplings as your

FOR SERVING

¼ cup (15 g) finely chopped dill

¼ cup (15 g) finely chopped flat-leaf parsley

¼ cup (15 g) finely chopped green onions

dinner guests can eat. Save leftover batter in the fridge to cook the next day.

When the dumplings are done, pull all the rabbit meat off the bone, roughly chop into bite-size pieces, and place the meat back into the pot. Taste the stew and adjust the seasoning.

Serve the stew in wide, shallow bowls with dumplings and garnished with lots of the dill, parsley, and green onions.

RABBIT HUNTING IN BAYOU LACACHE

Bayou Lacache, or Hidden Bayou, has given way to coastal erosion. My dad remembers casting a paupière for shrimp on the long-gone bayou in his outboard when he was young, but by his thirties it was just a lake. Bayou Lacache was once about sixteen feet wide and pretty deep, but when the tide was low, there was a mudflat, and rabbits would come out of the woods to drink from the bayou and unfortunately meet their death by shotgun. At that time the bayou was flanked by solid marsh, oak, and cypress trees—not an open lake or gulf as it is today.

After the hunters killed the rabbits, they would wash them free of mud in the bayou, butcher them, and pass them out to family. Folks cooked panfried rabbit, smothered rabbit, rabbit sauce piquant, rabbit stew, and fried rabbit (like fried chicken). Rabbit was a delicacy for everyone to eat.

Rabbit- and duck-hunting seasons are both in winter. In the days before refrigerators and freezers, it was important to hunt during the cold months to keep the rabbit meat fresh. Rabbits also taste better in winter because of their diets. They are still hunted all over South Louisiana with a season starting in October and ending in February.

Afternoon Pecan Cake

SERVES 8 TO 12

The great pecan tree that stood towering over my grandparents' home in Chauvin produced a plethora of pecans. It was a fall ritual for Dad to dutifully pick multiple five-gallon buckets' worth of pecans with ease, then crack them by hand the old-fashioned way for us to eat throughout the year. We lost the tree in Hurricane Ida. It's sad to lose the trees that fed us and kept traditions going without breaking the bank. I miss the process, the ceremony, and the communion with a tree that has a defined seasonal cycle, from the stringy long flowers to the green pods that ripen to a woody brown and to cracking and enjoying the nuts. Pecans, like most nuts, are expensive, and every year we use them to make candy, pies, and cakes that are worth all the effort of shucking them.

This pecan cake has minimal ingredients and is a one-layer affair. It is delicious on its own and does not need frosting.

⅔ cup (90 g) pecans

1 cup (125 g) all-purpose flour

8 ounces (225 g) unsalted butter, at room temperature, cut into small cubes

¾ cup (150 g) raw sugar

3 eggs, at room temperature

1 teaspoon baking powder

½ teaspoon kosher salt

1 teaspoon pure vanilla extract

Powdered sugar, for dusting (optional)

Preheat the oven to 350°F (180°C). Grease a 9-inch (23 cm) round cake pan with oil or pan spray.

In a food processor, pulse the pecans and ½ cup (65 g) of the flour until they turn into a fine meal like almond meal, stopping before they turn into a paste or nut butter.

In the bowl of a stand mixer fitted with the paddle attachment or in a large bowl using a handheld mixer, beat the butter and raw sugar, starting on low speed and gradually moving to high speed, until light and fluffy, 5 to 10 minutes. Scrape down the bowl with a silicone spatula, paying special attention to the center bottom of the bowl, where ingredients get stuck. Add the eggs one at a time, beating well and thoroughly scraping down the bowl after each addition, until fully incorporated. →

In another bowl, whisk or sift together the remaining ½ cup (65 g) flour, the pecan-flour mixture, baking powder, and salt. Add these dry ingredients to the egg mixture and beat just until incorporated.

Add the vanilla and mix for 10 seconds on low speed. The cake batter will be thicker than a regular cake batter. It's not pourable, and you will need to use a silicone spatula to scrape it from the mixing bowl and spread it in the prepared pan, smoothing it out a bit on top.

Bake for 45 minutes, gently turning the pan every 15 minutes, until golden on top and a cake tester inserted in the center comes out clean; alternatively, press down on the cake—if it springs back, it's done. Let the cake cool, then turn it out onto a cake stand or flat plate and serve. You can dust with powdered sugar, if you like, but it's not necessary. Pecan cake keeps for a couple days in a sealed container at room temperature.

LOVE

———— · ı ˎ ˏ ı ı ———

I HAD THE GREAT PRIVILEGE to grow up around love: for my Cajun culture and traditions, for our fisheries, for my relatives and friends, and for food. For me, food and love are intrinsically linked. I didn't come from a perfect family—there was generational trauma from hurricanes and death, from money or lack thereof, and the compounded trauma from trauma not being recognized and healed. I had people close to me who didn't know how to show affection, yet I knew I was surrounded by love, security, and protection. My father showed love through his work, having multiple jobs so he could take care of us, and he loved my mother. We knew they were in love, and we saw love between them. My mother showed love domestically by making us breakfast, lunch, and dinner. I felt love from my grandparents, aunts, and uncles who lived next door to us. I am aware that love is a privilege and growing up surrounded by it is a luxury.

The holidays bring out the giving and sharing side of love, and the great act of cooking for others. We plan our holiday menus, start shopping and prepping weeks in advance. Then we set out to make fabulous meals for our families and friends, splurging on ingredients. A simple crab dip, perfectly fried oysters in a winter grapefruit salad, or a soup with precious turtle meat can all communicate love. When a time-consuming holiday dressing or cabbage rolls make an appearance, we understand the hours and patience involved. All the dishes that come together to make a holiday meal are acts of love. What matters is that you put love into the act of preparing them and that you share them with people you love.

Lump Crab, Spinach, and Artichoke Dip

SERVES 6 AS A SNACK

The holidays call for special dishes, and adding jumbo lump crab to any dish signals something special. Not only is it delicate and elegant, but crab must be meticulously picked and is legitimately pricey because of that. This dip is a crowd-pleaser; putting out this bubbling cassoulet of spinach, artichoke, and crab dip says "let's celebrate."

Warm a heavy-bottomed Dutch oven over medium heat for 1 minute, then add the butter. When it has melted, add the garlic, ¼ teaspoon of the salt, and the red pepper flakes and cook, stirring often, until the garlic is fragrant and shows a little color, about 2 minutes.

Add the spinach a handful at a time and let it completely cook down, about 5 minutes. Once the spinach is wilted, add the artichokes, lemon juice, black pepper, and the remaining 1 teaspoon salt and stir to combine. Add the cream cheese and stir continuously until melted. Add the sour cream and stir until completely combined; you should have a beautiful dip now.

Remove from the heat and mix in the crabmeat, cayenne, and nutmeg; stir until combined. Taste and adjust the seasoning if necessary. Transfer the dip to a heatproof serving dish that's the right size for dipping, and serve immediately with toast points.

2 tablespoons unsalted butter

1 tablespoon finely chopped garlic

1¼ teaspoons kosher salt

⅛ teaspoon red pepper flakes

8 ounces (225 g) fresh spinach, roughly chopped into 2-inch (5 cm) square pieces

8.5 ounces (240 g) frozen or canned artichoke hearts, drained

1 tablespoon fresh lemon juice

¼ teaspoon cracked black pepper

6 ounces (170 g) cream cheese, cut into small chunks

½ cup (120 ml) sour cream

1 pound (455 g) jumbo lump crabmeat, picked clean of any shells

¼ teaspoon cayenne pepper

⅛ teaspoon freshly grated nutmeg

Toast points, for serving

Fried Oyster, Radicchio, and Grapefruit Salad

SERVES 4

Although salads do not count as Cajun food per se, chicories make the perfect dinner salad to serve with seafood. When the weather cools off, the radicchios start showing up at Louisiana farmers' markets. If you can find Bel Fiore radicchio, use it here; it is crunchy and mildly bitter, light green and white, with specks of burgundy throughout. Source a perfect winter Ruby Red grapefruit and plump salty oysters, and this will be a perfect salad for a special occasion or dinner.

Prepare a tabletop fryer with canola oil and heat to 350°F (180°C). Alternately, fill a large heavy-bottomed pot with 4 inches (10 cm) of oil and heat the oil over medium-high heat to 350°F (180°C).

Cut the radicchio into manageable bite-size pieces, then wash and dry. (If you have smaller radicchios, you can leave them whole or simply slice them in half.) Place in a salad bowl and season with the kosher salt and black pepper.

Use a sharp knife to segment the grapefruits over the bowl of radicchio so you capture all the juice (see page 258), letting the segments drop into the bowl. After you have released all the segments, squeeze the rind of the grapefruit over the bowl to get the last drops of juice. Gently mix the radicchio and fruit together with your hands or salad tongs.

In a small bowl, mix together the vinegar, shallot, and honey.

Drizzle the olive oil over the radicchio. Add the vinegar mixture and gently toss with your hands or salad tongs.

In a medium shallow bowl, season the cornmeal with a touch of cayenne and kosher salt and black pepper to taste. Dredge the oysters in the mixture. →

Canola oil or peanut oil, for frying

1 head radicchio (about 13 ounces/370 g)

1½ teaspoons kosher salt, plus more as needed

¼ teaspoon cracked black pepper, plus more as needed

1 pound (455 g) Ruby Red grapefruits

2 tablespoons white wine vinegar or apple cider vinegar, plus more as needed

1 tablespoon finely diced shallot

2 teaspoons honey

2 tablespoons olive oil or canola oil, plus more as needed

2 cups (320 g) cornmeal, preferably Bayou Cora Farms heirloom cornmeal

Cayenne pepper

20 to 24 oysters, shucked (reserve the liquor for another use)

Sea salt

1 ounce (30 g) Parmesan, shaved

Working in batches of 10 to 12, add the oysters to the hot oil and fry for 2 minutes. You will hear whistling and popping noises when the oysters enter the oil; this will cease quickly as oysters cook quickly. When the oil quiets down, the oysters are near done.

Use tongs to transfer the cooked oysters to a paper towel–lined plate or brown paper bags to absorb excess oil. Sprinkle them with a bit of sea salt and place on top of the salad immediately.

Top the salad with the Parmesan. Taste and season with more sea salt and black pepper, if needed. If the salad seems too dry, add a little more olive oil and vinegar.

HOW TO SEGMENT A GRAPEFRUIT OR OTHER CITRUS

Holding the grapefruit (or orange or lemon), slice off the stem end and then the opposite end to give you flat ends. Place one flat end down on the cutting board and, using a very sharp knife, begin to remove the peel and pith of the grapefruit. Do this by carefully running your knife down the grapefruit, following the curve, and finding the sweet spot between the flesh and the pith. You should be able to release all the flesh with eight peelings. Take your time when you do this.

Now hold the grapefruit in your hand and use a very sharp paring knife. I cannot express how important *sharp* is; if you do not have a sharp knife, you will mush the grapefruit instead of releasing the segments. There are natural lines between each segment, so bring the knife as close as possible to each line and carve down to the center, releasing the segment. You will be cutting in a triangular fashion. Do all of this over a bowl so you capture the grapefruit juice as well.

Turtle Soup

SERVES 8

Turtle sauce piquant and turtle soup were served at Lagniappe on the Bayou, a long-gone tiny fair that was a culinary destination for many in Louisiana every October. My family helped make the fair happen so everyone could pass a good time. Turtle soup was served in Styrofoam bowls at the fair, but it also sits on some of the most elegant menus across New Orleans and throughout France. Turtle soup was made by American Indians. This thread linking us back to our roots is so important in understanding Cajuns' place in this world. The soup is easy to make; it contains onions, bell peppers, and celery, plus beef stock for a rich, decadent meal.

NOTE: *You can source Louisiana turtle meat online (see Resources, page 359).*

Place the turtle meat in a bowl and pour the lemon juice over it, coating it evenly. Add the hot sauce, salt, black pepper, and cayenne and mix well. Let tenderize overnight in the refrigerator.

The next day, remove the turtle meat from the refrigerator and let it come to room temperature while you cook the vegetables.

Warm a heavy-bottomed 8-quart (7.5 L) pot or Dutch oven over medium heat, then add the oil and heat for about 30 seconds. Add the yellow onions and green onion whites and cook for 10 minutes, stirring occasionally. Reduce the heat to medium-low and cook, stirring occasionally, until the onions are caramelized, about 1 hour. Pour in a little of the stock or sherry or water to deglaze the bottom of the pot whenever the onions start to stick.

Add the celery, bell pepper, and bay leaves, stir well, and cook until the vegetables have softened and lost their bite, about 20 minutes. If the mixture looks too dry, reduce the heat to low, cover, and let the

1½ pounds (680 g) turtle meat, cubed

2 tablespoons fresh lemon juice

2 tablespoons hot sauce, preferably Original Louisiana Hot Sauce

2 tablespoons kosher salt

2 teaspoons cracked black pepper

½ teaspoon cayenne pepper

¼ cup (60 ml) canola oil or olive oil

2 pounds (910 g) yellow onions, finely diced

½ cup (30 g) finely chopped green onion whites (chop and reserve the greens for garnish)

2½ quarts (2.5 L) beef stock (page 347) or chicken stock (page 348), at room temperature

Sherry, for cooking and serving

½ cup (50 g) finely diced celery

½ cup (75 g) finely diced green bell pepper

3 bay leaves

1 cup (180 g) coarsely chopped ripe tomato

1 tablespoon tomato paste

6 thyme sprigs

¼ cup (15 g) finely chopped flat-leaf parsley

vegetables smother. Add the tomato and tomato paste and cook for 20 minutes more, stirring and deglazing the bottom of the pot, if necessary.

Add the turtle meat, stir to incorporate, and cook for 5 minutes over medium heat. Add the stock and thyme, bring to a simmer, and adjust the heat as needed to maintain a simmer until the turtle becomes tender, about 2 hours.

Taste and adjust the seasoning. Garnish the soup with the parsley and green onion tops and serve with a shot of sherry on the side.

Turnip Gratin

SERVES 8 AS A SIDE DISH

Growing up, we ate a lot of potato gratins, but you can use turnips in the same preparation and get all their earthy, spicy flavor. The gratin is inspired by the Acadians, who grew turnips because they are easy to store throughout the winter. During baking, the mixture may bubble over, so place the pan on a sheet pan to catch any spillage and keep your oven clean. I like to serve gratin with a vinegary cabbage salad to cut the richness of the dish.

Preheat the oven to 350°F (180°C). Butter a deep 8-inch (20 cm) round cast-iron pan or deep casserole dish.

In a large bowl, season the turnips with the salt, white pepper, and mustard powder. Arrange the turnips in layers in the prepared pan, spiraling them out from the bottom and layering until all the turnips are used.

Warm a heavy-bottomed 4-quart (3.8 L) saucepan over medium heat for 2 minutes, then add the butter and flour simultaneously and cook, stirring continuously, for 2 to 3 minutes to make a blond roux. Slowly stream in the milk while whisking constantly and bringing the mixture to a simmer, then remove the pan from the heat and stir in the 4 ounces (115 g) grated cheese. Add the thyme leaves, cayenne, and a touch of nutmeg to the cheese mixture and stir well. Pour the mixture over the turnips in the pan.

Place the pan on a rimmed sheet pan and bake for 30 minutes. Sprinkle the remaining 2 ounces (60 g) cheese evenly on top of the turnips, crown the gratin with the thyme sprigs, and return the pan to the oven. Bake for 20 to 25 minutes more, until the top is golden brown, the turnips are al dente (not mushy), and the liquid has been absorbed. Let the gratin sit at room temperature for 15 minutes before serving.

2 ounces (60 g) unsalted butter, cut into cubes, plus more for the pan

1½ pounds (680 g) turnips, peeled and cut into ½-inch-thick (1.3 cm) rounds

2 teaspoons kosher salt

¼ teaspoon ground white pepper

¼ teaspoon mustard powder

¼ cup (30 g) all-purpose flour

2 cups (480 ml) whole milk

4 ounces (115 g) grated Swiss cheese or Gruyère, plus 2 ounces (60 g) for topping

1 tablespoon fresh thyme leaves, plus 3 to 5 sprigs

⅛ teaspoon cayenne pepper

Freshly grated nutmeg

Chicken-Fried Quail

MAKES 8 QUAILS

I love cooking small birds. It reminds me of the ones my dad brought home from hunting trips, seemingly so exotic to a kid watching her mom cook them. Quails are plentiful in the South but can be found in almost all cuisines. Little birds can have slightly tough meat, so look for smaller quails and give them a good overnight soak in buttermilk to help tenderize them. I like to fry quails or stuff them with whatever is in season, like rice and pecans or citrus and greens. They take well to a sweet sauce or just a drizzle of honey or cane syrup.

In a large, high-rimmed baking dish, soak the quails overnight in the buttermilk, hot sauce, 1 teaspoon of the kosher salt, and thyme. Soak for at least 12 hours.

In a large bowl, mix together the flour, paprika, baking soda, black pepper, cayenne, and remaining 2 teaspoons kosher salt.

Remove one quail from the buttermilk at a time and immediately dredge it in the flour mixture. Be sure to get flour in all the nooks and crannies. Set the quail aside on a lightly floured sheet pan. Repeat with the remaining quails.

Prepare a tabletop fryer with oil and heat to 350°F (180°C). Alternatively, fill a large heavy-bottomed pot with 4 inches (10 cm) of oil and heat the oil over medium-high heat to 350°F (180°C).

Working in batches, place 2 quails in the hot oil and fry until golden brown on both sides and a thermometer inserted in the breast registers 165°F (74°C), 4 to 5 minutes total. Use tongs to transfer the quails to a paper towel–lined plate, brown paper bags, or a rack fitted in a sheet pan. Season with the sea salt.

Serve immediately with a drizzle of honey.

8 whole quails (about 2½ pounds/1.1 kg)

2 quarts (1.9 L) whole-fat buttermilk

¼ cup (60 ml) hot sauce, preferably Original Louisiana Hot Sauce

3 teaspoons kosher salt

6 thyme sprigs

2 cups (250 g) all-purpose flour, plus more for dusting

2 tablespoons paprika

1 teaspoon baking soda

¼ teaspoon cracked black pepper

¼ teaspoon cayenne pepper

Canola oil or peanut oil, for frying

1 teaspoon sea salt

Honey, for drizzling

HOLIDAYS AT HOME ON THE BAYOU

LOVE IS SPACE AND TIME MEASURED BY THE HEART.

—*Marcel Proust*

When I was a child, "home" was easy to understand; it was a tiny place surrounded by family. Home was a street with four aunts and a grandmother, a bayou that ran perpendicular to the street, a lake just past the woods, and a place with no fences. Home was a church, bridges, and community buildings, mom-and-pop gas stations serving po'boys and biscuits, a bar parents could bring their children to while two-stepping to Cajun and swamp pop music and drinking from an overflowing pirogue filled with beer. Home was my mom's kitchen and my dad's boat, my aunt's shrimp platform, and my uncle's garage, where we smashed cans for hours to make pennies.

Home took on a new meaning as I became an adult and moved farther and farther from the place where I felt safe and warm, from a place of belonging. I still return home for the holidays. It's the time I can inhabit my young self, just for a moment. We try to slow down and recapture a much simpler time.

Holidays are spent in the house where my parents still reside in Chauvin. It is a brick ranch, not a picturesque Cajun cabin on the bayou. My parents have lived under the same roof—although it's been replaced after hurricanes—for the last fifty-six years, and between the same walls that raised six kids and have been demolished and rebuilt. They cook in a kitchen that has seen many facelifts, on floors that have been covered in floodwater.

At Christmas my mother decks every corner of the home with lights and decorations, making it a wonderland. My dad decorates our family's communal gazebo. With trees and colorful lights, he makes a cozy place for slowing down. There is a spot on the gazebo's concrete pad that is worn away from the years my grandmother spent swinging while she folded clothes and peeled potatoes, snapped beans, shucked corn, and did whatever else my mother needed to tame a household of six kids. The gazebo is still a place for communing with family and making the veille: sitting a spell and just hanging out, taking time for each other, during the day and into the late hours.

On the bayou, Christmas has a Cajun theme. We have our own *Cajun Night Before Christmas* tale, where alligators named Gaston, Tobey, Pierre, Alcée, Ninette, Suzette, Celeste, and Renée pull Santa and his sleigh. Santa imbibes blackberry wine and sherry. There is a Cajun French version as well as a version that's not politically correct but that we found endearing growing up. It has a combination of French and Cajun English dialects—a language unto itself. Our librarian would read *Cajun Night Before Christmas* in her perfect Cajun French dialect, and we would read the altered version to ourselves. No matter the version, the story was true to a young girl who believed in Jolly Old Saint Nick. Forget reindeer: We had flying alligators on the bayou. And we had a Santa who spoke our language.

I remember how during the week of Christmas, the captains of trawlers, crab boats, and oyster luggers decorated their hulls with Christmas lights and flags and paraded down the bayou. (This still happens today in a smaller fashion.) Even if the weather was warm, we drank hot cocoa with marshmallows to toast the season. We caroled to our neighbors, went to midnight Mass, and came home to the honey-cooked ham that my aunts and uncles made in large pots outside on propane burners. We snacked on ham sandwiches on fresh French bread and ate tarte à la bouillie pie before bed.

My mom remembers her own holiday traditions from before we kids came along, such as her mom's oyster dressing. My grandmother would parboil oysters and grind them in a hand-crank meat grinder. My mom would help make the time-consuming dish. One of her most vivid memories is the beautiful Nativity pop-up book that my grandmother took out every year, and today at Christmas my mom puts out no less than twenty-four Nativity sets, including an almost life-size one in the yard. We are celebrating the Advent and not the commercial side of Christmas.

These days, marking a holiday with a big Cajun family is a bit chaotic. Comfort gives way to togetherness. My mother always picks a large tree and decorates it with care and makes sure each crevice of the house is festive, down to the holiday linens on the twin beds in our childhood bedrooms. My siblings and nephews sleep everywhere, shoving air mattresses in any available nook and cranny of the house and filling sofas and beds.

Our immediate family comprises more than twenty people, so we certainly can't go out to eat unless we do so in groups. Instead, we cook and eat an abundance of food at home. Our family holiday traditions taught me about production cooking, list preparation, long cooks that can be done ahead of time, short cooking, and last-minute cooking. Cajun holidays taught me sweet and savory production. They have shown me the power of women working in unison to cook for large families.

On Christmas Day, we feast on chicken gumbo, beef roast, stuffed peppers, rice dressing, mashed potatoes, petits pois, roasted turkey, honey-roasted ham, spinach and artichoke dip, oyster soup, potato salad, winter greens salad, and smothered cabbage. We have cakes, pies, cookies, and fudge. We take turns serving ourselves, and scatter between the kitchen, dining room, and gazebo, eating on TV trays. This is normal and this is home.

For children, if they are lucky, holidays are a time of magic. For adults, holidays open us up. From the marking of All Souls' Day until the ringing in of the new year, we go into a trance, undergo a metamorphosis of the soul. Holidays are not easy emotionally, but we adorn our homes until they sparkle with joy. We bake together and laugh together, gather to be together, gather to be home. We enter the new year with our spirits changed. The holidays will be back in a year's time, and we will gather then, too, allowing the magic of the season to transform our souls once again. We will come home.

Holiday Dressing

SERVES ABOUT 12 AS A SIDE

Making holiday dressing is a labor of love. It's my family's favorite accoutrement to turkey, duck, quail, or roast beef with a side of peas and green beans. To re-create my grandmother's dressing, my mom and I talked to her sisters and sisters-in-law, trying to remember all the steps and ingredients that my grandmother used. The recipe includes oysters, beef, pork, chicken livers, chicken gizzards, rice, onions, bell peppers, and celery, but it need not be made in one day. You can take it in steps, then finish the dressing on the day you'll eat it. Like any labor of love, the hard work is worth the effort, and there are bound to be leftovers. The holidays are a perfect time to remember loved ones by bringing their recipes to life.

Place the gizzards in a small bowl, cover with 2 inches (5 cm) of cold water, and add 1 teaspoon of the salt. Let sit for at least 2 hours and up to overnight, then drain and rinse the gizzards. In a medium pot, cover the gizzards with 2 inches (5 cm) of water and bring to a boil over high heat, then reduce the heat to medium and maintain a hard simmer for 30 minutes, skimming off any scum or foam that rises to the surface. Strain and cool.

Rinse the livers. Fill a medium pot with enough water to cover the livers by 4 inches (10 cm), add 1 teaspoon salt, and bring to a simmer over medium-high heat. Cook for 15 minutes, skimming off any scum that develops during cooking. Drain and cool.

Strain the oysters and reserve the oyster liquor (the water that is in the oyster container or in the shell when shucking). Rinse each oyster to remove any fragments of shell. In a medium pot, bring the oyster liquor to a boil. If you do not have enough oyster liquor to cover the oysters and for them to move freely while cooking, add enough water to cover (up to 2 quarts/1.9 L) and up to 1 tablespoon salt. Add the

½ pound (225 g) chicken gizzards

3 teaspoons kosher salt, plus more as needed

½ pound (225 g) chicken livers

2 pounds (910 g) shucked oysters

1 pound (455 g) ground beef

1 pound (455 g) ground pork

½ teaspoon cracked black pepper

½ teaspoon cayenne pepper

¼ cup (60 ml) canola oil

2 cups (250 g) finely diced yellow onions

½ cup (75 g) finely diced green bell pepper

½ cup (50 g) finely diced celery

¼ cup (15 g) finely chopped green onion whites (chop and reserve the greens for garnish)

2 cups (400 g) cooked rice

¼ cup (15 g) finely chopped flat-leaf parsley

oysters and simmer for 5 minutes, skimming off any scum or foam. Strain the water and reserve for another use, if you like.

Using a meat grinder or a KitchenAid mixer with the meat grinder attachment, grind the livers and gizzards together on a coarse small die and place in a bowl. (Alternatively, you can hand-chop them with a sharp knife.) Using the same grinder, grind the oysters and set them in a separate bowl in the fridge. No need to clean the grinder in between.

In a bowl, season the beef and pork with the remaining 1 teaspoon salt, the black pepper, and the cayenne. Warm a heavy-bottomed 12-quart (11 L) pan over medium-high heat, then add the oil and heat for 2 minutes. Add the beef and pork and sauté until no longer pink, about 10 minutes. Add the ground livers and gizzards and stir.

Stir in the yellow onions, bell pepper, celery, and green onion whites. Cover, reduce the heat to low, and smother together until the meat gets really tender and the vegetables soften and have little bite, 2 hours. Stir in the chopped oysters and rice, then taste the dressing: Does it need more salt, black pepper, or cayenne? If so, add some.

Serve topped with the parsley and green onion tops. The dressing will keep for up to 4 days covered in the fridge.

Fried Turkey

SERVES 12

Fried turkey is a party in itself. Many folks in South Louisiana prefer it over roasted turkey for Thanksgiving, Christmas, and New Year's Eve. A bunch of my uncles whom I have never seen cook in the kitchen will gather outside drinking beer around a large pot of boiling oil and watch a whole turkey fry. When I was little, I thought these men were knowledgeable and in control. Now that I'm an older, wiser chef, I can't believe we made it through a holiday with limbs intact. Let's face it: Frying a whole turkey is a dangerous thing. That much heated oil in a Cajun fryer without a thermometer is downright maniacal. But I live to tell the tale.

If you want to fry a turkey, be very safe and fry it the right way. I use a dry cure to keep the bird as dry as possible. It's important to note that when frying a turkey there is a lot of carryover heat, meaning after you remove the bird from the boiling oil, it will continue cooking for quite some time. That's why in this recipe I ask you to remove the bird before it's normally considered done, because it will eventually reach the desired temperature range of 175° to 180°F (79° to 82°C). Cooking time will depend on the outside temperature, of course; if it's cold outdoors, the air will cool your pot down. The general culinary rule for frying turkeys is that it takes three to four minutes per pound (450 g), but frying outside in Louisiana will be in stark contrast to frying outside in Minnesota.

Prepare a dry cure by mixing together in a bowl the sugars, salt, black pepper, cayenne, and thyme. Crinkle the bay leaf in your hand, then mix it in.

Put the turkey on a pan that will fit in your refrigerator. Pat the turkey inside and out with clean, dry rags until completely dry, then thoroughly rub the turkey with the dry cure. Loosely cover the bird with a towel and place the pan in the refrigerator for 24 to 48 hours,

FOR THE DRY CURE

½ cup (100 g) raw sugar

½ cup packed (110 g) brown sugar

¼ cup (35 g) kosher salt

2 tablespoons freshly ground black pepper

1 teaspoon cayenne pepper

Handful of thyme stems (about 20)

1 bay leaf

8- to 10-pound (3.6 to 4.5 kg) turkey

2½ gallons (9.4 L) peanut oil, for frying

then remove the turkey and give it another rubdown with rags. You want the turkey to be completely dry when you fry it. Bring the bird to room temperature to help keep the frying temperature consistent.

Select a pot at least 8 inches (20 cm) taller than the turkey so that the frying oil will not rise to the very top of the pot (I use an 18-quart/ 17 L stockpot). Fill the pot halfway with oil and clip a deep-fat thermometer to the side. Carefully set the pot on a propane burner outside in a safe location and heat the oil to 325°F (170°C). It should take about an hour to bring the oil up to temperature.

Have a table set up nearby with all your equipment. I use a basket insert to fry the turkey because I believe it is safer, and I like to have welding gloves available as well as large tongs, a meat thermometer appropriate for turkey, a pan fitted with a draining rack, a fire extinguisher, and a friend.

Begin with the basket insert out of the heated oil. Turn off the flame. Place the turkey in the basket and carefully lower it into the hot oil. Turn the fire back on medium-low and maintain the temperature at 325° to 350°F (170° to 180°C). The oil should rise to cover the turkey. If it does not cover the turkey completely, add more oil to cover. Don't worry if the extra oil starts out cool; it will warm up rapidly. Make sure the basket handle stays visible and preferably out of the oil.

Fry the turkey for 30 minutes, then carefully lift the basket and insert a meat thermometer into the thickest part of the bird and take a reading. Then take a second reading in another spot; the temperature will not be the same in the breast and legs, but you'll want it in the 155° to 160°F (68° to 71°C) range so that the carryover heat will get it up to 175°F (79°C). Working with a second person, carefully remove the insert with the turkey and place it on the pan fitted with a draining rack. After 10 to 15 minutes, check the temperature again to confirm it's at least 175°F (79°C). If it isn't, carefully place the turkey back into the oil, cook for 10 to 15 minutes more, and check the temperature again.

Let the turkey rest for 30 minutes, then carve and enjoy. You did it.

Happy New Year Cabbage Rolls

MAKES 16 CABBAGE ROLLS

In a photo of my grandmother sitting in her wheelchair pulled close to my mom's kitchen table, she is opposite my sister Maria, and they are making cabbage rolls together. My grandmother, in her eighties, looks a bit frail but is focused on her task. Cabbage rolls are a New Year's tradition, like tucking a small piece of dried cabbage in aluminum foil and handing it out to relatives on New Year's Day. The cabbage is supposed to bring you money all year long.

This is a simple recipe for a delicious meal. Make a casserole of cabbage rolls and eat them all week. Cabbage rolls can easily be made vegetarian; swap out the beef and pork for a stuffing of rice and beans.

NOTE: *You'll need three pots going on your stove to make this recipe: one for boiling cabbage, one for smothering meat and vegetables, and one for making tomato sauce; alternatively, you can make the tomato sauce or smother the meat a day ahead.*

Bring a pot of salted water to a boil. Core the cabbage and gently pry off the leaves. Blanch them in the boiling water until wilted, soft, and pliable, about 5 minutes. Use tongs to transfer the leaves to a colander to drain and cool.

In a large bowl, combine the pork, beef, 1 tablespoon of the salt, 1 teaspoon of the black pepper, and the cayenne.

Warm a small heavy-bottomed pot over medium heat. Add the meat mixture and 2 tablespoons of the oil, then cook, browning, for about 4 minutes. Reduce the heat to medium-low and cook for 6 minutes more, stirring to break up the meat. Remove the mixture to a fine-mesh strainer over a bowl to drain excess oil and set aside.

In the same pot over medium heat, pour in the remaining 2 tablespoons oil and heat for 1 minute, then add the onions and cook until translucent

1 to 2 heads very large cabbage, like napa or Savoy (about 2½ pounds/ 1.1 kg)

½ pound (225 g) ground pork

½ pound (225 g) ground beef

2 tablespoons kosher salt

1½ teaspoons cracked black pepper

¼ teaspoon cayenne pepper

4 tablespoons canola oil or olive oil

1 pound (455 g) yellow onions, finely diced

¼ cup (35 g) finely diced green bell pepper

¼ cup (25 g) finely diced celery

2 ounces (60 g) unsalted butter or olive oil

2 (28-ounce/795 g) cans crushed no-salt-added San Marzano or other good-quality tomatoes

6 teaspoons raw sugar

1 cup (180 g) diced ripe tomato

2 cups (400 g) cooked rice

¼ cup (15 g) finely chopped flat-leaf parsley

Parmesan, for finishing

and taking on a golden hue, about 20 minutes. Add the bell pepper and celery and cook until they are soft and have lost their bite, another 20 minutes. Stir often and turn the heat down, if necessary, so the vegetables don't stick and burn. If needed, add a splash of water to deglaze the pot and scrape up any bits stuck to the bottom.

Meanwhile, warm a medium heavy-bottomed pot over medium heat for 1 minute, then add the butter. When it has melted, add 3 cups (675 g) of the crushed tomatoes and 2 teaspoons of the sugar and cook for about 8 minutes, letting the sauce start to brown on the bottom of the pot. Add another 2 cups (450 g) crushed tomatoes and 2 teaspoons sugar and repeat the browning process. Add 1 cup (225 g) crushed tomatoes and the remaining 2 teaspoons sugar and repeat the process one more time. Season with the remaining 1 tablespoon salt and ½ teaspoon black pepper.

To the pan of onions, bell pepper, and celery add the reserved meat and diced tomato. Stir and cook together over medium-low heat for 5 minutes. Remove from the heat and let cool for about 15 minutes. Add the rice and stir.

Preheat the oven to 350°F (180°C).

To stuff the rolls, hold a large cabbage leaf in your nondominant hand. Scoop ¼ cup (60 g) of the filling and place it in the center of the leaf—do not overstuff. Cup the leaf in both hands, as if you were trying to hold water. Now think of your cupped hands as a compass: Use your thumbs to fold the east and west sides of the leaf into the center. Then fold the south side of the leaf over the two pressed-down sides and roll toward the north side. (Alternatively, you can place each leaf on a cutting board to fill and roll it.) Place the cabbage roll seam-side down in a large casserole dish. Repeat with the remaining leaves and filling, placing the rolls snug against one another.

Pour the tomato sauce over the cabbage rolls and bake for 30 to 45 minutes. The sauce should be thick and slowly bubbling.

To serve, sprinkle with the parsley and top with a grating of Parmesan.

Black-Eyed Pea Soup

SERVES 10 TO 12

Every New Year's Day my mom makes a spread of cabbage rolls, black-eyed pea soup, smothered cabbage, roast, and rice. She often fries shrimp, oysters, or fish to accompany them. This soup combines black-eyed peas, greens, and a Cajun's favorite, salt pork. It is easy to make and stocks you with leftovers that just get better the next day. It's also a great way to use any ham hocks or ham bones you have saved in the freezer.

You can double the batch and give soup to your family and friends as an act of generosity on New Year's Eve. It's a soup that's a whole meal in one.

Warm a heavy-bottomed 8-quart (7.5 L) Dutch oven over medium heat, then add the oil and heat for 30 seconds. Add the salt pork and cook, turning as needed to brown it on all sides, about 8 minutes. Carefully drain off all but ¼ cup (60 ml) of the fat.

Add the onions and cook until they are translucent, starting to caramelize, and taking on a golden hue, about 20 minutes. Add the celery and bell pepper and cook for 20 minutes, uncovered, stirring frequently.

Add the black-eyed peas and carrots, stir well, and season with the salt, black pepper, cayenne, hot sauce, and bay leaf. Pour in the chicken stock, reduce the heat to its lowest setting, and simmer together uncovered. Now is the time to toss in any ham hocks or ham bones, if using.

When the black-eyed peas are al dente, taste the soup: Does it need more salt or black pepper? Add some. Does it need more heat? Add cayenne. Does it need acid? If so, add a squeeze of lemon juice, a dash of vinegar, or more hot sauce. Right before serving, stir the chopped greens into the soup. Happy New Year!

¼ cup (60 ml) canola oil

1 pound (455 g) salt pork, diced

2 pounds (910 g) yellow onions, finely diced

½ cup (50 g) finely diced celery

⅓ cup (50 g) finely diced green bell pepper

1 pound (455 g) dried black-eyed peas, rinsed

½ cup (70 g) carrots, diced into small cubes

1 tablespoon kosher salt

¼ teaspoon freshly ground black pepper

¼ teaspoon cayenne pepper

1 tablespoon hot sauce, preferably Original Louisiana Hot Sauce, plus more as needed

1 bay leaf

3 quarts (2.8 L) chicken stock (page 348) or vegetable stock

Ham hocks or ham bones (optional)

Lemon wedges or vinegar (optional)

1 small bunch (225 g) hearty greens (collards, mustard, or curly kale), chopped into small pieces

Gateau Nana

SERVES 8 TO 12

Nancy Brewer of the Kitchen Shop in Grand Coteau, Louisiana, is a professionally trained baker who had an epiphany in baking school when tasting pâte sucrée. She realized it was the same dough as in her grandmother's sweet pies. It's a wonderful feeling as a chef to hit on something so far away that brings you right back to home. Nancy has created a tradition in her tiny community of Grand Coteau that has reverberated worldwide. She makes and ships pies on a grand scale during the holidays and is known for her Cajun treats that combine the best of her professional training and her knowledge from her grandmother's kitchen. Nostalgia drives those of us chasing a specific flavor. Nancy and I both believe in these little things that are so important to a season and a community and how to bake them into dough for celebration. This Gateau Nana, inspired by Nancy and the coasts of Brittany and Basque country, is filled with a Louisiana pecan frangipane.

Make the crust: In the bowl of a stand mixer fitted with the paddle attachment or in a large bowl using a handheld mixer, cream together the butter and superfine sugar, starting on low speed and gradually moving to high speed, for about 5 minutes, occasionally scraping down the sides. Add the egg yolks and mix just until combined. In a small bowl, mix together the flour and salt, then add the flour mixture to the egg mixture. The dough should come together quickly and be soft, pliable, and forgiving. Separate the dough into two equal portions and place in a bowl with a towel on top. Let rest in the refrigerator.

Make the filling: In a food processor, pulse the nuts, raw sugar, and salt until they turn into a fine meal, stopping before they turn into nut butter. Add the butter and combine. Add the egg, egg yolk, and vanilla and combine. Add the flour and pulse until incorporated, scraping down the sides of the bowl once or twice. →

FOR THE CRUST

8½ ounces (240 g) unsalted butter, at room temperature

½ cup (100 g) superfine sugar

6 egg yolks

2½ cups (310 g) all-purpose flour

½ teaspoon kosher salt

FOR THE FILLING

2 cups (214 g) pecan pieces or whole nuts

½ cup (100 g) raw sugar

1 teaspoon kosher salt

3 ounces (85 g) unsalted butter, at room temperature

1 egg plus 1 egg yolk

½ teaspoon pure vanilla extract

2 tablespoons all-purpose flour

FOR THE EGG WASH

1 egg yolk

Heavy cream

Assemble the Gateau Nana: Preheat the oven to 350°F (180°C). Line the bottom of a 9-inch (23 cm) springform pan or tart pan with a removable bottom with parchment paper and grease it. Press one portion of the dough into the bottom of the pan. Spread the frangipane filling on top in an even layer. Pop the pan in the freezer for about 15 minutes to chill.

Roll out the remaining dough into a 9-inch (23 cm) circle. Move quickly so as not to warm the dough, and remember if the dough falls apart that it is very forgiving.

Remove the pan from the freezer and press the top layer of dough into the frangipane layer, pressing on the border gently to seal it. Gently drag the tines of a fork over the top crust to create a decorative crisscross pattern.

In a small bowl, make an egg wash by whisking together the egg yolk and a splash of cream. Brush the top of the dough with the egg wash.

Bake for 45 to 50 minutes, until the top is golden brown. Cool to lukewarm before slicing and serving. The pie keeps for 3 to 4 days but is best when freshest.

Alberta Songe's Red Velvet Cake

SERVES 12

Alberta Songe grew up on a citrus orchard in Chauvin. The orchard was for picking, and you could procure orange trees there, too. She shared her recipe for red velvet cake with my aunt more than fifty years ago, written in blue ink on paper that my aunt laminated. With the Louisiana weather, humidity got into the paper, blurred the ink, and made the recipe difficult to decipher. My sister and I were determined to save it, and this is the recipe we settled on. We kept the Crisco shortening but cut the amount in half and added butter to give flavor to both the cake and frosting. If you want to proceed with just Crisco, then omit the butter and use the same amount of Crisco.

Alberta's frosting is an "ermine frosting." An ermine is a white mink known for its soft, fluffy, shiny coat. The frosting will resemble whipped cream and won't be too sweet. Ermine frosting is sometimes called a "roux" frosting because you start it like a blond roux, with a little bit of milk and flour, cooking it until it thickens like pudding.

NOTE: *Alberta said to use four bottles of red food coloring, and she wasn't kidding! If you use concentrated red gel food coloring, you won't need as much. If you want to stay au naturel, use beet powder—but you won't ever achieve that yuletide red without the food coloring.*

Make the cake: Preheat the oven to 350°F (180°C). Thoroughly grease and flour two 9-inch (23 cm) cake pans. (I also cut out 9-inch/23 cm parchment paper rounds and press them into the bottom of the pans for extra sticking protection.)

In the bowl of a stand mixer fitted with the whisk attachment or in a large bowl using a handheld mixer, whisk the eggs on medium speed until light and fluffy, about 7 minutes. Add the raw sugar and whisk together, starting on low speed and gradually moving to high speed, until the mixture is thick, 3 to 4 minutes. Be sure to scrape down the

FOR THE CAKE

2 cups (250 g) all-purpose flour, plus more for the pans

2 eggs, at room temperature

1½ cups (300 g) raw sugar

4 ounces (115 g) Crisco (see headnote) or leaf lard

4 ounces (115 g) unsalted butter, at room temperature

1 tablespoon baking powder

1 tablespoon unsweetened cocoa powder

½ teaspoon kosher salt

1 cup (240 ml) whole-fat buttermilk, at room temperature

Up to 4 tablespoons red food gel (see Note)

1 teaspoon apple cider vinegar

1 teaspoon baking soda

FOR THE FROSTING

1½ cups (360 ml) whole milk

½ cup (65 g) all-purpose flour

Kosher salt

4 ounces (115 g) Crisco

4 ounces (115 g) unsalted butter, at room temperature

1 cup (195 g) superfine sugar)

½ vanilla bean, split lengthwise and seeds scraped out, or 1 teaspoon pure vanilla extract sides and middle bottom of the bowl—that's where ingredients seem to get stuck. Add the Crisco and butter and whisk until combined.

In a large bowl, sift or whisk together the flour, baking powder, cocoa, and salt. Add one-third of the flour mixture to the bowl with the eggs, sugar, and fat. Mix just until combined and scrape down the bowl and whisk. Add half of the buttermilk and mix until combined. Scrape, scrape, scrape! Add another one-third of the flour mixture, mix until combined, and scrape. Add the remaining buttermilk, mix, and scrape, then add the remaining flour mixture, mix, and scrape. When the flour and buttermilk are combined, add the food coloring to reach your desired shade. It will be lighter after the cake bakes.

In a small bowl, mix together the vinegar and baking soda, then immediately add to the batter and mix for 60 seconds.

Pour the batter into the prepared pans and bake for 30 to 35 minutes, turning the cakes halfway through the baking process, until a cake tester inserted in the center comes out clean. Let the cakes cool before you remove them from the pans. The cakes are very delicate.

Make the frosting: In a medium saucepan, bring the milk, flour, and a dash of salt to a simmer over medium-low heat. Stir together with a wooden spoon or heatproof spatula and stir constantly until the mixture comes together and resembles thick pudding, 5 to 10 minutes.

Transfer the mixture to a wide bowl and let cool to room temperature before you finish the frosting. It's very important that the pudding and the Crisco and butter be at the same temperature for optimal frosting success.

In the bowl of a stand mixer with the whisk attachment or in a mixing bowl with a handheld mixer, whisk the Crisco and butter together on medium speed until completely combined, about 3 minutes. Add the superfine sugar, then cream together for 3 minutes, starting on low speed and gradually moving to high speed. Scrape down the sides and middle bottom of the bowl. Add the pudding to the fat and whisk together until the texture is light and airy, like a silky whipped cream,

3 to 5 minutes. Add the vanilla and gently combine with the mixer on low speed for about 15 seconds. If the frosting is too loose, refrigerate for 15 minutes, then whisk again.

When the cake is completely cooled, it's ready to frost; using an offset spatula is your best bet. First, divide the frosting in half. Keep half out and reserve half in the refrigerator. Plan to use the first half of the frosting to do a crumb coat, a thin layer that functions like a paint primer to ready the cake for the final coat of frosting. This will keep your cake smooth and beautiful.

Place one layer of the cake on a cake round, flat plate, or cake stand for frosting. Using an offset spatula, place two-thirds of the unchilled frosting in the center and smooth out the frosting to cover one even layer about 1 inch (2.5 cm) thick. Place the top cake layer on top of the frosting and use the remaining frosting (not the reserved batch) to apply a thin layer all around the cake, making sure to smooth the frosting into any cracks and crevices. Rotate the cake as you frost it, so all sides are equally coated with frosting. Let the cake rest in the refrigerator or freezer for 45 minutes to 1 hour. After the rest time, let the reserved half of the frosting sit out at room temperature for about 5 minutes or until soft, then, using a clean offset spatula, do a final frosting all over the cake. Finish with some nice swooping motions to create some movement on your cake. 'Tis the season, so decorate with a Christmas theme. Alligators pulling a sleigh, maybe?

Serve the cake immediately or refrigerate for 3 to 4 days. Just be sure to take it out 10 to 15 minutes before serving to take the chill off and let the crumb relax.

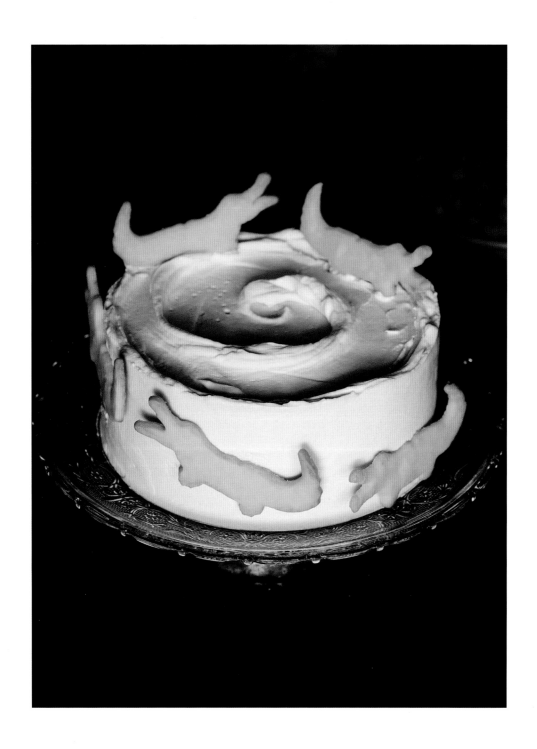

Pecan Crescents

MAKES 30 CRESCENTS

I found a recipe for pecan crescents in the cookbook *Cuisine à la Piquante*. The recipe was from the 1979 Queen Sauce Piquant, Miss Jan Veulman. I updated her recipe with ingredients I love. This cookie is light and sandy, and the recipe is easily altered for different flavor profiles like almond and lemon extract. It also makes use of the pecan, which is one of the few nut trees native to North America. This is a great everyday afternoon cookie, and also a great addition to a Christmas cookie box.

Preheat the oven to 300°F (150°C). Line a sheet pan with a silicone mat or parchment paper. In a small bowl, whisk together the flour and salt.

In the bowl of a stand mixer fitted with the paddle attachment or in a large bowl using a handheld mixer, mix the butter on medium speed until light and fluffy, about 5 minutes. Add the superfine sugar and mix, starting on low speed and gradually moving to high speed, until combined. Add the water and vanilla and mix until combined. Turn the mixer off, then add the flour carefully in three parts, mixing it in on low speed so you don't have a puff of flour all over your face and kitchen.

Place the pecans in a food processor and pulse a couple times, just until they are ground into a fine meal, stopping before they turn into a paste or nut butter. Add the pecans to the flour mixture and mix to combine.

Remove the dough, place it on a sheet of parchment paper, and refrigerate for about 30 minutes so it is easier to work with. Form small dough logs 1½ inches (3.8 cm) long and shape them into crescents or into the shape of the letter C. Place the cookies on the prepared sheet pan and bake for 45 minutes, or until golden brown.

Sift the powdered sugar liberally over the cookies. The cookies will keep for 1 week in an airtight container.

2 cups (250 g) all-purpose flour

½ teaspoon kosher salt

8 ounces (225 g) unsalted butter, at room temperature

¼ cup (50 g) superfine sugar

1 tablespoon water

2 teaspoons pure vanilla extract

1 cup (115 g) pecans

1 cup (125 g) powdered sugar, for dusting

A CAJUN FAREWELL

In the summer of 2019, my aunt Brenda, who was my godmother, or nanny, ended her battle with cancer. After ten years of treatment, including some experimental procedures, there was nothing more doctors could do. Brenda Cecile Lirette, a woman of strength and faith, decided she was done fighting. She would enjoy as many months as she could with her family and wait for the cancer to metastasize and end her life. My godmother had lost her fifteen-year-old son to leukemia, her husband had passed twenty years before her from a heart attack after living ten years with a heart transplant, and she'd lost her twenty-three-year-old grand-daughter to a drunk driver. She had known suffering her whole life.

My mom, Maxine; my nanny, Brenda; their sisters Christine, Laverne, and Linda; and my grandmother have all lived next door to each other for fifty years, and my aunt Earline lived just across the bayou. Growing up, every time I saw my nanny cross the street to visit, I got so excited. She was fun. We called my mom the Queen of No. But my nanny was a "yes" mom. She had traveled the world, and she emitted a certain ineffable joy. She had a saying, "So be it," and she lived by that mantra. Life is uncontrollable. We must lean in or we will never survive. When asked to write about my heroes growing up, I always wrote about her.

The last conversation I had with my godmother, in my mother's kitchen, was almost impossible. I attempted not to fall apart but shuddered, and tried to hide the panic on my face that weighed down my whole body, the panic that I still feel, years later, penning this memory. We knew she would be gone soon. It was a living farewell. I asked my nanny about her pecan pie. I could have easily asked about her red beans, shrimp gumbo, boulettes, or spicy spaghetti, but pecan pie came to my mind. It's a dessert she always baked for holidays. She easily rattled off the ingredients and method. Our last conversation was a list and a recipe, honed and perfected for years, to put together a treat to share with others. No one makes pie just for themselves.

My nanny was still lucid and laughing on All Hallows' Eve. For All Saints' Day, as tradition dictates, my family went to the cemetery to clean the tombstones and graves of our loved ones and friends. We made sure there were glowing candles and fresh bouquets of flowers. Then we rang in All Souls' Day at Mass in remembrance of those gone before us.

I spent the day watching my godmother breathe her last breaths and listening to my aunts and cousins talk. They yapped about little things: Instant Pots, ranges and hoods, cooking and gardens. I overheard my aunt Christine say, "We have to put some holy water in our okra and see if they gonna make some more," referring to her garden behind her house. There was an LSU football game blaring on the television, which my godmother would've loved. It was not a peaceful, quiet scene. My mom and her sisters are loud, and they tend to just get louder and louder and talk over each other. They talk about whose recipe is better and which place sells the best meat. (There was a proclamation at some point that a particular big-box store has superior meat, and I kept my mouth shut.) My nanny was being rocked to sleep in the normal chaos she had grown to love—touchdowns, food, laughter, and her family's voices.

Across the street, my mother's house was set up as the main kitchen. Everyone would hold vigil with my nanny and then cross the street for nourishment. They joked about how much weight they were going to gain with Aunt Maxine's cooking. The hospice nurse said it could be any time, but the days kept passing and everyone kept eating:

Monday: Fried fish, white beans
Tuesday: Roast beef po'boys
Wednesday: Beef and vegetable soup
Thursday: Chicken gumbo
Friday: Shrimp spaghetti and mashed potatoes
Saturday: Shrimp and okra gumbo, roast, rice, and mashed potatoes
Sunday: Leftovers and fried shrimp po'boys from Marty J's

My mom and her sisters are all excellent cooks. Their mom cooked for nine children and for hungry fishermen. Fishermen's daughters, they grew up surrounded by seafood and gardens, and they know their way around a kitchen. If you are in their presence in their kitchen, you are in a good place. Many Cajuns are also devout Catholics and have immeasurable faith, a faith that carries them through extreme suffering and incredible joy. They say the rosary daily and have used these beads as meditation and ritual. My mom considers her faith her armor.

On my nanny's last day, I was able to hold her hand and kiss her, sit on the couch and be present, and listen to the chatter of family all around me. It was almost midnight and her sisters had retired to their homes across the street to get some rest. My mother and three remaining sisters were phoned when my nanny took her last breath. One by one, each made her way to sit vigil by their sister's side. Aunt Earline, who lives across the bayou, arrived so swiftly we joked that she rode her broom over. Nanny's sisters surrounded her with the love she was privy to her whole life, and they said one last rosary with her, a proper send-off for a Cajun matriarch in the witching hours of November 22, 2020, in Chauvin, Louisiana.

Like most Cajun funerals, hers was a Catholic Mass with a huge Catholic family, the rosary, and beautiful eulogies to her strength and kindness. My brother and sister sang the hymns she had picked out, "Ave Maria" and "On Eagle's Wings," and my mother read the passages she had chosen from the Bible. An accordion player followed the casket as we made our way into Saint Joseph Cemetery, where she was buried beside her husband, overlooking her son's grave and near her parents, brother, sister, and brother-in-law.

Chauvin is a small universe. Back in the street, there was enough food for a large wedding: gumbos, jambalaya, beans, fried seafood, and enough rice cookers to require the use of a generator. We all feasted and remembered a woman who will be forever etched into our memories. We said our Cajun Farewell.

RESILIENCE

———— ·'⸲'' ————

THE SIMPLE NATURE OF AN ONION echoes resilience, the layers of being human, and the work behind reaching full expression. Each year on the bayou, our life unfolds layer by layer as the seasons take us through time. We tread through slowly, moment to moment, year to year, sharing in communion with one another through joy and hardships. Just like we prepare onions—slow and steady, with a bit of tears and patience. Onions are at the foundation of Cajun food and a mainstay in the Cajun larder.

Let's unpack the many ways we can prepare and push an onion. Onions lend a sweet and savory note to any dish. They can play a leading role, holding up a whole dish inconspicuously, or stand behind the scenes. The steps and methods of bringing onions to their full potential are expressed in dishes from quick pickled onions and shoestring onion rings to burnt onions nestled in butter or performing as the foundation of an entire jambalaya. It takes time and patience to take an onion to its greatest expression, and you can't skip steps. Onions represent the human capacity for flavor, frugality, and survival. They are the building blocks for a multitude of dishes around the Cajun and global tables.

Quick Pickled Yellow Onions

MAKES 4 CUPS (660 G)

Quick pickles are meant to be used immediately and not canned and stored for a long time. Use them for salads and for garnish on dishes. You can quick pickle just about anything. I adore quick pickled yellow onions, but you can use this same technique on beets, bell peppers, carrots, radishes, jalapeños . . . you name it.

1 pound (455 g) yellow onions, thinly sliced

1 cup (240 ml) white vinegar

1 tablespoon raw sugar

1½ teaspoons kosher salt

1 bay leaf

Pinch of coriander seeds, toasted

Place the onions in a lidded jar with the vinegar, sugar, salt, bay leaf, and coriander.

Let sit at room temperature for 15 to 20 minutes. Use right away or store in the refrigerator for up to 6 months.

Corn Bread with Dark Onion Butter

SERVES 8 TO 12

At some risk to my reputation, I offer a corn bread recipe. My corn bread wish is to make a dish with ingredients of integrity that tastes like the corn bread from the Jiffy box of my childhood, a box that also held a blueberry muffin mix upon which I will spend a lifetime trying without success to improve. I love corn bread, and I really, really love corn bread with onion butter. This recipe makes a lot of corn bread because people including yourself eat a lot more corn bread than you can imagine, because let's face it, corn bread is delicious.

Preheat the oven to 350°F (180°C). Grease a 9½-inch (24 cm) square pan with melted butter or baking spray.

In a large bowl, combine the cornmeal, flour, baking powder, and salt. Whisk or sift together until thoroughly combined.

In the bowl of a stand mixer with the whisk attachment or in a large bowl using elbow grease, whisk the eggs on medium speed until light yellow and fluffy, 5 to 7 minutes. Add the sugar and whisk until thick and fluffy like Marshmallow Fluff, scraping the bowl halfway through, for about 4 minutes.

Add the butter and mix in three additions, scraping down the bowl between additions and paying special attention to the middle bottom of the bowl, where things tend to get stuck. Mix until just combined. Add the buttermilk and mix in three additions, scraping down the bowl between additions. Mix until just combined.

Remove the bowl from the mixer and carefully fold in the cornmeal mixture, using a large silicone spatula and starting from the bottom. *Do not overmix!* The batter does not need to be smooth and shiny. →

4 ounces (115 g) unsalted butter, melted and cooled, plus more for the pan

2 cups (320 g) fine cornmeal

2 cups (250 g) all-purpose flour

2 tablespoons baking powder

2 teaspoons kosher salt

4 eggs, at room temperature

1 cup (200 g) granulated sugar

2¾ cups (660 ml) whole-fat buttermilk

Dark Onion Butter (recipe follows), for serving

Use a silicone spatula to scrape all the batter from the bowl into the prepared pan. Smooth out the top slightly.

Bake for about 45 minutes, or until the corn bread springs back when pressed down or a cake tester inserted in the center comes out clean. Don't overcook—you don't want to dry out your corn bread.

Spread a lavish amount of dark onion butter on a piece of corn bread and enjoy. Corn bread is best eaten the day it's made, but you can toast day-old pieces. Store in an airtight container.

DARK ONION BUTTER
MAKES 1 POUND (453 G)

Warm a heavy-bottomed soup pot or Dutch oven over medium heat for 3 minutes, then add the oil and heat for 1 minute. Add the onions to the pot and stir, stir, stir. This starts the very long process of browning the onions. Cook the onions for 1 to 1½ hours, depending on how hot your stove runs. Watch the onions very closely and stir every 2 minutes. If the onions start to stick too much, add a little bit of water to loosen them, then stir to incorporate the browner onions and scrape up any stuck-on bits from the bottom of the pot. Stir, stir, stir. If you're worried about the onions burning, reduce the heat. Don't walk away from the pot at any point. This is your time with your onions. Stir until the onions are deeply caramelized and resemble dark chocolate in color. Let the cooked onions cool completely.

In the bowl of a stand mixer fitted with the paddle attachment or in a mixing bowl using a wooden spoon, mix together the cooled onions, butter, and cane syrup until everything is properly distributed and there are no streaks of syrup. Place the onion butter in a container with a lid and sprinkle the salt over the top. Cover and refrigerate for up to 2 weeks or freeze for up to 3 months. Take out and let soften before using on corn bread or biscuits or to make omelets.

2 tablespoons canola oil

½ pound (225 g) yellow onions, finely diced

8 ounces (225 g) unsalted butter, at room temperature

1½ teaspoons cane syrup

1 teaspoon kosher salt

THE MIGHTY ONION

When you see a recipe that requires two or three pounds of onions, don't wince and turn the page. Take it instead as a sign of good things to come: Onions, a big pile of them, enough to make your eyes twitch and spill endless tears, are the building blocks for great dishes. The heat and humidity of a Cajun summer is not for the faint of heart, and neither is cutting three pounds of onions, which we do many times a week in bayou kitchens.

When you start a recipe with onions, you're connecting to a long tradition. The onion is more than 7,000 years old, its roots spanning the globe from Egyptian tombs to Indigenous American diets. The Old Testament makes reference to the onion, and Shakespeare invokes onions several times as a means to feign grief. Onions have helped sway political elections and have been used to negotiate in war. In "Valentine," former poet laureate of Scotland Carol Ann Duffy calls an onion a moon wrapped in brown paper. She describes how an onion's concentric circles break down to the size of a ring to slide on a finger—much more potent than a diamond. Onions have been used to dye Easter eggs and to darken broths. The onion family of wild and cultivated alliums numbers in the thousands, including garlic, chives, scapes, ramps, the revered and pricey shallot, and perfect yellow onions.

An onion grows thirteen dark green leaves one by one. They stand erect until they wither a bit and droop. Each leaf is responsible for transferring energy to the bulb and providing another circle to its center. Thus, a perfectly grown onion harvested at peak time has thirteen circles. When the onion can no longer support the weight of its leaves, all its life experiences resting on its shoulders, it is ready for its purpose. The onion is then harvested and allowed to cure. We purchase cured onions that need to be kept in a cool, dry place but not in the refrigerator—they'll get mushy.

Go ahead and cry when you're chopping onions. Cry because your tear ducts are being invaded by tear-jerking acid, or cry because the world is a complicated place and everyone needs a good cry. It's okay if you can't put your finger on what you're crying about. Keep chopping and come to the other side; there are good things waiting. A good sharp knife for quick, clean cuts helps, too—a dull knife mushes the onion and releases more acid.

The onion has so many tricks up its sleeve if handled properly. It's all about just two elements: cutting them and cooking them.

CUTTING ONIONS

Most of the recipes here, and throughout Cajun cooking, start with diced onions. My mother carefully dices onions with a small paring knife. I prefer an eight-inch (20 cm) chef's knife. If you are using a carbon steel knife, keep it clean between uses or the onions will take on a gray color from oxidation.

To dice an onion, first cut off the root side, then the opposite side, where the leaves were attached. Then cut the onion in half through the root ends and you will see all its beautiful concentric circles. (If your recipe requires a lot of diced onions, cut all your onions this way first.) Next, peel off all the skins and deposit in your compost. Clean your cutting board and wipe your knife.

Dice the onion by placing it flat-side down on the cutting board. Cut all the way through, following its natural lines and making smaller cuts for a smaller dice and larger cuts for a large coarse chop. Then turn the onion 90 degrees and cut in the opposite direction. The pieces should fall into a rustic dice. Some chefs keep the root end intact to hold the onion together and first cut parallel slices, then horizontal slices, and then come in for the final dice. You can choose what method suits you. If you have a dice that is uniform, the cooking time will be consistent.

COOKING ONIONS

Sometimes I'm asked how a particular dish got its color, or what makes a dish so sweet. In much of Cajun cooking, the answer to both is onions. Onions have that umami flavor from careful cooking. Pushing them to a desired golden, café au lait, or dark and decadent color is achieved through cooking time. All those pounds of chopped onions will cook down to less than half their size. The timing can differ for each stove, pot, and person. I generally cook onions using a Magnalite pot and a large stainless-steel spoon with a long handle, or a flat wooden paddle.

Place a heavy-bottomed pot over medium-high heat for about two minutes. If it's too hot to touch, it's ready for the fat to be added. The fat can be canola oil or olive oil; chicken, duck, or pork fat; butter; or Crisco. Let the fat heat up for another minute and test with a couple pieces of onion—you want to hear a sizzle. If it's not properly heated, your onions immediately go into the stewing phase rather than the sautéing phase. If you don't hear the pot and onions verbalize that they're ready, then wait. The sizzle is the sign.

Add the onions and stir to coat them with fat. Then proceed according to what you're cooking. Sautéed onions that have lost their bite but don't have much color take about 20 minutes. Getting onions to this translucent place is great for fennel, oyster, and fish soups where you need the yellow onions for building flavor but you're not necessarily looking for a lot of color or thickening power. Keep close watch and lower the heat so browning doesn't start to occur. If it does, no big deal—lower the heat or just keep stirring and keep learning.

To get more color and sweetness, cook the onions, stirring frequently over medium heat, for about 30 minutes total. For cabbage rolls, stuffed peppers, and crab cakes, you'll want your onions to achieve a golden hue. Onions with a richer, medium color will take 30 to 45 minutes. These are great for stews and shrimp étouffées.

To push onions as far as they can go is to take them to a shade that is very dark, a place that many high-end restaurants would call "burnt onions" and incorporate in a lovely butter to be paired with perhaps a sourdough boule. Dark onions take patience and time—don't commit to cooking them unless you have both. If you do, you will be rewarded with so much flavor and color. Stand watch, cooking and perhaps lowering the heat at times, for up to 90 minutes. Stir frequently and add tiny touches of water to deglaze the bottom of the pot and keep the onions from sticking and burning.

Deeply caramelized onions are sweet and the color of black coffee. As they develop that rich, nutty color, the sugars keep concentrating and concentrating until they have the power to hold up a whole soup, a hearty jambalaya, or the best gumbo you've ever made. The flavor is magical and your dishes will shine.

Shoestring Onion Rings

SERVES 8 AS A SNACK

When I was growing up, there was one takeaway restaurant in Chauvin, Danny's Fried Chicken. It was across from Bayou Petit Caillou, and I daresay it must have made a killing. When my mom wanted a break from cooking on Sundays, we stood in line to get a bucket of fried chicken and livers, rice dressing, rolls, and their shoestring onion rings. I have since been on a quest to re-create and celebrate a delicious meal from Danny's. The perfect thing about Danny's was the women working there—we knew them all and they knew us. They meant business and were slightly mean in the best way. From ordering in the tiny space to waiting until you were handed a warm orange-and-blue paper bag to hold in your lap until you made it home, time stood still. The nostalgia in those memories is palpable. It was the only takeout I knew as a kid.

If you have a basic Japanese mandoline, this recipe will be easier and result in perfectly sliced onions. I don't recommend a mandoline for many things. It is a dangerous contraption that, if not used correctly, can result in a trip to the ER. However, it's definitely the way to get perfectly cut onions. You'll need to soak the onions for at least 6 hours in this recipe.

2 pounds (910 g) yellow onions

4 cups (960 ml) whole-fat buttermilk

2 tablespoons hot sauce, preferably Original Louisiana Hot Sauce

Canola oil or peanut oil, for frying

2 cups (250 g) all-purpose flour, plus more for dusting

2 cups (260 g) cornstarch

1½ teaspoons kosher salt

¼ teaspoon finely ground black pepper

⅛ teaspoon cayenne pepper

Cut each onion in half through the center (not from end to end). Peel the onions. Using a very sharp knife, slice them about ⅛ inch (3 mm) thick or use a Japanese mandoline to thinly slice them. You want the onion slices to be long and a consistent size.

Place the sliced onions in a container and cover them with the buttermilk and hot sauce, then weigh down the onions with a plate to submerge them and let marinate in the refrigerator for 6 to 8 hours or up to overnight. →

Prepare a tabletop fryer with oil and heat to 350°F (180°C). Alternatively, fill a large heavy-bottomed pot with 4 inches (10 cm) of oil and heat the oil over medium-high heat to 350°F (180°C).

Remove the onions from the refrigerator. In a large colander fitted with a bowl underneath it, strain the onions and reserve the buttermilk for double dredging.

In a medium bowl, mix together the flour, cornstarch, 1 teaspoon of the salt, the black pepper, and the cayenne. Now it's time to double-batter the onion rings. Place half the onions in the flour mixture and dredge well. Put the dredged rings aside on a lightly floured sheet pan. Repeat with the rest of the onions.

Now dredge the onions again, first in the reserved buttermilk and then again in the flour, and return them to the floured sheet pan. Be sure that all the onions have taken on enough flour. If you see some spots where flour has flaked off, pass the onion back through the flour mixture, really patting the flour onto the onion.

Working in small batches, add the onions to the hot oil and fry until browned and crispy, 4 to 5 minutes. Use the fryer onion basket or a spider to transfer the fried onions to a bowl. Immediately toss with the remaining ½ teaspoon salt. Let the oil come back to temperature before you add another batch. Consume immediately.

French Onion Soup

SERVES 8

Few ingredients have as much flavor as an onion. This is a soup that has traveled the globe and is a testament to what an onion can do to feed a family frugally. You'll need a heavy-bottomed pot. If you can master this recipe, you can make the basis for almost all Cajun recipes.

NOTE: *You need very good beef stock to make this recipe. Look for beef bone broth or make a homemade stock.*

Make the soup: Warm a heavy-bottomed 8- to 10-quart (7.5 to 9.5 L) soup pot over medium-high heat, then add the olive oil and heat for 2 minutes. Add the onions and stir to coat with the oil. Cook for about 10 minutes, stirring frequently, then reduce the heat to medium, add the garlic, and cook for 60 to 80 minutes more to slowly caramelize the onions. You need enough heat to make the transition happen but not so much that the onions start to burn. Stir frequently, and constantly deglaze the pot with some of the stock or a bit of sherry, or both, if the onions stick. Add a little bit of the butter every 10 minutes, reserving 2 pieces to finish.

Warm the remaining stock in a separate medium saucepan over medium heat. When the onions are caramelized, stir in the stock, then add the thyme, bay leaf, salt, black pepper, and cayenne and bring to a low simmer for 10 minutes over medium-low heat. Turn off the heat, add the remaining 2 pieces butter, and let the pan sit, uncovered, for 1 to 2 hours to allow the flavors to marry.

When you're ready to serve the soup, preheat the oven to 375°F (190°C).

Warm 8 cups (1.9 L) of soup for your meal in a separate pot over medium heat. (Store the rest in an airtight container in the refrigerator. It will keep for 1 week.) →

FOR THE SOUP

¼ cup (60 ml) olive oil

5 pounds (2.3 kg) yellow onions, thinly sliced

12 garlic cloves, minced

2 quarts (1.9 L) very good beef stock (page 347)

¼ cup (60 ml) sherry, for deglazing the pan, as needed

4 ounces (115 g) unsalted butter, cut into 8 pieces

6 thyme sprigs

1 bay leaf

1 tablespoon kosher salt, plus more as needed

1 teaspoon cracked black pepper

¼ teaspoon cayenne pepper

FOR THE CROUTONS

8 slices sourdough or ciabatta, about ½ by 3 inches (1.3 by 7.6 cm)

2 ounces (60 g) unsalted butter, at room temperature

¼ cup (60 g) homemade mayonnaise (page 338)

8 ounces (225 g) Gruyère, freshly grated

Whole nutmeg

Meanwhile, make the croutons: Place the bread on a sheet pan and brush with the butter. Toast in the oven for 5 minutes, or until golden. Remove from the oven and spread the mayonnaise on the toast, then mound the Gruyère on top, forming a dome shape with the cheese.

Set the broiler to high. Place eight oven-safe soup crocks or bowls on another sheet pan. Fill each with 1 cup (240 ml) soup, grate some nutmeg over each, place a cheesy crouton on top, and broil for 1 to 2 minutes. When the cheese is bubbling and browning, carefully remove the crocks from the oven and serve.

Hamburger Steaks, Caramelized Onions, and Gravy

SERVES 8

This recipe is my mom's favorite. When we were little, we would make the gravy from a packet. Lord, was it good. I haven't had a dinner made with that packet in a long time, and there's no judgment here, but I believe we can do better than packaged gravy. Good gravy is not difficult to make, and it is a great accompaniment to hamburger steaks and caramelized onions.

¼ cup (60 ml) canola oil

3 pounds (1.4 kg) yellow onions, thinly sliced

1 tablespoon plus ½ teaspoon kosher salt

2½ cups (600 ml) plus 2 tablespoons rich beef stock (page 347)

1½ pounds (680 g) grass-fed ground beef

1 teaspoon cracked black pepper

½ teaspoon mustard powder

Pinch of cayenne pepper

1 tablespoon Worcestershire sauce

2 tablespoons all-purpose flour

2 tablespoons unsalted butter

1 tablespoon sherry, Steen's cane vinegar, or apple cider vinegar

Mashed potatoes or crisp green salad, for serving

Warm a wide, heavy-bottomed 10-quart (9.4 L) pot or roasting pan over medium heat for 2 minutes, then add the oil and warm for about 15 seconds. Add the onions and ½ teaspoon of the salt and cook until the onions are limp and darkly caramelized, about 45 minutes. Stir often while the onions are caramelizing. If they start to stick too much, deglaze the pot with some of the stock but don't add so much that the onions get soupy.

In a large bowl, mix together the beef, black pepper, mustard powder, cayenne, Worcestershire, and the remaining 1 tablespoon salt. Let marinate at room temperature while you cook your onions, then form the mixture into 8 hamburger patties about 6 inches (15 cm) in diameter.

Move all the onions to one side of the pot and position the pot side with the onions slightly off center on the burner so they are not getting direct heat. Make sure there is no stock left in the pan. Put the hamburger patties in the pot and press down on them to ensure flat surfaces and even cooking. If you can't fit all the patties in your pot, cook in batches of four at a time. Cook over medium-high heat for the first minute, then reduce the heat to medium for the remainder of the time. Cook for about 6 minutes, 3 minutes on each side. Remove the patties from the pot. →

Make a beef slurry by stirring together 2 tablespoons of the stock and the flour with a fork in a coffee cup. Immediately deglaze the pot with this slurry, scraping up all the meat bits and stirring in the onions. Add the remaining stock and simmer for about 3 minutes. Mix in the butter and sherry. Then add the patties back in, covering each one with gravy and onions and letting the flavors marry for another minute. Serve with mashed potatoes or a salad.

Fried Chicken Livers, Caramelized Onions, and Rice

SERVES 8

Liver is one of the most nutritionally dense foods you can eat from an animal. If you're a discriminating meat eater, you might extend your horizon to include liver in your diet. On the bayou, we use liver in boudin and country pâté, rice dressing, and stuffed peppers, and eat it fried with caramelized onions and rice.

When you get a whole chicken, it comes with the liver. You can start saving them in the freezer to fry later or you can buy chicken livers at a butcher shop. The livers in this recipe are soaked in buttermilk, although you can skip this step. But I love a soak in buttermilk for just about any ingredient. Buttermilk is acidic and helps tenderize meat. You'll want to marinate the livers for at least six hours for this recipe.

In a colander, rinse the chicken livers really well and separate the lobes. Pat dry, season with 2 teaspoons salt, and place in a medium bowl. Cover with the buttermilk and hot sauce. Let sit for 6 to 8 hours or up to overnight in the refrigerator.

Warm a large sauté pan over medium-high heat for 2 minutes, then add ¼ cup (60 ml) oil and heat for 30 seconds. Add the onions, stir well to coat them evenly with the oil, and cook for 2 minutes, then reduce the heat to medium and stir the onions every 2 or 3 minutes while they caramelize. If the onions begin to stick, deglaze the pan with a little of the stock, just enough to release the onions, and continue cooking until the onions are the color of milk chocolate, about 45 minutes. We are not trying to take them to dark chocolate, although you can if you'd like; that would just require a little more time and stirring. Once the onions are done, add the butter, season with salt to taste, and let them cool down.

When you are ready to fry the chicken livers, pull the bowl from the refrigerator and let the livers come to room temperature. →

2 pounds (910 g) chicken livers

5 teaspoons kosher salt

2 cups (480 ml) whole-fat buttermilk

2 tablespoons hot sauce, preferably Original Louisiana Hot Sauce

Canola oil or peanut oil, for frying

2 pounds (910 g) yellow onions, sliced into long strips

2 cups (480 ml) rich chicken stock (page 348)

1 tablespoon unsalted butter

2 cups (250 g) all-purpose flour, plus more for dusting

¼ teaspoon cracked black pepper

⅛ teaspoon cayenne pepper

2 cups (400 g) cooked rice, for serving

Finely chopped flat-leaf parsley and green onion, for garnish

Prepare a tabletop fryer with oil and heat to 350°F (180°C). Alternatively, fill a large heavy-bottomed pot with 4 inches (10 cm) of oil and heat the oil over medium-high heat to 350°F (180°C).

In a medium bowl, mix together the flour, 2 teaspoons salt, black pepper, and cayenne.

Remove a couple livers at a time from the buttermilk, dredge them in the flour mixture, and space them apart on a floured sheet pan. Repeat until they are all thoroughly coated with an ample amount of flour. You can double batter them if you'd like, but it's not necessary.

Working in batches, use a spider to gently lower 6 to 8 livers at a time into the hot oil. Be careful—these livers are full of moisture and will pop, so lower them and stand back. Fry until crisp and golden brown, about 5 minutes. Use the spider to transfer the livers to a paper towel–lined plate to drain. Let the oil come back to temperature and repeat with the remaining livers.

Season the fried livers with the remaining 1 teaspoon salt. Plate them with the caramelized onions and rice, garnish with the parsley and green onion, and serve.

Seven Steaks

SERVES 4

A seven steak is a shoulder steak from either a cow or a pig. It is an inexpensive piece of meat but it can be one of the best if treated properly. Seven steaks get the low-and-slow treatment in this simple dish that we enjoy down the bayou. Be sure to give the steak a nice sear on both sides before the stovetop braise; you really want to seal in the seasonings before the long cook. Start with a hot pan, and when you put the steaks in, press down on them to make firm contact with the pan. Season liberally and take your time, and you won't be disappointed. Serve with rice or mashed potatoes and a green salad.

Thoroughly rub the steaks with the vinegar, salt, and black pepper, then leave them on a plate to come to room temperature. (If you have time, you can refrigerate the seasoned steaks overnight, then bring to room temperature before cooking.)

Turn on your stove hood or a fan, or open a window. Warm a heavy-bottomed 8-quart (7.5 L) Dutch oven or wide pot over medium-high heat for 4 minutes. Right before the pot begins to smoke, add the oil and watch out for popping. Place the steaks in the oil and press down to make firm contact with the pan. Cook until seared on both sides, about 4 minutes on each side. Reduce the heat to medium after the first 4 minutes if the steaks start to burn.

Once the steaks are beautifully seared on both sides, set them aside on a plate, reduce the heat to medium, and add the yellow onions and bay leaf to the pot. Stir the onions for about 1 minute to pick up all the meaty goodness left behind from searing. Cook the onions until deeply caramelized and dark brown, about 60 minutes, stirring and deglazing with some of the stock if they begin to stick too much. Add the bell pepper, celery, tomato, and garlic and cook until the celery and bell pepper have softened and lost their bite, about 20 minutes. →

2 seven steaks (about 2 pounds/910 g)

½ cup (120 ml) white wine vinegar or sherry vinegar, plus more to finish

1 tablespoon kosher salt, plus more as needed

1 teaspoon cracked black pepper

¼ cup (60 ml) canola oil

2 pounds (910 g) yellow onions, finely diced

1 bay leaf

2 cups (480 ml) rich beef stock (page 347)

½ cup (75 g) finely diced green bell pepper

½ cup (50 g) finely diced celery

½ cup (90 g) torn tomato pieces

6 garlic cloves, finely chopped

¼ teaspoon cayenne pepper, plus more as needed

2 tablespoons finely chopped flat-leaf parsley, for garnish

2 tablespoons finely chopped green onion, for garnish

Return the steaks to the pot and add the remaining stock and the cayenne. Bring the stock up to a simmer and gently simmer until the steak easily comes apart, 2½ to 3 hours. Do not let the liquid boil; you want it shaking, with tiny bubbles rising from the bottom of the pan, not a rolling simmer or boil. Find the sweet spot on your stove with the pot you are using. I find having a diffuser (see page 19) over a gas flame helps regulate the heat for gumbo, soups, smothering, and stovetop braises.

By the time the steak is tender, the liquid should have reduced and formed a rich oniony sauce. Taste the dish. Does it need more salt? Add some. Heat? Add cayenne. Garnish with the parsley and green onion. I like to finish the steaks with a splash of vinegar before serving.

Velma Marie's Oyster Jambalaya

SERVES 8 TO 12

This jambalaya is a simple recipe made with oysters, salt pork, onions, and rice. It is a traditional recipe from my grandmother, Velma Marie, who worked as an oyster fisherman and often had more oysters than she knew what to do with. She was privy to oyster water and the freshest seafood, and she needed to feed a family of eleven, plus any visitors, whom any good Cajun will accommodate. This dish tastes like seawater: sweet, salty, and savory all at once. It is rich and filling. It reminds me of a time that is lost and almost forgotten. Take it slow when you make this recipe; you can't rush a jambalaya.

Enjoy this rich, silky rice dish with a crunchy salad.

Warm a heavy-bottomed 12-quart (11 L) Dutch oven over medium heat, then add the oil and heat for 2 minutes. Add the salt pork, turning as needed to brown it on all sides, about 8 minutes. Add the yellow onions and stir, stir, stir. This starts the very long process of browning the onions. Cook them for 1 to 1½ hours, depending on how hot your stove runs, watching them very closely and stirring every 2 minutes. If the onions start to stick too much, add a tablespoon or two of water to loosen them, then stir to incorporate the browner onions and scrape up any stuck-on bits from the bottom of the pot. Stir, stir, stir. If you're worried about burning, reduce the heat (see Cooking Onions, page 306). Don't walk away—focus on stirring your onions.

Add the celery, bell pepper, and bay leaf to the pot and stir. Cover, reduce the heat to low, and cook for 15 minutes, stirring every 5 minutes.

Meanwhile, put the oysters in a large bowl and season with the black pepper, cayenne, and hot sauce. Set aside to marinate at room temperature while the vegetables cook. →

2 tablespoons canola oil

½ pound (225 g) salt pork, diced

1½ pounds (680 g) yellow onions, finely diced (about 5 cups)

½ cup (50 g) finely diced celery

½ cup (75 g) finely diced green bell pepper

1 bay leaf

1 pound (455 g) shucked oysters, liquid reserved

¼ teaspoon cracked black pepper

¼ teaspoon cayenne pepper

1½ teaspoons hot sauce, preferably Original Louisiana Hot Sauce

2 cups (370 g) long-grain white rice, rinsed

Up to 5 cups (1.2 L) oyster liquor or water

½ cup (25 g) finely chopped flat-leaf parsley

½ cup (30 g) finely chopped green onions

Kosher salt (optional)

Add the rice to the pot with the vegetables and stir to combine. Raise the heat to medium and cook, uncovered, letting the flavors mingle and marry, for 5 minutes. Add the oysters and stir to incorporate them.

In a separate saucepan, bring to boil the reserved liquor from the oysters plus enough additional liquor to total 5 cups. Add the liquor to the jambalaya pot and return the jambalaya to a boil, then reduce the heat to low and simmer until the liquid has almost completely evaporated or looks like little puddles of water, about 10 minutes. When you're at the point of puddling—this is a judgment call based on temperature, pot size, and your stove—put the lid on the pot and reduce the heat to its lowest setting. From here, the cooking time will be 45 minutes total, and you can't remove the lid the entire time. This is a tough, long 45 minutes. But trust yourself. You'll want to peek, but don't.

Set a timer for 20 minutes. When it goes off, turn the heat off and let the jambalaya sit, covered, for 25 minutes before you lift the lid.

After 45 minutes, uncover the pot. Add the parsley and green onions. Taste and add salt if needed. Stir the jambalaya and serve.

Chicken and Smoked Sausage Gumbo

SERVES 8 TO 12

You can find chicken and sausage gumbo all over Louisiana—tucked away in home kitchens, on menus in tiny mom-and-pop restaurants, and in dining spots like chef Donald Link's New Orleans bakery La Boulangerie. It's one of my favorite treats. Making a chicken and sausage gumbo is a bit less expensive than making an elaborate seafood gumbo. In this classic, you'll need a medium roux and smoked sausage.

NOTES: *The sausage you use can be andouille or whatever is available in your neck of the woods. Sausage is so complex and delicious that you won't go wrong.*

There are different ways to go about making a roux. You can start over very high heat, whisking vigorously for a couple of minutes until the roux starts taking on color, then reduce the heat to medium-low and stir until it's the color of peanut butter. You must be very attentive and not leave the roux's side; this takes about 10 minutes. Those first 10 minutes are crucial; because cooking fat and flour on a high setting can cause some burns, be very careful if you choose this route. Alternatively, you can slowly cook the roux over medium-low heat for 20 to 30 minutes and achieve the same color. I've even seen people cook their roux on the stove until it reaches the color of peanut butter, then put it in the oven, coming back to stir it every so often.

Transfer the chicken pieces to a large bowl. Season with the hot sauce, salt, black pepper, and cayenne. Let the chicken come to room temperature.

Warm a large heavy-bottomed soup pot over medium-high heat, then add 1 teaspoon of the oil and heat for 1 minute. Add the sausage, reduce the heat to medium, and sear the sausage until brown on both sides, 2 to 3 minutes per side. Transfer the sausage to a bowl and set aside. Add a little stock or water to deglaze the pot and scrape up

3- to 4-pound (1.4 to 1.8 kg) chicken, skin removed, broken down into 4 to 6 pieces, with back and neck

2 tablespoons hot sauce, preferably Original Louisiana Hot Sauce

1 tablespoon kosher salt

½ teaspoon cracked black pepper

½ teaspoon cayenne pepper

1 cup (240 ml) plus 1 teaspoon canola oil

1 pound (455 g) smoked sausage, cut into 1-inch (2.5 cm) rounds (see Notes)

2 quarts (1.9 L) chicken stock (page 348)

1 cup (125 g) all-purpose flour

3 pounds (1.4 kg) yellow onions, finely diced

1 cup (100 g) finely diced celery

1 cup (145 g) finely diced green bell peppers

1 bay leaf

Cooked rice, for serving

1 tablespoon finely chopped flat-leaf parsley, for garnish

1 tablespoon finely chopped green onion, for garnish

any bits stuck to the bottom, then pour the deglazing liquid over the sausage. Clean the pot and return it to the stove.

Warm the pot over medium-low for 2 minutes. Add the remaining 1 cup (240 ml) oil and heat for 20 seconds. Stir in the flour, then continuously stir the mixture for 20 to 30 minutes so you don't burn the roux and it develops flavor. This will give you a peanut butter–colored roux.

Add the yellow onions and cook for 5 minutes, stirring often, over medium-high heat. Reduce the heat to medium-low and cook, stirring every couple of minutes, for 30 minutes more, to let the onions caramelize. Do not let the onions burn or you will ruin all your hard work on the roux (see Notes). If the onions start to stick too much, deglaze with a little of the stock.

Push the onions to the side of the pot and place half of the chicken on the bottom of the pot. Rearrange the onions so they cover this first batch of chicken, then add the remaining pieces of chicken to the pot. Don't worry about moving every piece of onion. Raise the heat to medium and brown the chicken for 4 minutes on each side, trying to keep the chicken skin in contact with the pot.

Add the celery, bell peppers, and bay leaf and stir everything together. Cover, reduce the heat to the lowest possible setting, and set a timer for 1½ hours. Halfway through the cooking time, stir the pot and make sure the heat is low enough to smother the chicken and not burn it. After 1½ hours, the chicken should be completely falling apart. Stir in the remaining stock and the reserved smoked sausage. Bring to a simmer and cook, without letting the gumbo boil, for 30 minutes. Just look for small bubbles rising from the bottom to the top, not a rolling boil.

Serve with the rice and garnish with the parsley and green onion.

Caramelized Onion and Fig Tart

SERVES 8 TO 10

In Louisiana we are graced with figs in July and early August. I normally spend my time eating the fruit straight from the tree in my backyard. However, when you have a plethora of figs, this tart paired with a salad and a crisp white wine makes for a perfect lunch. It's also a great starter course for a lengthy harvest dinner. A caramelized onion tart marries sweet and savory in the most decadent way.

Warm a heavy-bottomed pot, preferably enameled cast iron, over medium heat for 2 minutes, then add the oil and heat for 30 seconds. Add the onions and stir to coat them with the oil. Add the thyme, then cook the mixture for 45 minutes to 1 hour, stirring occasionally at first and then more frequently as the onions take on color. As you stir, scrape up the bits sticking to the bottom of the pot; this is the fond. If needed, add water 1 tablespoon at a time to loosen and scrape up all the delicious brown bits. If the heat is getting too intense, reduce it. Thirty minutes into the cooking time, add the butter (to deepen the flavor and color), 1 teaspoon of the salt, and ⅛ teaspoon of the black pepper. When the onions are a deep dark brown, remove the pot from the heat. Let the onions cool in the pot, then stir to loosen any bits on the bottom and incorporate them.

In a medium mixing bowl, stir together the cream, mustard, the remaining 1 teaspoon salt and ⅛ teaspoon black pepper, and the cayenne. Add the cooled onions and mix thoroughly. Add the goat cheese to the bowl and fold in.

Dust the tart dough with a bit of flour and roll the dough out between two layers of plastic wrap into a 12-inch (30 cm) disk. Flip the dough into a 10-inch (25 cm) tart pan and fit it completely into the pan, gently pressing the dough against the fluted edges. Use scissors or a knife to cut any excess dough off the edges. If you

¼ cup (60 ml) canola oil

3 pounds (1.4 kg) yellow onions, halved and sliced thinly from root to stem

Small bunch of thyme sprigs or 1 tablespoon chopped fresh thyme

2 tablespoons unsalted butter

2 teaspoons kosher salt

¼ teaspoon freshly ground black pepper

1 cup (240 ml) heavy cream

1 teaspoon Dijon mustard

¼ teaspoon cayenne pepper

2 ounces (60 g) crumbly goat cheese

1 recipe Tart Dough (recipe follows)

All-purpose flour, for dusting

½ pound (225 g) fresh figs

¼ cup (60 ml) honey

1 teaspoon apple cider vinegar

are baking in a warm climate, chill the dough in the freezer for 30 minutes before proceeding.

Pour the onion mixture into the tart crust, spreading the filling out evenly.

Preheat the oven to 400°F (200°C).

Slice the figs either widthwise or lengthwise into ¼-inch (6 mm) pieces. In a small bowl, mix the honey and vinegar. Dredge each fig slice in the honey mixture, then place on top of the onion mixture to create a pretty pattern. Set the tart pan on a sheet pan and bake for 30 to 45 minutes, rotating the pan once after 20 minutes. The tart is done when the figs look jammy and a knife inserted in the center of the tart comes out clean.

TART DOUGH

MAKES ONE 10-INCH (25 CM) TART

In a large bowl, whisk together the flour and salt. Using a pastry cutter or your fingers, work the butter into the flour mixture. Add the lard and cut it in with your fingers until the fats are covered in flour and are in pieces smaller than peas. Slowly add the ice water, 1 tablespoon at a time, and mix gently with a silicone spatula until the dough begins to come together. Form the dough into a disk, wrap in plastic wrap, and place in the fridge to firm up for at least 30 minutes before rolling, or store for up to 24 hours in the fridge or up to 3 months in the freezer.

2 cups (250 g) all-purpose flour

½ teaspoon kosher salt

3 ounces (85 g) unsalted butter, cut into small cubes and chilled or frozen

3 ounces (85 g) lard, very cold or frozen

3 to 4 tablespoons ice water

ROOTS

HERE ARE SOME PANTRY STAPLES to build recipes and round out meals. Having homemade mayonnaise available for a quick dipping sauce is key. Keeping stock and smothered okra in your freezer allows you to pull together a gumbo with ease. Quick pickles to use as garnishes and sides are always a treat to have in your pantry.

Mayonnaise

MAKES 2 CUPS (460 G)

Mayonnaise is a perfect base for seafood dips and dressings, and it's great slathered on a sandwich.

In a food processor, combine the lemon juice, vinegar, mustard, egg, and salt.

While the processor runs, slowly drizzle in the oil until the mayonnaise comes together. There is a point where the mayonnaise seems to be getting more liquidy, but keep adding the oil and watch: The mayo will thicken right up and start pulling away from the sides of the bowl when it is cohesive. Store in an airtight container in the refrigerator for up to 1 week.

2 tablespoons fresh lemon juice

2 tablespoons malt vinegar or white vinegar

2 teaspoons Dijon mustard

1 egg, at room temperature

1½ teaspoons kosher salt

1½ cups (355 ml) vegetable oil or canola oil

Lemon Aioli

MAKES 3 CUPS (690 G)

This is a great dipping sauce for seafood and vegetables.

In a large bowl or mortar, pound the garlic and salt with a wooden pestle until the mixture resembles a paste. Add the egg yolks and pound and mix together well. Start adding the olive oil 1 teaspoon at a time by pouring the oil on the upper edge of the bowl and letting it slowly run down the side of the bowl and into the egg and garlic mixture. Mix with a fork or the pestle and continue to drizzle the oil until all of it is incorporated. Use a bit of the lemon juice to thin it if it becomes too thick. When the consistency is that of a slightly thin mayonnaise, stir in the remaining lemon juice and a touch of cayenne. Store in an airtight container in the refrigerator for up to 1 week.

4 garlic cloves, finely chopped

1 teaspoon sea salt

4 egg yolks, at room temperature

2 cups (480 ml) olive oil

3 tablespoons fresh lemon juice

Cayenne pepper

Drawn Butter with Lemon and Bay

MAKES 1 POUND (455 G)

Make this the night or morning before you boil crabs, and warm it before serving.

1 pound (455 g) unsalted butter

Peels from 1 lemon

1 bay leaf

Make a double boiler by placing a heatproof bowl on top of a pan with 2 inches (5 cm) of boiling water in it. Set the double boiler over medium-low heat. Place the butter, lemon peels, and bay leaf in the bowl over the boiling water. Let the butter melt completely and the lemon peels steep in the butter for 10 minutes. Remove the bowl from the double boiler and let cool slightly. Skim off the foam that has risen to the top, then chill the bowl in the refrigerator for about 6 hours. If water forms in the bowl, just drain it out before reheating the butter in a small saucepan when you're ready to serve it. Remove the peels and bay leaf immediately before serving the warm melted butter.

Shrimp Butter

MAKES 8 OUNCES (225 G)

A compound butter is butter mixed with something else. It could be sweet or savory. This shrimp-infused butter adds an extra layer of sweet richness to any dish.

8 ounces (225 g) unsalted butter

½ pound (225 g) shrimp heads and shells

In a large sauté pan, melt the butter over medium-low heat. Add the shrimp heads and shells and let simmer for 30 minutes, then strain the butter through a fine-mesh sieve into an airtight container. Discard the shrimp. Store, covered, in the refrigerator for 1 week or in the freezer for 3 months.

Small-Batch Boiled Shrimp, Head On

MAKES 3 POUNDS (1.4 KG)

This recipe can easily be doubled or tripled. It is a basic tried-and-true recipe for boiling a small or large amount of shrimp. Watch the salt; it should not be added until the water is turned off.

Pour the water into a heavy-bottomed pot. Add the onions, celery, lemons, parsley, bay leaves, peppercorns, and cayenne. Bring to a boil over high heat, then reduce the heat to low and simmer until the vegetables are soft, 45 minutes to 1 hour. You can really smell the aroma when the stock starts building flavor. Taste the stock; it should have a subtle, bright vegetable flavor and taste clean, with hints of onions, celery, lemon, and pepper. If it's checking those boxes, you're ready to cook the shrimp. If not, cook it a bit longer to develop flavor.

Rinse the shrimp briefly under cold water and drain. Add the shrimp to the boiling stock and push them down into the stock with a large slotted spoon. Increase the heat to high, bring the stock back to a boil, and cook the shrimp for 4 minutes, until bright pink and firm. As soon as the shrimp are done, turn off the heat and stir in the butter and 3 tablespoons of the salt. Soak the shrimp with the salt for about 8 minutes. Taste the shrimp: If you would like them to be saltier, add the remaining 1 tablespoon salt and soak for 5 minutes more, then taste again. Continue adding salt and soaking until the desired flavor is achieved. You can also add more cayenne if you'd like more heat.

When the seasoning feels balanced, strain the shrimp. If you'll be eating them right away, transfer them to a large platter and enjoy. To use later, transfer them to a sheet pan to cool for about 15 minutes, then refrigerate in an airtight container for up to 1 week.

1.5 gallons (5.7 L) water

2 large yellow onions (about 600 g), peeled and quartered

8 celery stalks, chopped into 4-inch (10 cm) pieces

4 lemons, cut in half

Stems from 1 bunch parsley

2 bay leaves

2 tablespoons whole black peppercorns

2 teaspoons cayenne pepper, plus more as needed

3 pounds (1.4 kg) head-on medium or large shrimp

2 tablespoons unsalted butter

4 tablespoons (60 g) kosher salt, plus more as needed

NOTE: *3 pounds (1.4 kg) of head-on shrimp will yield 1½ pounds (680 g) of peeled shrimp.*

Pickled Mustard Seeds

MAKES ½ CUP (140 G)

Mustard is made by grinding mustard seeds with oil, vinegar, and spices. Pickling mustard seeds is the step before making mustard. These pickled seeds add texture and crunch to salads, deviled eggs, charcuterie, and cheese boards.

¼ cup (42 g) dry yellow mustard seeds

2 cups (480 ml) water

½ cup (120 ml) apple cider vinegar

2 teaspoons kosher salt

2 teaspoons raw sugar

In a small saucepan, bring the mustard seeds and 1 cup (240 ml) of the water to a boil. Boil for 1 minute, then strain through a fine-mesh sieve. Return the seeds to the pan, add the remaining 1 cup (240 ml) water, and bring to a boil. The seeds will expand, mellow in flavor, and get a little viscous. Strain the seeds and transfer to a small mixing bowl. In the same saucepan, bring the vinegar, salt, and sugar to a boil. Pour this over the seeds. Cover and let sit until it cools to room temperature. Store in an airtight container in the fridge indefinitely.

Quick Pickled Red Onions

MAKES 1 CUP (230 G)

These vibrantly colored pickled onions are a great garnish for salads, sandwiches, and seafood, to name a few.

1 cup (125 g) thinly sliced red onions

½ cup (120 ml) apple cider vinegar

½ teaspoon raw sugar

In a small bowl, stir together the onions, vinegar, and sugar. Let sit for at least 5 minutes before using. Store in a lidded jar in the fridge for up to 1 year.

Quick Pickled Red Blackberries

MAKES 1 CUP (220 G)

These pickled blackberries are an ode to Camille Fourmont's beloved La Buvette café in the 11th arrondissement on rue St. Maur in Paris. Her pickled cherries paired with pâté and saucisse reminds me of all the lovely vegetables and peppers we pickle on the bayou. Red unripe blackberries should be foraged and pickled in spring and brought out to pair with hog's head cheese, boudin, and sausages in fall. They're excellent tossed in salads, too.

2 tablespoons rice wine vinegar

2 tablespoons water

1 bay leaf

2 tablespoons raw sugar

¼ teaspoon kosher salt

¼ teaspoon cracked black pepper

1 cup (140 g) red blackberries

In a small saucepan over medium heat, warm the vinegar, water, and bay leaf. Add the sugar and salt, bring to a simmer, and simmer for 1 minute or until the sugar and salt have dissolved. Add the pepper, stir, and let the mixture cool down. Toss the blackberries into the vinegar mixture and let sit for 1 hour or up to overnight in the refrigerator. Store pickled blackberries in an airtight container in the refrigerator for up to 1 year.

Smothered Okra

MAKES 1 CUP (240 G)

Smothering okra is not a quick task—it's a commitment, something you do when you have a whole day to stir and watch your pot. It will take at least 9 hours from start to finish.

About 2 tablespoons canola oil

2 pounds (910 g) okra, trimmed and cut into ¼-inch-thick (6 mm) rounds

1 small ripe tomato, diced

Warm a heavy-bottomed pot large enough to hold all the okra over medium heat. Pour in just enough of the oil to coat the bottom of the pot so the okra won't stick. Add the okra, reduce the heat to its lowest setting, and cover. Cook, stirring every 15 to 20 minutes, for a total of 6 to 8 hours. The covered pot will create steam and the steam will drip into the okra, keeping it from sticking to the bottom of the pot. If you feel your pot is not creating enough steam, add a tablespoon of water when you stir.

When your okra has completely broken down and is dark green and only small pieces of green fibrous material and okra seeds remain, stir in the tomato; this will neutralize the slime. Smother for another hour.

The final product should be a mess of dark swampy-green okra and pale pink seeds. Let the okra cool in the pot with the lid slightly ajar until it is completely cool, then freeze in a ziplock bag or use it to make gumbo. Okra holds its flavor and texture in the freezer for up to 1 year.

Shrimp Stock

MAKES 1 GALLON (3.7 L)

I make stock when I clean out my fridge. Half of a yellow onion in a pint container, onions that don't look that great, wilted parsley, sad celery? Check. I'm not saying you should cook with vegetables gone bad, but when your produce has simply seen better days, it's the perfect time to make a quick stock.

Preheat the oven to 400°F (200°C).

Place the shrimp heads and shells on a sheet pan and roast until they turn pink and aromatic, about 30 minutes.

Place the onions, celery, bell peppers, parsley stems, bay leaf, peppercorns, and salt in a 10-quart (9.4 L) or larger stockpot. Add the water and bring to a boil, then reduce the heat and simmer gently for 2 hours. Keep the stock at a steady simmer but not a full boil: You want gentle little bubbles making little sounds and giving off steam, not a rolling boil. Add the shrimp heads and shells to the pot and continue to simmer gently for 1 hour more.

Strain and let cool. Use immediately, refrigerate in an airtight container for up to 5 days, or freeze for up to 6 months.

2 pounds (910 g) shrimp heads and shells (about 1 gallon/3.7 L)

3 pounds (1.4 kg) yellow onions, peeled and quartered

3 celery stalks, roughly chopped

2 green bell peppers, halved

Stems from 1 bunch parsley

1 bay leaf

2 tablespoons whole black peppercorns

Pinch of salt

1½ gallons (5.7 L) water

Pork Stock

MAKES 1 GALLON (3.7 L)

Sure to add flavor to any dish, pork stock is great to have in the freezer. You can pull it out for gumbos, soups, and stews, and you can branch out and make other dishes like ramen and pho with it, adding shrimp or chicken. It is versatile, tasty, and highly gelatinous.

NOTE: *You can source pork bones from a butcher or farmers' market vendor who sells pork products.*

5 pounds (2.3 kg) pork bones

4 pounds (3.6 kg) yellow onions, peeled and quartered

1 pound (455 g) celery stalks, roughly chopped

1 pound (455 g) green bell peppers, roughly chopped

3 bay leaves

2 gallons (7.6 L) water

Wash the pork bones really well. Place the bones, onions, celery, bell peppers, and bay leaves in a large stockpot. Add the water to the pot, bring to a boil over medium heat, and simmer for 6 to 8 hours.

In the first hour, skim and discard any scum that comes to the surface; continue skimming as needed throughout the cooking process. Keep the stock at a steady simmer but not a full boil: You want gentle little bubbles making little sounds and giving off steam, not a rolling boil. After 6 hours, taste the stock to see if it has developed enough flavor; go longer for a richer stock. It takes time for bones to release all their goodness. When you are happy with the flavors, strain it through a fine-mesh sieve and let the liquid cool.

Leave the stock uncovered in the refrigerator after it has cooled, then skim off the fat the next day; it will all rise to the top. You can discard the fat or save it for another use, like frying potatoes or starting a roux. Pour the cooled stock into containers and use within a day or two or freeze for up to 6 months.

Beef Stock

MAKES 1 GALLON (3.7 L)

Beef stock adds richness to stews and soups. Ask a butcher for soup and meat bones to make stock for braising or sipping.

Place the beef bones on a sheet pan, pat dry, and season with the pepper and salt. Heat a 12-quart (11 L) or larger pot over medium heat for 2 minutes, then add the oil and heat for 30 seconds. Gently place the bones in the hot oil and cook, turning as needed to brown on each side, about 3 minutes per side. Remove the bones and set aside; then place the yellow onions in the pot. Let each side of the onions caramelize and even blacken a bit, about 2 minutes per side. Then begin adding the tomato, using a wooden spoon to smash each piece against the bottom to deglaze the pot. After about 5 minutes, when the tomato begins to stick as it cooks down, add the celery and carrots and give the mixture a stir, scraping up the fond (the bits sticking to the bottom of the pot). Pour the water into the pot. Scrape the bottom of the pot again to loosen up the fond. Add the bell peppers, green onions, parsley stems, bay leaf, and thyme and return the bones to the pot. Bring to a boil, reduce the heat to low, and simmer for 5 hours. Keep the stock at a steady simmer but not a full boil: You want gentle little bubbles making little sounds and giving off steam, not a rolling boil.

Taste the stock. When you are happy with the flavors, strain it through a fine-mesh sieve and let the liquid cool. Use immediately, refrigerate in an airtight container for up to 5 days, or freeze for up to 6 months.

4 pounds (1.8 kg) meaty beef bones

1 tablespoon freshly cracked black pepper

1 teaspoon kosher salt

¼ cup (60 ml) canola oil

2 pounds (910 g) yellow onions, peeled and quartered

1 large ripe tomato, quartered

3 celery stalks, roughly chopped

4 ounces (115 g) carrots, roughly chopped

2 gallons (7.6 L) water

2 green bell peppers, halved

6 green onions, roughly chopped

Stems from 1 bunch parsley

1 bay leaf

Several thyme sprigs

Roasted Chicken or Duck Stock

MAKES 1 GALLON (3.7 L)

Always save chicken or duck carcasses to make stock. Not only is it economical, it's delicious. Poultry stock is in my top ten most important pantry staples for a quick and delicious meal.

Preheat the oven to 400°F (200°C).

Place the chicken feet, offal, and necks on a sheet pan and roast until they turn golden brown, about 1 hour. The time will vary based on the size of the bones, so start checking at 30 minutes.

Place the roasted chicken parts, carcasses, onions, celery, bell peppers, parsley stems, bay leaves, peppercorns, and salt in a 12-quart (11 L) or larger stockpot. Use a bit of water to deglaze the sheet pan, scraping up all the sticky bits or fond and adding that to the pot. Then add the remaining water and bring to a boil. Turn the heat down and simmer gently for 4 hours. Keep the stock at a steady simmer but not a full boil: You want gentle little bubbles making little sounds and giving off steam, not a rolling boil. Taste the stock. When you are happy with the flavors, strain it through a fine-mesh sieve and let the liquid cool. Use immediately, refrigerate in an airtight container for up to 5 days, or freeze for up to 6 months.

2 pounds (910 g) chicken or duck feet

½ pound (225 g) chicken or duck offal and necks

2 pounds (910 g) chicken or duck carcasses or cages

3 pounds (1.4 kg) yellow onions, peeled and quartered

3 celery stalks, roughly chopped

2 green bell peppers, halved

Stems from 1 bunch parsley

3 bay leaves

2 tablespoons whole black peppercorns

Pinch of kosher salt

1¾ gallons (6.6 L) water

Candied Pecans

MAKES 3 CUPS (215 G)

These candied pecans are glossy and shiny from the egg white. It's a slightly larger recipe so you can share some with friends, put them out as snacks with a cheese tray, or save them in your freezer to use another time.

1 cup (200 g) raw sugar

1 rosemary sprig (optional)

1 egg white, at room temperature

1½ teaspoons kosher salt

⅛ teaspoon cayenne pepper

3 cups (215 g) pecan halves

If you wish, the night before, place the sugar and rosemary sprig in a small bowl. Rub the rosemary into the sugar to release its essence. Let the sprig sit in the sugar overnight and discard the rosemary before proceeding.

Preheat the oven to 225°F (110°C). Line a sheet pan with a silicone mat.

In a medium bowl, whisk the egg white just until foamy, about 2 minutes. You don't want any peaks to form. Whisk in the sugar until just incorporated. Add the salt and cayenne, then fold in the pecans.

Spread the pecans out on the prepared sheet pan. Cook for about 1 hour, stirring the pecans and rotating the pan every 15 minutes. Check to see if the pecans are dry and beginning to get crunchy. If not, continue checking every 10 minutes. Let the nuts cool, then store in an airtight container for up to 1 week.

I KNOW HOW THIS ENDS

One of the things we've held dear at Mosquito Supper Club is going to the source for superior ingredients. That means weekly trips to Higgins Seafood in Lafitte, Louisiana, for crab and to Wilson's in Houma, Louisiana, to pick up oysters. My electric hatchback can hold four large ice chests. The guys at the docks always tell me I need a truck, but my MPG says different. Houma is about an hour southwest from New Orleans, an easy drive to get the best product for my grandmother's oyster soup recipe. I pick up enough oysters to fill two large ice chests each week to treat Mosquito Supper Club guests to her brilliant soup. I love this ritual, as it brings me home.

On my foraging trips down Bayou Petit Caillou, the best lunch spot is my mother's kitchen. There are always leftovers in the icebox. One day, my dad and I head down to Cocodrie after lunch to look at a camp for sale. My mom grew up in Cocodrie when it was a hardscrabble peasant town, a fishing village, and eventually she saw it shoulder a bit too much oil industry. The camp is situated on land that was owned by numerous oil companies from 1936 to 1990. A home was built on it, and later that home—like almost all the residential structures around here—became a base for sport fishing, and a home became a camp. Folks with disposable income could own a camp, and those who grew up there and stayed—because this was home—got involved in the fishing industry or catered to sport fishermen.

Our visit is post–Hurricane Ida, and there are still capsized boats in the bayou and loads of debris from houses, barges, cranes, and camps. The town looks like it's been weed-whacked. The community will recover, but it will not be the same. We have never been able to afford property in Cocodrie, even though it is my mom's native home. It's where her father carried her, holding a purple toy poodle, out of floodwaters. It's where she grew up and lived with cistern water and no air-conditioning until she married my father and moved a couple miles up the bayou. But after the hurricane there are camps that need roofs and walls. They're inexpensive, and with a little elbow grease, the dream of having our own place in Cocodrie is suddenly viable.

To get to Cocodrie, you need to take the Boudreaux Canal swing bridge, still operated by a human; it connects the landmass of Chauvin, Robinson Canal, and Cocodrie. Once you cross the bridge, the real estate almost triples in price. It's a wonder the bridge hasn't been condemned. It's a mess, and as we drive over, my dad laughs and says, "I guess one day we might go in the drink." This innate knowledge of a life lived in one place warms me. I often tell my parents: "If I could make y'all younger we could have some businesses." I dream of culinary immersions in Cocodrie where I cook for people and my dad takes people fishing so they, too, can hear his stories. I want people to really understand about bayou people, bayou ways, and bayou food. How it all happens naturally, how this was a perfect ecosystem, a vast permaculture of sea and land, a sophisticated culture, and an Eden of resources. Now we hold on to only threads of it.

It seems ill-advised, a bit reckless, to look at real estate in a place that is eroding faster than almost anywhere else in the world, a place that can see a Category 5 hurricane any year coming. At this point, buying anywhere on the Gulf Coast bears the same risk, though. Even so, buying a camp in Cocodrie still seems like a beautiful endeavor. I dream of a place my family and friends can gather for boiled shrimp and crabs caught from our dock, endless fish fries, countless pedro (a Cajun card game) tournaments, nights dancing to the sounds of a swamp pop band at the Bayou Bar, and days of joy and laughter.

After our real estate adventure, trays of freshly boiled spicy crabs and shrimp await us at home and we settle in for a seafood feast. My dad and Uncle Gordon tell stories of when they were young, how my dad would hang on to the back of the boat motor so the weight distribution would help the boat go faster, or the time he accidentally ran over my mom with the boat, or the time Uncle Gordon's nets filled with so much drum that his boat started moving backward from the sheer strength of nature. My dad and Uncle Gordon still fish together as many times a week as the weather will allow. My mom and I wish we could put a GoPro on my dad's trolling motor to see what shenanigans they get up to.

No amount of money can conjure up nostalgia or communion; it is embedded in our senses and only in this place. I say to myself, I love this place. So I put an offer on the camp. We're all pretty sure we know how it ends, and there is beauty in that.

RESOURCES

INGREDIENTS

BEANS

L. H. Hayward and Company (Camellia Brand beans)
camelliabrand.com

Rancho Gordo (heirloom beans)
ranchogordo.com

CORN HUSKS

Mex Grocer
mexgrocer.com

FILÉ

Penzeys
penzeys.com

FRESHLY MILLED CORNMEAL AND FLOUR

Anson Mills
ansonmills.com

Carolina Ground
carolinaground.com

HOT SAUCE

Original Louisiana Hot Sauce
louisiana-brand.com

LEAF LARD

Fannie and Flo
fannieandflo.net

LOUISIANA CANE SYRUP AND CANE VINEGAR

Poirier's Cane Syrup
realcanesyrup.com

Steen's Syrup
steenssyrup.com

LOUISIANA RICE

Anson Mills
ansonmills.com

Baker Farms
campbellfarms.com

LOUISIANA SEAFOOD

Anna Marie Shrimp (shrimp)
annamarieshrimp.com

Louisiana Crawfish Co. (crabs, crawfish, shrimp)
lacrawfish.com

Louisiana Direct Seafood (crabs, fish, oysters, shrimp)
louisianadirectseafood.com

Sea to Table (fish, shrimp)
sea2table.com

SALT PORK

Wellshire
wellshirefarms.com

TURTLE MEAT

Cajun Grocer
cajungrocer.com

Exotic Meat Market
exoticmeatmarkets.com

EQUIPMENT

CRAWFISH BOILERS

Bayou Classic Depot
bayouclassicdepot.com

SKILLETS AND POTS

Cajun Cast Iron (McWare products)

Lodge Cast Iron
lodgecastiron.com

Seasoned (Magnalite cookware)
seasonednola.com

ACKNOWLEDGMENTS

Making a cookbook is an insane task. There are no rulebooks or apps or how-tos; you just dive in and hope you make it out years later. You organize, reorganize, forget how to organize, reinvent organizing, break your computer, and organize again. There are so many people who dive in with you, treading water violently, second-guessing the organization or measurements. Those are the people who deserve the most thanks. If I could add more names to the cover of the book, they would be Anne Churchill, CJ Lotz, Judy Pray, and Denny Culbert. These are the fabulous four.

Anne Churchill worked tirelessly creating and testing recipes, measuring and measuring again, running around South Louisiana for ingredients, working at the restaurant, and cooking us staff meal (the best staff meal).

CJ Lotz kept me creatively sailing: steering and righting. You need a first mate to hold your hand and deal with the flotsam and jetsam; even when throwing your darlings overboard is painful, you must slash and burn.

Judy Pray is a dream editor. I am forever grateful she gave me a chance and humors my ideas.

The shooting of a cookbook is another insane task. Denny Culbert is the calmest, coolest photographer you'll ever meet, and he shows up to the gig with pizza, tinned fish, kombucha, and cases of natural wine.

To the shoot crew: Joe Vidrine, Suzanne Sterling, Bronwen Wyatt, Erin Quon, Anne, my parents, and anyone else who stopped by to lend a hand one way or the other, I have so many thanks. We basically did three straight weeks of camp together. Suzanne, thanks for Christmas; it was magical.

Rémy Robert graciously tested all the recipes in her home kitchen in New Orleans while having a social life and many high-profile jobs and teaching bar.

Thanks to Cecil Lapeyrouse for letting me come over to the store and take over at a moment's notice.

Cassi Dymond and Cara Lambright, thanks for the dates. Tara Jensen, the world is a better place with you. Betsy Lindell, you are my work wife.

Leslie Stoker of Stoker Literary, thanks for staying the course with me. Thank you to Artisan for taking another chance on this book and to the incredible team I got to work with: Allison McGeehon, Lia Ronnen, Bella Lemos, Brooke Beckmann, and Nina Simoneaux.

To my long-term Mosquito Supper Club staff: Donnelle Williams, Maritza Howard, Esme Curran, Emily Pilkington, Camille Cook, and Nola Carpenter. Great books get made by chefs when they have great restaurant staffs. Thanks for making Mosquito sing.

I would like to thank all the amazing women who led me to Crawford House in Franklin, Louisiana, where we photographed so much of this book. Especially Malachi Garff and her late mother, Ann Caffery Garff, known as "Sister," whose vision and spirit drew us together with an invisible string.

My art would not be possible without the love and support of my family. Thank you to everyone who answers the phone and listens. To my mom, Maxine, and my dad, Chucky: Thanks for getting on board always. You are amazing parents and there is never a day that goes by without a reflection of how lucky I am. To Maria and Ben Davis: Thank you for the countless meals, conversations, and endless support. Mallory Martin, Lee Martin, Leslie Martin, Lance Martin, and the "SOCKS," thanks for being an incredible family.

Kaia Martin, Dillon Stave, Saga, and Jackson, it's been a WILD RIDE; thanks for making me a grandparent. I love each and every one of you.

No thanks to Cocodrie, Ezra, and Eggy "The Professor" Martin, who just barked and destroyed things while I tried to work. ISJ, you're the best. RAJ, nothing without you.

INDEX